Depression After Childbirth

How to recognize, treat, and
prevent postnatal depression

FOURTH EDITION
Katharina Dalton with Wendy Holton

OXFORD
UNIVERSITY PRESS

OXFORD
UNIVERSITY PRESS

Great Clarendon Street, Oxford OX2 6DP

Oxford University Press is a department of the University of Oxford.
It furthers the University's objective of excellence in research, scholarship,
and education by publishing worldwide in

Oxford New York

Athens Auckland Bangkok Bogotá Buenos Aires Calcutta
Cape Town Chennai Dar es Salaam Delhi Florence Hong Kong Istanbul
Karachi Kuala Lumpur Madrid Melbourne Mexico City Mumbai
Nairobi Paris São Paulo Singapore Taipei Tokyo Toronto Warsaw

with associated companies in

Berlin Ibadan

Oxford is a registered trade mark of Oxford University Press
in the UK and in certain other countries

Published in the United States
by Oxford University Press, Inc., New York

A catalogue record for this title is available from the British Library

Library of Congress Cataloging in Publication Data
Dalton, Katharina, 1916-
Depression after childbirth : how to recognize, treat, and prevent postnatal depression/
Katharina Dalton, with Wendy Holton.—4th ed.
Includes bibliographical references and index.
1. Postpartum depression. 2. Puerperal psychoses. I. Holton, Wendy M. II. Title
RG852 .D34 2001 618.7′6—dc21

1 3 5 7 9 10 8 6 4 2

ISBN 0 19 263277 9 (Pbk)

Typeset by Florence Production Ltd, Stoodleigh, Devon

Printed in Great Britain on acid free paper by
Biddles Ltd., Guildford & King's Lynn

Foreword to the first edition
Esther Rantzen

I am one of the thousands of women who have suffered from postnatal depression. I know, from my own experience, how unprepared you feel, and your family feels, when depression descends. I know how lonely I felt, surrounded by all the other happy, competent new mothers who clearly had not the slightest difficulty managing their homes, their work, their new babies, or themselves. So at least it looked to me at the time.

I also know from my own experience how humiliating it is to confess that one has had any kind of mental breakdown, no matter how temporary. Mental illness has become a taboo subject. When colleagues of mine decided to make a programme about postnatal depression, they could not find any woman in public life who was prepared to admit that she had suffered from it. But as a result of that programme, which was broadcast on BBC television, hundreds of letters poured in from women who were suffering from depression. The recurring theme in all those letters was that each woman had thought she was alone.

I took part in that programme, along with Mary Whitlock, who now runs the Meet-a-Mum Association of postnatal self-help support groups, and so did Dr Katharina Dalton. I am completely unqualified to judge her treatment of postnatal depression in medical terms. I am not, of course, a doctor. But I do know how tremendously impressive it was to meet her, because she has a complete understanding of depression, which feels like a physical illness and yet is so often dismissed as just another irrational female complaint.

Reading her book, I once again felt that enormous reassurance and relief. Here is someone who not only knows exactly what depression feels like, but has been able to treat it successfully. The silliest comment I ever heard about depression was that reading about it causes it. The reverse is true. Reading about postnatal depression in this book can only bring comfort to families who might otherwise feel isolated and hopeless. It makes those of us who have suffered from it feel less ashamed to admit it, and let us hope it makes those who dismiss it reconsider. After all, it is an illness that can and should be taken seriously. Thousands of women already have reason to thank Dr Dalton for her work. After this book many thousands more will have reason to thank her.

Preface to the fourth edition

It is now twenty years since the first edition of *Depression After Childbirth* was published. During the intervening years there have been many advances in the understanding of postnatal depression. The taboo surrounding the subject has lifted somewhat, and the problem is now discussed more openly among mothers and in the media. However it is still a subject not much mentioned to pregnant women; the attitude that if you don't know about postnatal depression then you can't suffer it, is still widespread. Sadly many women will confirm that this is untrue, and that some unfortunate women can and do experience either postnatal depression or the more extreme postnatal psychosis, also referred to as puerperal psychosis. It is estimated that there are one thousand new cases of postnatal depression in Britain each week.

Now in the early twenty-first century there is a recognition of postnatal depression and health professionals are on the alert to spot early signs to ensure effective help is available. The Edinburgh Postnatal Depression Scale can effectively identify those who may be experiencing postnatal depression at around six weeks postnatally. It is used by health visitors throughout the country. Unfortunately there are some mothers who do slip through the net and whose postnatal depression is not caught in the early stages.

Today mothers take a far more proactive approach to their pregnancy and childbirth; they are involved in the actual planning of their delivery. This enables those mothers who have previously suffered postnatal depression, or who have a high probability of suffering postnatal depression, to ask for preventive treatment to be included in their birth plan.

All the chapters have been fully revised and brought up to date with the most recent scientific research and findings. We have included a new chapter on the animal studies that are being undertaken worldwide and their relevance to postnatal depression. Several new chapters mark some of the changes in society over the past two decades. There is a chapter concerned with the complexities of combining motherhood with a career, as well as chapters on the three-hourly starch diet and stress. We also have a new chapter written specifically for the new fathers who today play a much more 'hands-on' part in parenthood.

The chapter 'Tales of three mothers' includes 'Nancy's tale' (which has appeared in all the editions of this book) and 'Pamela's story' highlighting her tortured thoughts whilst suffering severe puerperal psychosis (which first appeared in the third edition). Also included from the third edition is 'Sally's report' of her two episodes of postnatal depression and her slow route to recovery.

For simplicity, throughout the book we refer to the baby as 'he', except when quoting people's exact words. Similarly we refer to doctors as 'he' rather than the remoter 'he/she'. The written assumption is that partners are male, although we accept that there are circumstances when the partner or father figure may in fact be female.

Eight years ago my husband, Tom, died. Not only was he my husband for forty-eight years, he was also the strongest supporter and critic of my work. It was his dearest wish that I continue with our life's work, and this I have done. Tom was also my ghostwriter for the first two editions of this book as well as my other publications, and his absence is sorely missed. I have been fortunate in our daughter, Wendy Holton, who has co-authored this book, along with much of my recent work. Her husband, David, has helped in dotting the 'i's' and correcting our many minor grammatical errors. To them I extend my grateful thanks.

Thanks also go to my granddaughter, Jennie Holton, who prepared the figures for the third edition which are contained herein. She also helped me with the complexities of the internet for sending and receiving draft chapters to and from Wendy. My thanks are also due to my granddaughter, Dr Sarah Holton, who meticulously searched for so many references.

I am grateful to the Editors of the *British Medical Journal* for the use of Figures 2 and 3 and to Peter Andrew Publishers of Droitwich for Figure 4.

Finally I would like to thank Martin Baum and his colleagues at Oxford University Press for enabling this new, fully revised edition to come to fruition.

Katharina Dalton
June 2000

Contents

List of figures

Abbreviations

APNI	Association for Postnatal Illness
CPN	community psychiatric nurse
DAD	depression after delivery
ECG	electrocardiogram
ECT	electroconvulsive therapy
EPDS	Edinburgh Postnatal Depression Scale
FSH	follicle stimulating hormone
GnRH	gonadotropin releasing hormone
HCG	human chorionic gonadotropin
HRT	hormone replacement therapy
ISPOG	International Society for Psychosomatic Obstetrics and Gynaecology
LH	luteinizing hormone
MAMA	Meet-A-Mum Association
MAOI	monoamine oxidase inhibitor
NCT	National Childbirth Trust
PANDA	Post and AnteNatal Depression Association
PET	pre-eclampsia (pre-eclamptic toxaemia)
PMS	premenstrual syndrome
PND	postnatal depression
PNI	postnatal illness
SAD	seasonal affective disorder
SSRI	selective serotonin re-uptake inhibitor
TSH	thyroid stimulating hormone

CHAPTER 1

Introduction

A single baby's bootee with the cryptic message 'Get knitting' was posted from London to each set of future grandparents in Adelaide.

'Test positive—champagne at eight' was how one high-powered executive learnt that he had been promoted to the ranks of a prospective grandfather.

These are two examples of how the good news of a confirmed pregnancy was announced. They were both from young couples filled with excitement and happiness at the news of the confirmation of their fondest hope, a much-wanted baby.

Once pregnancy is confirmed, labour is inevitable, but the unknown factors include when, where, and how. If it was unplanned, an early and difficult decision may be whether or not to continue with the pregnancy. After the initial excitement at the realization that she is pregnant, a woman and her partner will find that the next few weeks are taken up with making decisions and planning for the future. The choice of a doctor, the place of birth, arrangements for housing, work commitment, maternity and paternity leave, and holiday schemes all need consideration. Then come thoughts about the baby, for example, wondering whether to breastfeed or bottle-feed and the future desirability of sending the child to a creche, play group, or nursery at an early age.

But after the safe arrival, what then? No woman ever gives a thought to the chance of becoming the one in ten who is later affected by postnatal illness (PNI). This unexpected gloom, which can descend on a new mother and transform her whole personality, leads innumerable husbands to announce that 'She's never been the same since the birth of our baby'. Yet such a possibility is far from the thoughts of the happy young couples.

Breaking the silence

This is, of course, as it should be, for needless worrying throughout pregnancy about the one-in-ten chance of developing PNI is obviously not a good thing. There are not many whose suffering is as severe and traumatic as some of the cases recounted here. But there is much that can be done about PNI once it has been spotted, and the earlier it is recognized, the easier it is to treat. This is one reason for writing this book: there is far too much silence about PNI, which is often considered to be just a foible of the weaker sex, a female fancy, or a feminine fantasy. The second reason is that, with our present knowledge, a recurrence of that unpleasant illness is virtually unnecessary.

The range of postnatal problems

PNI covers a range of afflictions, from sadness to infanticide, which start after childbirth (see Box). Although the symptoms vary from the mildest blues to the blackest of black depressions, they tend to be lumped together under such euphemisms as 'mental exhaustion', 'nervous debility', or merely a 'breakdown'. PNI does not necessarily occur immediately after childbirth, but within a few weeks or months it can have changed the mother's behaviour, personality, and outlook. It is convenient to divide these manifestations into groups according to severity, but in practice the conditions merge imperceptibly into each other. The groups are the blues, postnatal depression, puerperal psychosis, and infanticide or homicide.

Incidence of problems after childbirth

Blues	8 in 10
Postnatal depression	1 in 10
Puerperal psychosis	1 in 200
Infanticide	1 in 125 000

The blues

The blues occur when the new mother cries suddenly for no good reason during the first ten to twelve days after birth. Her dilemma is fully discussed in Chapter 4. Nowadays it is increasingly thought that, as these are tears of emotion rather than sadness, and as they can occur in up to 80 per cent of new mothers, the blues are physiological rather than pathological. This tiredness is not necessarily unnatural or pathological; rather it is natural or physiological, in much the same way as tiredness after a good day's work is natural. So, while the blues should be recognized, and partners, parents, and friends should be educated about the condition, they are generally not included under the heading of 'PNI' or 'postnatal depression'.

Postnatal depression

Postnatal depression (PND) is more rigidly defined as 'the first occurrence of psychiatric symptoms severe enough to require medical help occurring after childbirth and before the return of menstruation'. It does not include the blues, which do not require medical help, and also excludes the condition of those who have previously sought psychiatric help because of other psychiatric illnesses such as schizophrenia, manic depression, depression, or drug abuse. Mothers with PND have symptoms which can occur in a mild form in healthy individuals but which, for them, are present in a severe form. These include complaints of exhaustion, irritability, insomnia, anxiety, and, of course, depression.

PND occurs in about one in every ten mothers. It may start immediately after delivery, carry on from the blues, stopping breastfeeding, or start any time during the first year after childbirth or up to the return of normal menstruation. In some mothers it is self-limiting and all is forgotten in a few weeks or months; in others, however, the changed personality and lifestyle may persist for twenty or more years, with the condition gradually changing into premenstrual syndrome. This is discussed in Chapters 5, 6, and 7, and 'Sally's tale' of depression is included in Chapter 11.

Postnatal depression

is the first occurrence of psychiatric symptoms severe enough to require medical help occurring after childbirth and before the return of menstruation.

Postnatal psychosis

Also included in the definition of PND is psychosis. Some mothers with PND have symptoms which do not normally occur in mentally stable individuals—symptoms such as delusions, confusion, visual or aural hallucinations, and rejection of their baby. These seriously ill mothers are fortunately few, but they have a form of PNI called 'psychosis', previously known as 'puerperal psychosis'. Because of the severity, hospital admission is usually necessary to protect the lives of, and possible harm to the baby, mothers, and others. Admission will preferably be to a mother and baby unit, as discussed in Chapter 18. The subject is covered in Chapters 9 and 10, and 'Nancy's tale' of psychosis is included in Chapter 11.

Infanticide

The most severe form of PNI is when the mother kills her baby. This can occur when the new mother is in such a bizarre mental state that there is a total absence of normal maternal instinct and behaviour. In many cases the hallucinating mother hears voices telling her to harm her baby, but she is able to fight the fears. Occasionally, instead of killing her own baby, she kills herself, other children, her husband, or her parent. This tragic state of affairs is dealt with in Chapter 10, and 'Pamela's tale' of the infanticidal voices is included in Chapter 11.

An unexpected illness

PND is an apparently inexplicable problem which few people seem to understand. It strikes without warning, bringing guilt, misery, and helplessness just when young parents should be experiencing great happiness. PND is no respecter of persons. It attacks, at random, royalty, nobility, and famous media personalities as well as the typist, the factory worker, and the shop assistant; it can affect the happily married woman, the single mother, the flat dweller, the squatter, and those caught in the poverty trap. The knowledge that Queen Victoria herself suffered is not much consolation. It strikes at those who have a much-wanted child, including women who have endured years of attendance at infertility clinics with relentless early morning temperature-taking, *in vitro* fertilization, and artificial insemination, and at those for whom the pregnancy was an unwelcome interruption in their well-ordered lives. It affects equally regular attenders at antenatal clinics and relaxation classes, and mothers who have spurned all medical help during their pregnancy. It comes unexpectedly into families who have a clean bill of health and have never before had to cope with a psychiatric illness. It can touch the few who have a stillborn baby but also the many who have a healthy child.

Unfortunately, PND can easily be missed and not recognized as an illness. All too often it is considered as a defect of personality which allows slovenliness, laziness, selfishness, and ingratitude to rise to the top. PND is, however, real, and it can be helped and treated once it is recognized as a hormonal illness which is preventable. See Chapter 3 on the hormones of pregnancy and Chapter 16 on progesterone preventive treatment.

Gradual recognition of PND

Until the mid-1960s there was little interest in this subject. Puerperal psychosis was recognized and was allowed a few lines in medical textbooks, but, as the disturbed, confused, or hallucinating new mothers showed the same diverse presentations as other men and women in the psychiatric wards, they tended to be treated in the same way, with the same drug therapy and/or psychotherapy, as other patients. At the other extreme there were the blues, long recognized by midwives, but only brought to the notice of psychiatrists by Dr Brice Pitt when, in 1964, he interviewed a hundred women at random at the Royal London Hospital between the seventh and tenth day after birth and found half had felt tearful or depressed since the birth. In most of the new mothers it was the usual fleeting, trivial blues, but in six women the dejection lasted a month or more. In 1973 Dr Pitt concluded in the *British Journal of Psychiatry*:

> The presence of confusional features and the absence of personality predisposition or special psychological stresses together suggest that the syndrome is organically determined. The lack of any significant association with the infection or other obstetric complications leaves the most likely factor the profound endocrine change which follows parturition. The occurrence of two-thirds of cases within four days of parturition, with a peak incidence on the third day, and the probably significant association with lactation problems among breast feeders, suggest that the relevant change might be the precipitate fall in the progesterone and oestrogen levels postpartum.

Emotional changes of pregnancy

'Novelists tell us that women blossom and exude happiness and vitality in pregnancy—do they?' This question was asked by Dr A.G. Mezey, a highly respected psychiatrist, at a medical luncheon at the North Middlesex Hospital in 1965. It provoked a heated discussion: 'Of course they do!' 'Certainly the majority of women have increased vitality at this time', asserted the female general practitioners, who in those days did many home deliveries. 'I never meet them', stated the psychiatrist and his colleagues.

Out of that exchange arose a research project that was for many doctors the introduction to a new interest in PND. I led a group of fourteen general practitioners and the psychiatrist in a study of the emotional changes of pregnant women. Special questionnaires were completed giving the age, occupation, and general health of the patient, previous psychiatric breakdowns in the patient and her family, as well as an assessment of her emotional state—happy, placid, normal, depressed, or anxious. When completed, the questionnaires were posted to a research secretary at the hospital to ensure that the doctor would not refer to them at the next antenatal visit, but the usual antenatal cooperation card giving particulars of blood pressure, weight, and growth of the foetus, was kept by the doctor.

Five hundred women were recruited and their particulars recorded at each antenatal visit, as well as at six days, six weeks, and six months after their baby's birth. The survey found that 7 per cent of the mothers developed PND severe enough to require medical treatment, although none needed hospital admission. What were the characteristics of those developing PND? They were those of the women who 'blossom and exude happiness and vitality in pregnancy'.

My findings of that study were published in the *British Journal of Psychiatry* in 1971. Psychiatrists and psychologists suddenly appreciated the vast amount of ill health that was suffered by new mothers which was more severe than the blues, and yet without the confusions, delusions, or hallucinations of women with psychosis. They learnt about the new mothers who had sought help from their general practitioners for their miseries and changed personalities. Intense study of PNI followed, aimed at early recognition, methods of diagnosis, treatment, and the effect of the illness on their children. Mother and baby units were developed and, in 1994, 19 per cent of all health districts in England and Wales had dedicated facilities for mother and baby admissions, and in half of these there was a local consultant with a special interest in PNI.

The Marcé Society, an international medical society founded in 1980 to further the study of PNI, has held conferences throughout the world. One of its past presidents was Dr Brice Pitt, who did so much to open up the subject in the 1960s. However, since the Marcé Society committee consists predominantly of psychiatrists, psychologists, and sociologists, with minimal representation by obstetricians and no gynaecological endocrinologists, it has failed to consider the hormonal aspects of PND or the preceding events of pregnancy. Psychiatrists never see the successes of preventive progesterone treatment; they see the many who have never received preventive progesterone. In this edition I want to emphasize the important hormonal changes of pregnancy and to remind readers that PND is a hormonal disease (Chapters 2 and 3), and that it can be prevented by progesterone intervention at the completion of the birth process (Chapter 16). The treatment of established PND is discussed in Chapter 15, and advice to those helping the mother is given in Chapter 18.

Public awareness

The problem of mental illness after childbirth was first brought to public attention in a BBC 'Man Alive' television programme entitled 'Baby Blues to Breakdown'. It produced a deluge of letters from sufferers relating their personal experiences. They expressed relief that the subject had at long last been opened up for discussion and the hope that their husbands and relatives might appreciate their personal problems and have more understanding of their altered behaviour.

Anna, who described herself as a long-suffering, overburdened housewife, pleaded:

> I am sure there are many of us needing help. I have suffered from these agonizing, unrecognized and untreated symptoms for what seems ages. It's so difficult to explain to others—no one really understands. Please educate everyone.

Brenda, a social worker, asked:

> How many women are warned that they might suffer these miseries during the first few weeks of baby's arrival? How many of those who thrive during their

pregnancy, and are filled with health and vivacity in spite of their awkward increasing shape, later think they are freaks when instead of sheer happiness at their perfect son they react with silent suffering and helpless depression.

Other letters emphasized the seriousness of the problem:

> I tend to have difficult pregnancies and complicated labours, but that wouldn't deter me from having children. However, with the depression experienced after this pregnancy I feel I could never have another one for this reason alone. I just long to get back to my own personality, my old energy and sex drive, and to be able to leave all this behind.

Then there were letters from those who had reached the point of desperation:

> I really need help. I can't spend the rest of my life as a psyche cripple. My problem is severe enough to prevent me living a normal life. I'm nearing the end of my rope.

The majority of women suffering from PNI do not even recognize that they are ill. They believe that they are just leading a lower quality of life, bogged down by utter exhaustion and irritability—a sadly changed character. It is all too easy to blame their condition on the extra work that their baby brings into their new life. However, once PND is recognized as a hormonal illness, different from typical depression, the outlook changes, for treatment needs to be specific and individually tailored—it is not enough to prescribe tranquillizers. Once the condition has been recognized and treated the husband will be able to declare: 'She's once again the woman I married.'

A doctor's personal experience

A doctor explained how experiencing PND herself changed her 'we-and-they' attitude to medicine. Previously she had thought of 'we' as those with self-control, who did not let themselves go, could control their tempers and tears, and were eternally grateful for their healthy children. Afterwards she felt that women with PND were truly ill, not just ungrateful and lacking moral fibre and self-control, and appreciated that they would not benefit from being told to 'pull themselves together'. It was only when women doctors who had themselves borne children became interested in PND that it began to be considered as a medical entity.

Unfortunately we cannot wait for all doctors to undergo that metamorphosis by personal suffering. This lack of interest by the medical profession is understandable for, with ever greater specialization, there is no room for a disease which falls between several disciplines with no one in overall control. PND belongs to the obstetrician, the psychiatrist, and the general practitioner, while the prevention lies with the community physician.

Approaching the doctor

Many letters refer to the difficulty that mothers experience when approaching their doctors. Carol, a mother of two children in Yorkshire, wrote:

> I always get the same answer—that it's one of those things—it's something you have to live with—no one dies of it and one doctor even suggested it might be psychosomatic. Well, after having realized what it meant, I was so upset and disgusted to think anyone could think you could imagine such an agonizing sickness. They are not programmed to see a woman as a natural person.

A husband, giving a full description of his wife's sufferings, ended:

> To make matters worse, although both of her parents are doctors themselves, Diane has an apparent fear or phobia about visiting doctors or hospitals and has on certain occasions begged me not to let anyone take her away. It's almost as if she believed that she was no longer in control of herself.

Continuous antenatal care is accepted as good medical practice; there are regular monthly examinations in early pregnancy increasing to weekly visits in the later months. Ultrasound scans ensure that the foetus is developing properly, thus ensuring a normal and safe delivery of a healthy baby. By comparison, postnatal care is perfunctory, with little thought or attention being paid to the mental well-being of the mother, apart from a pat on the shoulder and an assurance that everything will settle down soon. This is based on the assumption that all that matters is the delivery of a healthy baby and that once labour is completed all that is needed is a postnatal examination at six weeks.

Help is available

The repercussions of the illness fall first on the father, who may already be caring for a family, and is now doing the housekeeping and has also to take care of the new baby, often putting his own job and earning capacity in peril. It is now legally possible for new fathers to take some paternity leave at this time, regrettably at present this is usually unpaid. It is interesting to note that Tony Blair, as Prime Minister, felt unable to do this and only placed himself on 'holiday mode', giving a few extra hours to the family each day. The problems of the father are discussed in Chapter 21.

In the earlier and milder cases of PND the general practitioner, with the help of the midwife and health visitor, will treat the mother. Only in the severest of cases will the psychiatrist be called in. On many occasions the first visit by the psychiatrist will be at home, to meet both the patient and her partner and possibly other members of the family. The psychiatrist will then be able to decide whether, in the special circumstances, the best progress will be made at home or by admission to a specialized mother and baby unit. The psychiatrist may arrange for regular visits and supervision by the community psychiatric nurse, who may have had special training in PNI. This important aspect of help for the new mother is discussed in Chapter 15.

Even if doctors and the public have been slow to recognize PNI, it is recognized by English law. The Infanticide Act of 1938 states that a mother cannot be found guilty of murder of her own child within twelve months of childbirth as 'the balance of her mind is disturbed by reason of her not having fully recovered from the effects of giving birth'. She can, however, be prosecuted for the lesser offence of manslaughter of her child, known as 'infanticide', for which a custodial sentence is not mandatory. Actually infanticide is quite rare; there were eleven reported cases in England and Wales during the four years 1995–8. This is dealt with in Chapter 10.

Historical reasons for neglect

For hundreds of years childbirth has been associated with a high death rate, especially due to puerperal pyrexia or septicaemia after the birth. The open area in the womb to which the placenta was attached provides an inviting entrance for infecting bacteria. There is little resistance to infection in the womb following delivery, so bacteria can quickly reach the abdominal cavity, causing the dreaded peritonitis and death. One of the early warning signs of puerperal pyrexia is confusion, delusions, and hallucinations, with a rising temperature, and in the absence of effective treatment death used to be expected to follow within two days. It was Dr Ignaz Semmelweiss (1818–56) who first stressed the importance of doctors washing their hands after visiting the mortuary and before delivering a baby. That was in the days when medical students learnt the art of delivering babies by practising in the mortuary on the bodies of women who had died in childbirth. His warning to wash hands went unheeded in Budapest and later in Vienna, until Professor Joseph Lister at the Royal Infirmary, Glasgow, showed the vital importance of avoiding sepsis in surgical operations by the use of crude antiseptics such as carbolic acid. The death rate has been further reduced, first of all dramatically by the discovery of penicillin by Professors Fleming and Florey, and since then by the discovery of many other antibiotics.

Today puerperal pyrexia no longer spells death, although it is still a notifiable disease, which in England and Wales must be reported to the Department of Health and Social Services if the mother develops a temperature of 38°C (100.4°F) or over during the first fourteen days after the birth of a child. It has been the removal of puerperal pyrexia from the hazards of childbirth which has uncovered the problems of PND.

Media exposure

The media regularly expose horrifying tragedies in which the verdicts in the coroner's courts state that PND was the cause. Examples of headlines over the years include:

Mother hanged herself
Mother of twins freed after stabbing
Mother drowns baby girl
Tragic dancer freezes to death
Train death of woman with PND
Mercy for mother who tried to drown her own daughters
Mum threw baby out of the window
Mum's frozen body found
Baby blues sparks bloody hammer rage
Mother of four takes overdose

Mother kills her three children
Wife stabs her husband
Death of burning Mum

In all these examples, severe PND went unrecognized by those close to the new mother.

When a well-known actress committed suicide shortly after her baby's birth, her husband stated that he had never heard of PND and certainly had not appreciated that it could have had such severe consequences. But there had been an early warning, as in all cases: the young mother had not been herself, she had been unusually irritable, no longer laughing, and had lost her bubbling vitality. Such symptoms are too easily blamed on loss of sleep with a crying newborn.

We must never forget the possibility that such symptoms could indicate PND. We all have a responsibility to be aware of the unexpected torment that can occur in a new mother's mind, leading her to act in the most unexpected manner when she is at the end of her tether. Husbands need to be warned during antenatal classes of the possibility of this horrible disease occurring and to appreciate that help is at hand, to know how to recognize it, and the need to summon assistance. More education of the public is required before there can be an end to these tragedies, which is the very reason for writing this book.

CHAPTER 2

The changes of pregnancy

During the fifties the American endocrinologist, Hans Selye (1907–1982) introduced the word 'stress' into medicine and was the first to demonstrate how the hormone, cortisone, was the body's natural defence to stress. He described the three stages of the general adaptation syndrome. With the initial stage of shock or damage, followed by the second stage of resistance if the stress was protracted, and ultimately the stage of exhaustion if stress was prolonged. It was the first occasion in which hormones were used to treat psychological symptoms. Selye suggested that when hormones were fully understood psychiatrists would not be needed. The result was that psychiatrists stopped studying hormones, nor were they interested in animals in relation to behaviour and hormones. Nevertheless in the interval many psychiatric diseases have been recognised as due to hormone imbalance and moved out of the realm of psychiatry to be treated by endocrinologists. These include the mental dullness and lethargy of thyroid deficiency, the anxiety of thyroid excess, and also the aggressive outbursts associated with low blood sugar. It is in this category that premenstrual syndrome and postnatal depression belong.

Reproduction is an essential characteristic of all living animals and vegetables. In lower animals reproduction is asexual, involving only one

---

Postnatal depression is a hormonal disease

Conception, maintenmance of pregnancy, birth, breastfeeding, and conversion to non-pregnant state are all under hormonal control.

Reproduction is a physiological process, not a psychological process.

Problems of reproduction are caused by hormonal imbalance, not psychological causes.

Postnatal depression is due to hormonal imbalance.

Events in the reproductive cycle

Menstruation

Ovulation

Conception

Pregnancy

Labour

Lactation

---

sex, but in higher animals it is sexual, with marked differences in the contributions of males and females. It must be appreciated that the initiation and maintenance of pregnancy, the birth process, and the conversion back to the non-pregnant state are all under hormonal control. So illnesses or abnormalities related to pregnancy are due to an imbalance of the hormones of pregnancy. Thus PND is essentially an abnormal hormonal disease. Although PND may have psychological symptoms and secondary psychological factors in its development, its cause is certainly not psychological. Mere power of the mind will not cause a pregnancy.

PND includes the rarer types of PNI occurring in other systems such as the lungs (with asthma) or the eyes (with rare ophthalmologic disease). PND covers the range of psychological symptoms which are by far the most common illnesses occurring after birth. In this book it is the psychological symptoms which are fully discussed.

PND is an exclusive disease. It cannot occur in men or children and is limited to mothers, coming after a series of events in the woman's reproductive cycle, all of which are under hormonal control.

To understand PND one needs also to understand the many bodily and psychological changes which precede the disease and to recognize the importance of alterations in levels of various hormones which stimulate

---

Ovulation

is the start of pregnancy

Menstruation

is a failed pregnancy

---

the numerous vital events which occur during pregnancy and labour. These events include cessation of menstruation, ovulation, conception, pregnancy, labour, the preparation for breastfeeding, and the return to a non-pregnant state.

Ovulation

Ovulation, or the release of an ovum (or egg), is the first essential event. Women who attend fertility clinics are sometimes surprised to discover that, although they have always menstruated regularly, they have not ovulated. For ovulation the ovaries need to be stimulated by two hormones from the pituitary (a gland situated directly below the brain which releases many hormones that pass to other parts of the body, such as the adrenals and pancreas). The two special hormones affecting pregnancy that pass from the pituitary to stimulate the ovary are the follicle-stimulating hormone (FSH) and the luteinizing hormone (LH) (see p. 189). If ovulation is not occurring naturally, then drugs can be used to stimulate the ovaries to mature an egg cell and then release it at ovulation. Indeed, if *in vitro* fertilization is planned, it is possible to administer hormone treatment designed to produce *super*ovulation, in which several egg cells are matured simultaneously. These can then be harvested, stored frozen, and used when required at a later date.

Conception

For conception to take place the male sperm must penetrate the egg cell. This means that the fallopian tubes, leading from the ovaries to the womb, must be open before the egg cell and sperm can meet. The fertilized egg must then become embedded in the spongy lining on the inside of the womb. At each menstruation this spongy lining is shed and a new lining is created, the process being stimulated by the joint action of the ovarian hormones, oestrogen and progesterone.

At conception there are immediate changes in the hormone level, even before the woman has missed her first menstruation or before the foetus has become embedded within the womb. This provides justification for those women who notice the difference and are sure that they are pregnant a day or two after conception and even before they have missed menstruation. As one expectant mother explained:

I knew I had conceived. First I had a terrible migraine, then within a day or two I started feeling sick and tired and my boobs became tender and bigger, but I still had to wait another seven days to see if my period would turn up. My husband didn't believe me, but I knew our baby was on the way.

Hormones

Hormones are chemical messengers in the body which produce changes in selected cells. The definition of a hormone, as given in *The Shorter Oxford Dictionary,* is: 'Substance formed in an organ serving to excite some vital process, as secretion.' *Hormone* is derived from a Greek word meaning 'to urge on', which is exactly what hormones do—they urge on certain cells to do particular tasks. Hormones are produced in one organ, called an endocrine gland, and pass into the blood to act on some other organ at a distant site. This is why those who specialize in the study of hormones are called 'endocrinologists'.

Hormones are very powerful and precise, and only minute quantities are needed to produce profound effects. They are also very selective, usually having only a few specific tasks to perform, and they are able to work only if conditions are exactly right. But problems occur if the wrong balance of hormones is present at the wrong time, either in the menstrual cycle or in the reproductive cycle. The problem caused by too much or too little of one particular hormone is out of all proportion to the actual amount of the hormone, which may be no greater than a single grain of salt.

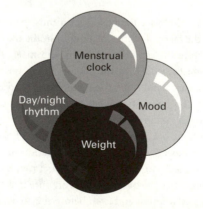

Fig. 1 Proximity of controlling centres in the hypothalamus

All the body's activities are controlled by hormones. They control our growth, temperature, reactions to stress, digestion, excretion, pigmentation, and many other functions, but in this chapter we are concerned only with the hormones involved in the purely feminine functions of menstruation and pregnancy.

The hypothalamus

The hypothalamus is a specialized part of the lower brain which contains many of the controlling centres of the body. These include the menstrual controlling centre, or 'menstrual clock', which controls the menstrual and pregnancy hormones (FSH, LH, progesterone, and oestrogen), as well as the centres controlling mood, weight, and day/night rhythm.

Imagine the centres being like a lot of snooker balls, all placed next to each other (Fig. 1). If one ball is disturbed, it tends to have a knock-on effect on the others. You can then understand why, when the menstrual controlling centre is suddenly affected by the abrupt fall in progesterone and oestrogen, such as occurs during labour, that there may be a subsequent upset of mood, sleep, and weight leading to PND.

In normally menstruating women the menstrual clock is responsible for releasing the necessary hormones to regulate the timing of ovulation and menstruation, and deciding the intervals between menstruations, but in pregnancy this controlling function is no longer needed as the control of the pregnancy hormones is taken over by the pituitary–foetal axis, and the menstrual clock enters a temporarily dormant phase.

In menstruating women the hypothalamus produces a very powerful hormone called 'gonadotrophin releasing hormone' (GnRH), which passes by a special pathway to the pituitary (Fig. 2).

The pituitary gland

The pituitary gland is a small, but vitally important, pea-sized organ, situated next to the hypothalamus. It was once called 'the leader of the endocrine orchestra' because it controlled so many hormones and was responsible for so many functions of the body. But now that we have a greater appreciation of the importance of the hypothalamus and its intimate relationship with the pituitary, we refer to the hypothalamic–pituitary

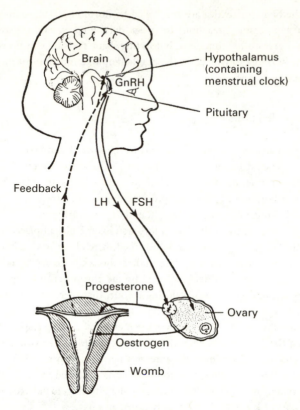

Fig. 2 Menstrual hormones from the hypothalamus and pituitary to the ovaries and womb

axis, and we are no longer sure which organ holds the seat of the greatest power (see Fig. 2). The pituitary produces many stimulating hormones which cause other glands, including the adrenals, thyroid, and pancreas, to produce their own specialized hormones, but here we will concentrate only on the hormones of menstruation and pregnancy.

When GnRH is released from the hypothalamus, it stimulates the pituitary to produce two menstrual hormones: follicle-stimulating hormone (FSH) and luteinizing hormone (LH). From the pituitary the FSH passes in the blood to the ovary, where it has two functions. It causes one of the thousands of immature follicles within the ovary to ripen and come to the surface of the ovary, where it appears like a little blister; within it is the egg cell. It also stimulates the ovarian cells to produce the hormone oestrogen. This oestrogen passes in the blood to the womb, where it rebuilds the inner lining of the womb, which disintegrated and was shed at the last menstruation (see Fig. 2).

The other hormone from the pituitary, LH, also passes to the ovary, where it acts upon the ripening follicle, causing it to burst and release the egg cell. This is known as ovulation and normally occurs about fourteen days before the onset of menstruation. The LH also causes special cells to be formed where the follicle burst, and these cells have the remarkable property of producing the hormone progesterone. Progesterone is present in the blood only after ovulation and until menstruation. It passes in the blood to the womb where it has the task of thickening the lining so that, if conception occurs, there is a comfortable soft lining inside the womb in which the fertilized egg can become embedded. Progesterone is known as the 'pregnancy hormone' because it prepares the womb for a possible pregnancy.

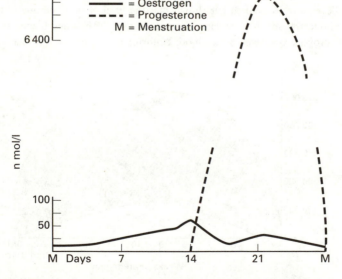

Fig. 3 Normal levels of oestrogen and progesterone during a menstrual cycle

Menstrual hormones

The levels of the various menstrual hormones vary throughout the menstrual cycle. Figure 3 shows the timing of the relative levels, but not the precise levels, for progesterone levels are measured in nanograms per millilitre, while oestrogen is measured in picograms per millilitre, which are a thousand times smaller.

The hormone LH is present in small amounts throughout the cycle, with a sudden high peak at ovulation. FSH is also present throughout the cycle, but its level varies. These hormones enter the bloodstream not in a continuous flow, but in spurts. For instance, it has been estimated that, in the case of progesterone and LH, the spurts occur at about twenty-minute intervals. Oestrogen is present throughout the cycle in varying amounts, having a higher level at the time of ovulation and again halfway between ovulation and menstruation. In contrast, progesterone is present in unmeasurably small quantities during the first half of the menstrual cycle, increasing only at ovulation. It rises to a peak halfway between ovulation and menstruation at about the twenty-first day, and then rapidly falls away and disappears at menstruation.

The hormone levels mentioned so far relate to the levels found in the blood by radioimmunoassays, but the work of Dr Kruitwagon and his colleagues in Rotterdam has shown that the level of progesterone in the peritoneal fluid after ovulation is on average fifty times higher than the progesterone level in the blood. Unfortunately, whereas it is relatively

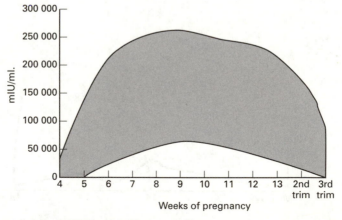

Fig. 4 Levels of HCG during early pregnancy

easy to obtain blood samples for hormone estimations, it is difficult to obtain peritoneal fluid from within the abdominal cavity.

Hormonal changes in pregnancy

Within hours of conception the fertilized egg cell affects the hormones. The levels of the ovarian hormones, oestrogen and progesterone, instead of dropping for menstruation, continue to rise, and unique new hormones are produced. They include human chorionic gonadotrophin (HCG), which is used as the basis for pregnancy tests. If present then the woman is pregnant. The level rises very rapidly, peaking at about the ninth week, and then decreases. It can be detected in the blood even before the first menstruation is missed (Fig. 4). Its function is to help in the formation of the placenta.

Gradually a new organ, the placenta or afterbirth, is formed. It is attached to the lining of the womb and passes nutrients and hormones via the umbilical cord to the foetus (Fig. 5). The placenta becomes a hormone factory producing massive amounts of progesterone and oestrogen under the partial control of the foetal adrenal glands.

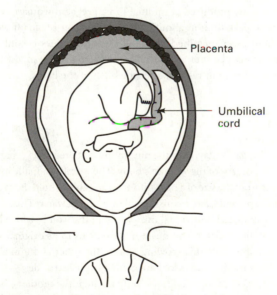

Fig. 5 Pregnant womb with placenta and umbilical cord

During the early weeks of pregnancy the progesterone and oestrogen are produced by the ovary, but gradually the placenta takes over the production, which causes the progesterone levels in the blood to rise to a level some fifty times higher than the normal peak level of progesterone occurring on the twenty-first day of a non-pregnant woman's cycle. By the sixteenth week of pregnancy the ovarian hormone production is no longer of importance, and indeed the ovaries can be removed without affecting the pregnancy. The increase in progesterone level during pregnancy is discussed further in Chapter 3.

Another hormone that shows a marked increase in output is prolactin, which is produced by the pituitary. The level becomes raised throughout pregnancy and is responsible for preparing the breasts for lactation. Even in the early stages of pregnancy one of the first symptoms may be an increase in the size of the breasts with the veins becoming visible, and it may be possible to express some fluid from the nipples as early as the sixth to eighth week of pregnancy.

During pregnancy the amount of hormones produced by the adrenals increases, so that twice as many corticosteroids are produced. In addition there is a change in the day/night rhythm in late pregnancy, so that more corticosteroids are produced at midnight in a pregnant woman, compared with the usual peak hour at about 9.00 a.m. in a non-pregnant woman.

Throughout pregnancy the level of all these hormones is controlled by the hypothalamus, placenta, and foetal adrenals, so that the menstrual clock rests until menstruation restarts after the birth of the baby.

Pregnancy

Very gradually, day by day, over the nine months of pregnancy, changes take place in all the organs of the woman's body. The womb gradually increases in size, growing from the size of a pear into an organ able to hold the ever-growing foetus, the placenta, and a considerable amount of water. This increase in size takes place in each individual muscle cell of the womb, which becomes more than 40 times larger, and never quite returns to its original size after birth. To accommodate this growing womb, the other abdominal organs, especially the intestines and colon, are gradually pushed aside.

The heart has to pump blood, not only through the mother's body, but also through to the placenta and foetus. The heart increases in size, increases

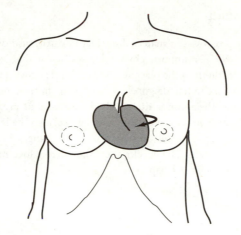

Fig. 6 Heart twisting round in pregnancy

its workload, and twists round, so that changes occur in the ECG pattern (Fig. 6). Cardiologists are still discussing how long it takes for these changes in cardiac output to return to normal after a pregnancy. Drs Eleanor Capeless and James Clapp reported in the *American Journal of Obstetrics and Gynecology* in November 1992 that about 10 per cent of physically fit and active women still had an increase in cardiac output six months later, whereas by one year they had all returned to normal.

During pregnancy the ribcage gradually enlarges as the lungs increase their oxygen intake to provide enough oxygen for both mother and the growing foetus. At the same time there is an upward pressure on the diaphragm, due to the enlarging womb. The kidneys are also called upon to increase their normal work of excreting the mother's metabolic waste and to take on the excretion for the foetus as well. Meanwhile the two ureters, which pass urine from the kidneys to the bladder, also increase in size and are misplaced by the enlarging womb. After pregnancy the ureters never quite return to their normal size.

Unseen changes also occur in cellular chemistry in relation to the maintenance of the blood glucose level. There are also changes in insulin resistance, which is discussed further in Chapter 3. Occasionally a special form of diabetes, known as 'gestational diabetes', develops; this needs treatment with insulin during pregnancy but clears up immediately after delivery.

Maternal instinct

As pregnancy progresses, a maternal instinct normally also develops. The mother's love for her unborn child increases, again due largely to the hormonal secretion from the placenta. Although pregnancy may have been unplanned and its initial diagnosis viewed with horror, most mothers gradually change their minds during the long weeks of pregnancy. This does not necessarily happen with the father, especially if he is not there to observe the gradual physical and psychological changes in the mother during the nine months. The development of maternal love and behaviour is discussed more fully in Chapter 3.

Birth

After nine months the unborn baby is fully grown and ready to leave the womb. First the door of the womb opens gradually, with contractions occurring about every ten to twenty minutes; when it is wide open, tremendous muscular contractions of the body of the womb push the baby out. The exact mechanism and control of labour are still not fully understood, but they are under hormonal control. At the baby's birth the placenta also comes away, which means there is an abrupt change in the levels of progesterone and oestrogen during the twenty-four hours after birth.

Puerperium

After the baby's birth the many bodily changes of pregnancy gradually return to the non-pregnant state. The womb shrinks rapidly in the first seven days and then more gradually over the next six weeks. The abdominal muscles gradually regain power and act to hold the abdomen in; this is helped by daily postnatal exercises. As the heart returns to normal there can be the occasional palpitation or irregular heartbeat, which may cause panic and anxiety, but this is nothing to worry about.

Once the blood levels of oestrogen and progesterone have dropped after delivery, the level of oestrogen remains low and there is an almost complete absence of progesterone. This is the resting or 'refractory phase'. During this phase the usual stimulants that are given to the pituitary or ovary—such as GnRH, LH, or fertility drugs (buserelin, goserelin, clomiphene)—will not produce the normal outpouring of menstrual hormones.

If the mother is breastfeeding, her prolactin level will remain raised until she stops feeding, and the refractory phase is likely to continue until then.

There are other occasions when the menstrual clock is dormant, such as before puberty, after stopping the Pill, or in anorexia nervosa, and in all these instances premenstrual syndrome (PMS) is likely to start after the dormant or refractory phase of the menstrual clock ends.

Lactation

The physiological changes of reproduction do not finish with the baby's birth, for the mother's body is then prepared for breastfeeding and looking after the baby for the first few months. This time it is the hormone prolactin which is involved; this is produced in plenty by the pituitary and stimulates the breast tissue to produce milk. The baby's sucking further stimulates the milk production. Breastfeeding also encourages the development of maternal instinct and the bonding of the mother with her child. It is at this time, after the birth but before the return of menstruation, that PND, in its many different presentations, first occurs.

Menstruation and ovulation

Menstruation and ovulation do not usually occur when the mother is breastfeeding fully. Although doctors are aware that there are exceptions to every rule and are taught 'never say never', it is agreed that occasionally ovulation does occur and another pregnancy can begin even before menstruation has restarted. So contraception is advised even when a mother is breastfeeding fully.

Menstruation usually starts again about a month after stopping breastfeeding, but it does not matter if it takes six months or longer to restart. If the mother has started a weight-reducing diet, menstruation is slower to resume. Menstruation may previously have been accompanied by spasms of pain, or spasmodic dysmenorrhoea, but after a full-term pregnancy this type of menstrual pain generally disappears. Some women develop PMS when menstruation restarts; this problem is covered in Chapter 14.

Upsets in the normal hormonal control of the reproductive cycle can occur at any stage in the reproductive cycle, as can psychiatric disturbances. PND should be seen as an illness which occurs towards the end of this reproductive cycle, because of an upset of the normal hormonal balance.

CHAPTER 3

Progesterone—its molecules and receptors

Progesterone is an essential pregnancy hormone. This point has been emphasized by *in vitro* fertilization. Oestrogen is needed for maturing the immature egg cell and for ovulation. It is possible to fertilize an egg outside the womb, but progesterone is essential for the successful implantation of the fertilized egg in the lining of the womb and for the continuation of the pregnancy. After ovulation, if conception occurs there is a rapid and massive increase in the progesterone blood level, first from the ovary and then from the placenta (Fig. 7).

It is important to appreciate that blood progesterone is measured in nanograms, whereas oestrogen is measured in picagrams, a measurement one thousand times smaller (see Box). Although pregnancy in all vertebrates and humans is associated with, and dependent on, marked hormonal changes it should be noted that psychiatrists involved in postnatal depression do not study endocrinology. Indeed even a modern textbook on postnatal depression for psychiatrists and authored by an authoritative professor in psychiatry contains a graph incorrectly giving both progesterone and oestrogen blood levels measured in nanograms. If oestrogen is measured in picagrams (which are one thousand to one nanogram), it

---

Oestrogen

blood levels are measured in picagrams

Progesterone

blood levels are measured in nanograms

1000 picagrams = 1 nanogram

In treatment the dose of progesterone may need to be one thousand times higher than that of oestrogen

---

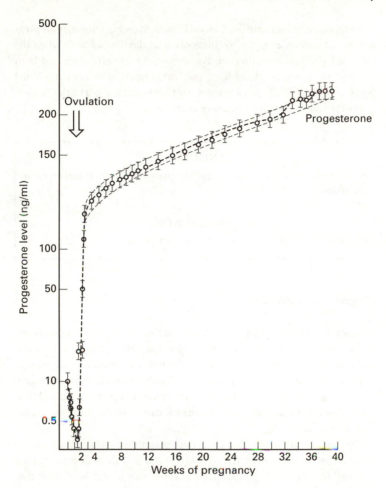

Fig. 7 Progesterone blood levels in a human pregnancy

follows that it is therefore impossible in any book to depict a graph to scale showing simultaneously progesterone and oestrogen levels.

The increase in the progesterone blood level reached during pregnancy is some fifty to one hundred times higher than that reached by a normal menstruating woman. There is also a rise in oestrogen level, but the progesterone blood level is still some fifty times higher than that of oestrogen.

The progesterone and oestrogen blood levels remain high throughout pregnancy, but sudden abrupt alterations occur at the time of birth when the baby and placenta are delivered. For almost nine months there has been this high progesterone blood level, but within hours of delivery the blood levels drop to insignificant amounts, with only minute quantities of progesterone and oestrogen circulating in the blood.

Oestrogen

is essential for ovulation and until the placenta is fully functioning at the sixteenth week

Progesterone

is essential for conception and throughout pregnancy

Progesterone molecules

Progesterone molecules are estimated to be five hundred million years old and are the basis of all other steroids. They are present in all vertebrates and humans of all ages and both sexes. Progesterone molecules are synthesized in the two adrenal glands and then converted into oestrogen, testosterone, and corticosteroids (stress hormones). It is not yet possible to do routine estimations of progesterone molecules or progesterone receptors in individuals.

The amounts are so tiny that progesterone is measured in nanograms per millilitre, or 'ng/ml', which is 1 / 1 000 000 000 of a gram of progesterone in a millilitre of blood. To give readers some idea of just how small that fraction is, if we equate one gram with ten million pounds sterling, then one nanogram would equal one penny. The progesterone level drops from about 150 ng/ml at the end of pregnancy to under 7 ng/ml on the third day after birth, and becomes unmeasurable by the seventh day after birth.

A mother's normal adjustment to such marked changes in hormonal levels at the time of birth is indeed heroic, and one should wonder at the large number of women who stand up to the changes without upset, rather than express surprise at the few who are disturbed by this hormonal upheaval.

The forgotten hormone

Progesterone is a hormone forgotten by doctors and public alike. It can be measured in the blood, but it is difficult to interpret the result. Progesterone enters the blood in spurts, so to get a reliable result one would need to collect several blood samples on the same day, which would be very expensive. Moreover, there is a lower progesterone level following a large meal, which should be considered when interpreting the results (Fig. 8).

Progesterone is present in measurable quantities during only half the menstrual cycle, and when it is present, after ovulation, it varies in amount depending on the number of days before menstruation, so to interpret the result of a test it is necessary to know both the date on which the last menstruation started and also the actual day the next menstruation starts. So one needs to wait until the next menstruation before the test can be interpreted. That is the only way to be precise as normal healthy women can have menstrual cycles of anywhere between twenty-one and thirty-five days. In a woman with a cycle of about twenty-eight days, the level will be highest on day twenty-one, and if above about 10 ng/ml it is assumed that normal ovulation has occurred. In short, while knowledge of progesterone levels is necessary for research purposes, a single routine test of progesterone blood level is of limited value. Progesterone estimations are of no value in the treatment of PMS or PND but are useful, in investigations for infertility, if taken seven days before the expected time of menstruation to determine whether ovulation has occurred.

Another problem is that progesterone cannot be given by mouth, or as a skin patch, but needs to be administered vaginally or rectally at least twice daily, or by intramuscular injections on at least alternate days. In fact, absorption of progesterone introduced to the body is so poor that 400-mg suppositories twice daily are the minimum effective dose, although the levels are measured in nanograms. Too often natural progesterone is confused with the artificial progestogens (see p. 36).

Often it is much easier to treat the patient with oestrogen and forget about progesterone.

Hormone receptors

Recent technology, and especially the electron microscope, have enabled molecular biologists to understand just how a molecule of a hormone

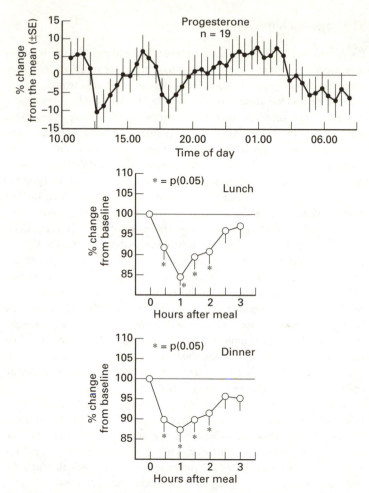

Fig. 8 Progesterone blood levels in relation to food intake. (Source: modified from S.T. Nakajima, T. McAuliffe, and M. Gibson, *Journal of Clinical Endocrinology and Metabolism*, **71** (1990), 345)

reaches the nucleus of a cell, and also the many chemical changes which occur within the cell's nucleus. They have isolated specific hormone receptors, which have the task of transporting a single molecule of their particular hormone through the cell substance and into the nucleus of that cell, where it binds to the DNA. There are special hormone receptors for each natural hormone—for instance, thyroid, insulin, cortisone, testosterone, oestrogen, and progesterone.

In the fifth edition (1994) of *Clinical Gynecologic Endocrinology and Infertility* the authors, Drs Leon Spiroff, Robert Glass, and Nathan Kase, remind us: 'We have entered the age of molecular biology. It won't be long before endocrine problems will be explained, diagnosed and treated at the molecular level. Soon the traditional hormone assays will be a medical practice of the past.' This comment is particularly apt in reference to progesterone. Scientists have isolated and found the complete formulae and molecular weight of many specific hormone receptors, including progesterone receptors.

Progesterone receptors

Progesterone receptors have been isolated in all vertebrate animals, including chimpanzees, pigs, dogs, cats, birds, fish, rodents, snakes, turtles, and frogs. In these animals the functions of progesterone are in brain chemistry, respiration, cerebral metabolism (especially preventing water retention), for cardiac muscles, inner lining of blood vessels, glucose metabolism, gall bladder muscles, ligaments, bone mineral density, gums, hair, and skin. It should be noted that progesterone receptors are not limited to menstruating animals.

In 1981, Jacobs and his team first isolated progesterone receptors in human cells. They have since been reported in most of the body's organs, with the largest concentration in the limbic area of the midbrain, the centre of emotion. This is the area which animal physiologists refer to as the 'area of rage and violence', for it is known that stimulation at this site results in violent behaviour. Other sites where progesterone receptors are found include the vagina, womb, eyes, nasopharyngeal passages, lungs, bones, breasts, liver, and urethra. These are all sites where symptoms of PMS may occur.

It now seems that in PND, postnatal psychosis, and PMS, the fault may lie in the receptivity of progesterone receptors. We now realize that it does not matter how many or how few progesterone molecules are present in the blood. What does matter is how many progesterone molecules reach the nuclei and are metabolized and used there.

The unique characteristics of progesterone receptors are being energetically studied by scientists worldwide. We now know that progesterone receptors will not transport the man-made, artificial progestogens, such as are present in all contraceptive pills (see p. 35). Progesterone receptors will not transport molecules of progesterone in the presence of adrenalin, which means that at times of stress the receptors transport corticosteroids rather than progesterone into the nuclei. Similarly, when there has been a long food gap and cells are short of glucose (sugar), the progesterone receptors transport glucocorticoids back into the cells in preference to progesterone (Fig. 9).

There is a marked similarity in the formula of progesterone receptors, which bind to the DNA at four sites, and that of the glucocorticoid receptors, which transport the glucose molecules and which bind to the DNA at three sites, one of which is a progesterone binding site. This means that in treatment it is of no value to administer progesterone to raise the blood level of progesterone unless one also ensures that there is adequate sugar in the cells. Unfortunately it is not yet possible to test the receptivity of progesterone receptors in the brains of living women.

Recognizing the function of progesterone receptors has helped us to understand why progesterone taken by mouth is not effective. Oral progesterone passes from the intestines to the liver, where there are many progesterone receptors which metabolize the progesterone before it has a chance to reach the systemic circulation and pass to the brain and other organs which require progesterone. Also progesterone does not pass easily through the skin into the blood and so is not suitable for administration by cream or patch.

Cellular action of progesterone

The molecular scientists have also increased our knowledge by showing the biochemical activity of progesterone at cellular level. In 1991, Professor J. Prior of British Columbia University showed how progesterone helps in the building of bones. More important to our subject has been the work of Professor Zuspan and his professorial team at Illinois University, who succeeded in culturing human placental cells and demonstrated that progesterone has an action in inhibiting the build-up of monoamine oxidase. For the last thirty years psychiatrists have been successfully using a group of drugs known as monoamine oxidase inhibitors (MAOIs) for atypical

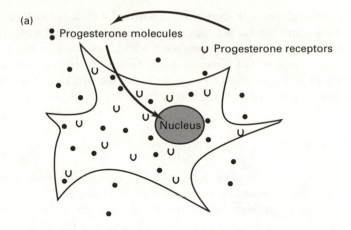

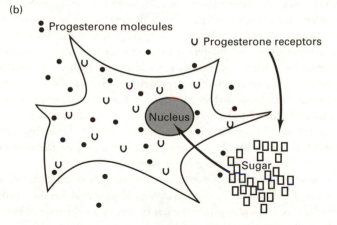

Fig. 9 Action of progesterone receptors: (a) normal conditions: the progesterone receptors transport progesterone molecules to the nucleus; (b) low blood sugar: the progesterone receptors transfer sugar into the cell

depression. Only now is it realized that progesterone can be considered nature's own MAOI or antidepressant.

Other teams working at the cellular level of the brain have isolated one of the neurotransmitters, called serotonin, which is involved in the dopamine pathway dealing with emotion and mood. Serotonin is decreased in platelets, plasma, and whole blood in sufferers of PMS, and in Chapter 14 the similarity between postnatal depression and premenstrual syndrome is discussed. The importance of serotonin is further discussed on page 176 because there now is a group of drugs, known as selective serotonin re-uptake inhibitors (SSRIs), which can rectify this deficiency. They are particularly useful for some sufferers of PND and PMS.

Hormone tests

A frequent request heard by doctors is 'Can I have my hormones tested please, so that I can find out exactly what's wrong with me?'

How one wishes the answer to PNI was as simple as that. If there is a disorder of the blood cells, then a blood test is invaluable. It will tell the exact number, size, and shape of your red cells, white cells, and platelets. If you are anaemic, a blood test will tell you exactly how much iron there is in your blood and how much iron is needed to bring your iron level up to normal. But hormone tests are different, particularly when testing the menstrual and pregnancy hormones. It does not matter how high the progesterone blood level is if there are insufficient progesterone receptors to transport the progesterone molecules to the cells' nuclei. Whereas blood samples measure the total amount of progesterone in the blood, including bound and free progesterone, a salivary test measures only the amount of free progesterone available for immediate use. There are no routine tests for the number or function of progesterone receptors or progesterone molecules.

Whenever a new hormone test is discovered, there is still a considerable amount of work needed at the developmental stage to determine what are the normal values and whether the test is affected by the time of the day, activity, sleep, sex (male or female), age, stress, food, alcohol, exercise, menstrual cycle, and different types of drugs being taken. Also it is important that other biochemists throughout the world are able to repeat the test and get the same results.

Progesterone levels in the blues

In 1976, Dr P.M. Nott and his associates from Oxford took progesterone blood samples every two or three days from healthy women for up to ten weeks following delivery and noted that the greater the progesterone drop, the more likely the women were to rate themselves depressed during the early days, but that they were less likely to complain of insomnia.

In 1994, the *British Medical Journal* published trials by Dr Brian Harris and his team from Cardiff on the levels of salivary progesterone in women who developed postnatal blues. The trials covered one hundred and twenty healthy women pregnant for the first time; they excluded thirty-six women who had a physical illness or required Caesarian section, as well as those who were homeless, those whose relationship with the father was reported as poor or fair, and those with financial difficulties. Salivary samples were used, which are considerably easier to collect than multiple blood samples, and which can be taken by the patient at home without supervision. The women were shown how to collect samples and instructed to collect two samples daily at set times until delivery, three times daily during the next five days, and then twice daily until they received a home visit between thirty-five and forty days after delivery. The samples were kept in the ice box of a fridge or in a deep freeze. The volunteers also completed self-ratings of mood each evening, while pregnant, for the first ten days after delivery, and again at the home visit when the samples were collected. The results showed that the mother's mood in the days after delivery is related to the withdrawal of naturally occurring progesterone. Those who suffered from the blues had higher progesterone levels in late pregnancy and a lower level in the days immediately after delivery, thus confirming that the blues are related to progesterone level.

This is now being repeated with a considerably larger sample in the hopes that some women who develop postnatal depression or psychosis will be included, but the results are still to be published. The blues are at least sixty times more common than postnatal psychosis, so at least ten thousand pregnant volunteers will need to be recruited and more than half a million salivary progesterone estimations will be required from volunteers in a clinical trial before there is definitive proof of the effectiveness of progesterone in the prevention of postnatal psychosis.

Progestogens

There is a vital difference between the natural progesterone and the synthetic compounds known as 'progestogens'. They are not the same, although many people think they are. The natural progesterone about which we have heard so much in this chapter cannot be given by mouth and if given by injection never lasts longer than forty-eight hours; if vaginal or rectal administration is used this needs to be at least twice daily. Certain other natural hormones, such as the insulin given to diabetics, cannot be given orally and frequent injections are needed.

In the 1950s, when scientists were working on an oral contraceptive pill, it was known that oestrogen could be used to prevent ovulation but that progesterone was required to cause menstruation. At that time progesterone could be given only as intramuscular injections, but this method of administration was not generally acceptable. Biochemists set to work to find a tablet which would do much the same as progesterone but could be taken by mouth. They developed several completely new drugs by slightly altering testosterone, the male hormone, and removing its masculinizing effects, and found these drugs to be effective contraceptives which could be given by mouth (Fig. 10). Furthermore, the drugs had the same effect

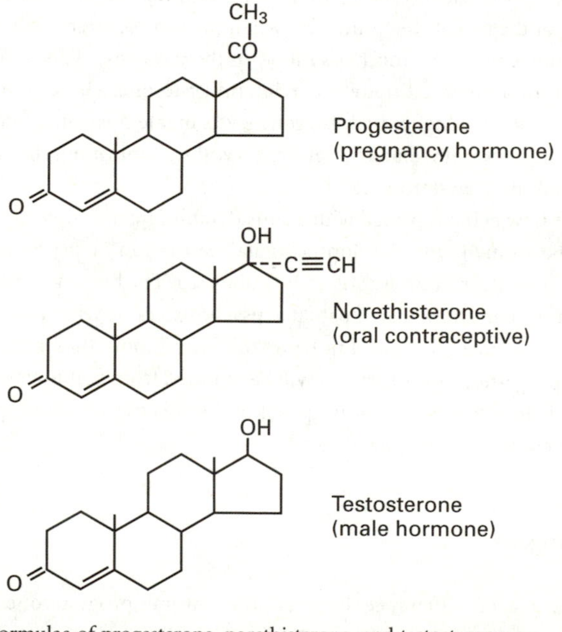

Progesterone
(pregnancy hormone)

Norethisterone
(oral contraceptive)

Testosterone
(male hormone)

Fig. 10 Formulae of progesterone, norethisterone, and testosterone

as natural progesterone, if given with oestrogen for some days and then stopped, of causing vaginal bleeding. They became the basis of the contraceptive pill, taken today by millions worldwide and the basis of a multimillion dollar industry.

As women did not like to be taking testosterone-type drugs, the drugs were given the more feminine-sounding name of 'progestogens' or 'progestins'. Figure 10 shows the formulae of natural progesterone and testosterone together with that of one of the first progestogens called norethisterone. However, the actions of natural progesterone and the artificial progestogens are completely different. Dr E.D.B. Johansson and his colleagues from Uppsala, Sweden, were the first to point out, as long ago as 1971, that norethisterone, and also the other progestogens, lower the progesterone blood level. Figure 11 shows the effect of norethisterone, also known as 'Primulut N', in lowering the progesterone blood level when given during the luteal phase, the days after ovulation until menstruation. This means that women suffering from the effect of the dramatic drop in progesterone after delivery are made worse by taking progestogens or the Pill, and so too are women suffering from progesterone-responsive illnesses, such as sufferers of PMS.

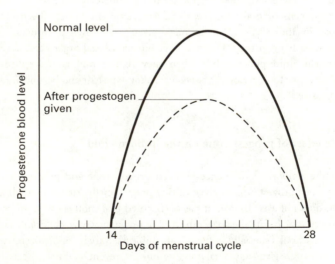

Fig. 11 Effect of progestogen on progesterone blood level

Progestogens in pregnancy

Another important difference between natural progesterone and man-made progestogens is the effect progestogens can have on the unborn child. If progestogens, with their similarity to testosterone, are taken in early pregnancy to prevent a miscarriage, they increase the male characteristics of the foetus. This does not matter so much if the child is a boy—he will become more masculine and muscular. But if the child is a girl, her external genital organs may be so changed that at birth it is difficult to decide the sex of the baby. As a girl she will tend to be a tomboy, and have male hair distribution and other characteristics.

Professor Goy, at the Primate Center at Madison, Wisconsin, has shown on videos the effect of progestogens administered during pregnancy on female offspring of rhesus monkeys. If progestogens are given in high doses to pregnant monkeys, they produce abnormalities in the female offspring's vagina, so that there may be doubts about the sex of the offspring at birth and the offspring may become more masculine and muscular. However, if only a small dose of progestogen is given, the young female monkeys have normal genital organs and develop normally until puberty, when they become unduly aggressive and adopt masculine behaviour and characteristics. These characteristics are increased if they are given progestogens or oral contraceptives. The same effects have been recognized in the offspring of humans given low doses of progestogens during early pregnancy. The girls have normal genital organs and develop normally until puberty, but when they receive oral contraceptives at puberty they too develop excessive masculine-type hair and become unduly aggressive.

The effect of progesterone on the unborn child

Another important difference between progesterone and progestogens is that when progesterone is given during pregnancy the risk of masculinization does not arise. Indeed it has been noted that mothers who are given progesterone before the sixteenth week of pregnancy have children who do well at school, especially in the science subjects. Surveys of children whose mothers were given antenatal progesterone to prevent habitual miscarriages or for excessive morning sickness have shown an educational enhancement at 9–10 years, at 'O' levels (the forerunners of the present GCSEs), and at 'A' levels, as well as at university entrance.

One study of thirty-four 'progesterone children' born in 1958–61 at the City of London Maternity Hospital showed that 32 per cent gained university admission compared with 6 per cent of control children. At that time 6 per cent was also the average for university admission in the borough in which most of the children lived and for the Inner London Education Authority, and was also the national average (Fig. 12). This work by Dr K. Dalton was awarded a BMA Prize in 1967. The benefit of progesterone was greatest if given before the sixteenth week of pregnancy, for at least eight weeks, and in high dosage.

Because of the many problems associated with testing progesterone blood levels in individual patients and the difficulty of administering progesterone, too many doctors take the easy line of prescribing either oestrogen or progestogens instead. But both these drugs have a completely different function and the result is quite different from that produced by natural progesterone.

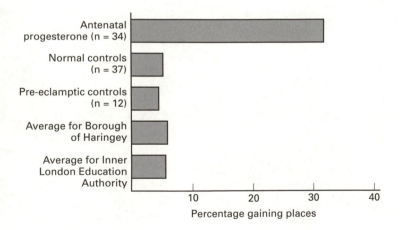

Fig. 12 'Progesterone children' and controls gaining university places, 1975/6. (Source: information from K. Dalton, *British Journal of Psychiatry*, **129** (1976), 438–42; figure from K. Dalton and D. Holton, *PMS: The Essential Guide to Treatment Options* (London, 1994), 155)

This chapter has emphasized the changes which occur in normal healthy women during and after pregnancy. Too often specialists looking after women during pregnancy are not those who care for them once the baby has arrived. So PNI is too often neglected or missed. The next chapters describe the many different presentations of PNI from the mild to the horrifyingly severe. But today there is an answer. By avoiding the sudden drop in progesterone which occurs when the placenta comes away, PND can be prevented.

CHAPTER 4

The blues

In the days when mothers stayed in hospital for a few days after delivery of their babies, the postnatal ward was referred to as the 'weeping ward' (in contrast to the antenatal ward, which is invariably a happy ward) and tales like that of Eileen's, which follows, were commonplace. Such events still occur today, but with the discharge of the mother within hours of the birth it is now only the father and relatives who appreciate the character change of the new mum.

Eileen was a telephone operator with an infectious laugh, guaranteed to keep the office happy, so not surprisingly when she left for her maternity leave she was showered with gifts of Babygros, baby powders, and lotions. She planned her nursery with care and was fully prepared for the greatest day in her life. The arrival of blue-eyed Adrian with a mop of black hair was witnessed by her husband Bill, a radio mechanic, who was normally squeamish at the sight of blood. This time it was different. They hugged, kissed, and congratulated each other on their big success, all 3 kilos (7 pounds) of him, during his first hour of life. The following evening the visiting hour was spent writing out the announcement cards, 'a bundle of Love has arrived', with more kisses and cuddles. But when Bill arrived on the third evening, clutching a bunch of red roses from their garden, Eileen had changed. Her face was no longer wreathed in smiles, but instead the tears had washed away the carefully applied mascara. She cried at the sight of the flowers and, when that was over, there was another five minutes of crying as he proudly showed his letter of appointment for his new job. Then she grumbled about the food, the nurses, the other patients, the postman, and even the diminutive paper-boy who had come too early. Dutifully and lovingly Bill listened, encouraged, sympathized, and helped her over the day's trivialities. Within two days she was herself again, the brief episodes of tears had passed, and she was ready for discharge and for the start of a new life at home on the eighth day.

There is nothing unusual or different about this story. Eileen, like at least half the other women in her ward, was suffering from the 'blues', a transient, self-limiting emotional upset which occurs during the days immediately following a birth.

Other names

The blues by any other name are just the same. They have always been well recognized by midwives, who have referred to them as 'baby', 'childbirth', 'puerperal', or 'postnatal' blues. Sometimes they are named as a reminder of the day of onset, such as 'three-', 'four-', or 'five-day blues', while others refer to them as the 'ten-day weepies', which represents how long this emotional upheaval usually lasts. In the nineteenth century they were known as 'milk fever', because they occurred during those days when milk was appearing in the breasts in quantity.

The characteristic crying

Crying is the most characteristic symptom of the blues. A new mother may start sobbing when she should be smiling joyously, or she might have an unexpected flood of tears, perhaps lasting less than five minutes, but maybe continuing for hours on end. Sometimes she successfully controls the tears and is merely constantly sniffing. Crying is babyish, and the new mother is regarded as mature. She is ashamed of herself and later she is apologetic for having appeared in public with tears running down her face. Worst of all is if her other children find her crying, for children know that mothers do not cry. In some instances, in addition to the tears, there are rapid mood changes from hearty laughter to uncontrolled sobbing.

The blues occur equally among women in hospital and those delivered at home, although mothers often say it is easier to hide the tears at home, and somehow the shame of crying in front of a ward full of other mothers is much worse. Also, like PND, which is dealt with in the next chapter, the blues occur equally in all cultures and are not related to social class, marital status, economic conditions, obstetric difficulties, or stressful life events. One wit of a husband suggested that the social services should be asked to provide professional shoulders for crying on! It is the few mothers who are still having crying episodes after ten days who are most likely to develop PND and to be in need of help.

Frequency of crying

In 1968, a team of four psychiatrists from Stamford Medical School, led by Dr Irvin D. Yalom, studied a group of thirty-nine women both before delivery and for the first ten days after birth. They found that two-thirds had episodes of crying lasting at least five minutes during those first ten days after birth, while five women cried continuously for more than two hours. Figure 13 shows the days on which the episodes of crying occurred: there was little difference during the first eight days and then a slight reduction. When this was compared with the ten-day period studied during pregnancy, the episodes of crying after birth were three times more frequent than those during pregnancy. Furthermore, during pregnancy the tears rarely lasted longer than five minutes.

Dr P.M. Nott and a team from Oxford studied healthy pregnant women and took blood samples to test the progesterone and oestrogen levels every two to three days for up to ten weeks after the birth. They noticed that the more the progesterone blood level dropped after delivery, the

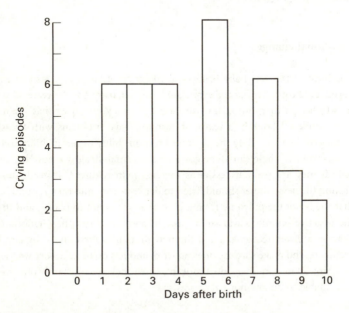

Fig. 13 Crying episodes in thirty-nine women after childbirth

more likely the subjects were to rate themselves as depressed, but they were less likely to report sleep disturbances. Their results in respect of progesterone were later to be confirmed by Dr Brian Harris and his Cardiff team (see p. 35).

Tears of emotion

The tears are those of emotion, not sadness. They are like the emotional tears often shed by the mother of the bride at her daughter's wedding. Psychiatrists who have studied the blues have noticed the great variety of reasons that mothers give for crying: when they read the birth announcement; when they received too much or too little attention from the nurses; when one of their room-mates left hospital; if they had insufficient milk; the ugliness of their baby; a sarcastic remark; relief that the long-awaited labour was over; perhaps they considered themselves a failure or had taken on more than they could cope with. Moreover, they were always oversensitive to minor rebuffs.

Emotional changes

The birth of the new baby brings out many emotions, both positive and negative. The mother may be very elated, excited, happy, with greater closeness to her partner, but at the same time she may feel upset that she did not complete labour in a textbook fashion, have problems with breast-feeding, or be worried by the increased responsibility or her inability to be a 'supermum'. These can all be considered normal, healthy emotions, and only if they are really excessive is medical help required. Instead, those around the new mother should listen to her concerns, and then remind her that she is not the only one feeling blue, that she is not to blame, and that the negative emotions will soon pass. In some cultures these emotional changes are well recognized and the new mother is surrounded by family members who make sure she does no work and has no unnecessary worries. In China all new mothers 'do a month', when they are constantly observed and unable to do any normal chores.

The nurse's view

Frances, an ex-nurse from Surrey, who described herself as a 'thoroughly normal mother and housewife', wrote:

> The most distressing thing about puerperal blues is the way one is treated in hospital while suffering from the blues. I felt like a naughty child who'd misbe-haved and must be chided or ignored until I behaved better, or worse still, was jollied/bullied along in the 'get-up-and-forget-about-it' attitude. The treatment of new mothers in many hospitals leaves much to be desired anyway, though I do remember that when I was nursing they were among my least favourite patients as they weren't really ill.

If the nurses are young they are often embarrassed by the floods of tears from mothers who are older than they are. In a hospital ward tears are infectious. The nurses in the postnatal ward may tell you that, if they happen to drop a cup or saucer, the whole ward will start crying in unison within a few minutes of the crash; or if one husband is as much as five minutes late at visiting time, all the mothers will react in sympathy. They may be exaggerating slightly, but there is more than an element of truth in such anecdotes.

Another difficulty for the new mother is that the nurses on the postnatal wards are not necessarily the same ones she had come to know so well on her frequent antenatal clinic visits. The bond that formed when the happy, carefree, mother-to-be joked with the nurses during those months of ante-natal examinations is broken abruptly when the mother is admitted to the postnatal ward with her baby. Now in her emotional state she is called upon to establish new relationships with a fresh set of nurses and this can produce special problems for the mother.

Other symptoms

Other symptoms of the blues which may occur during these immediate postnatal days are fatigue, poor concentration, slowness to learn (particu-larly such skills as bathing and feeding the baby), as well as confusion, anxiety (especially over the baby), and hostility directed towards the father. One mother referred to it as 'a fit of the fed-ups which goes before it comes'. I remember my mother saying that during those first few days a baby is a full-time job. But these are all transient conditions which have disappeared by the tenth day or by the time the midwife stops her home visits.

Sometimes the baby is a source of anxiety: the crying disturbs the new mother and feeding difficulties may assume unreasonable proportions. Those who have already decided not to breastfeed may be unduly disturbed by the milk continuing to come and causing breast pains. In the past, oestrogens or bromocriptine were used to halt the unwanted breast milk, but now that the side-effects of these medications are better understood the new mother is encouraged to let it settle naturally.

The mother may be upset on realizing that the blotchy, red-faced newborn is very different from the ones seen in photographs, or she may be disturbed by the excessive interest and cooing over the baby when visitors come.

Women who usually suffer from migraine or asthma are often freed from these problems during the last few months of pregnancy but, alas, they may return with a vengeance during the third to seventh day after childbirth. Dr George Stein and five colleagues in London and Hamburg studied a hundred normal mothers during the first seven days after birth and noted that thirty-three complained of headaches. The headaches were particularly common among those with a previous or family history of migraine or PMS, and those who had already had more than one child.

The majority of women suffering from the blues will find their predicament soon vanishes and their problems are solved. But careful observation and follow-up is necessary for the unfortunate few whose crying continues after the first two weeks, for they may gradually develop other symptoms of PND. This is dealt with in the next chapter. Guidance about the help others can give and further advice on the handling of those with the blues are to be found in Chapter 21.

CHAPTER 5

Black depression

The term 'postnatal depression' is used by many different people in numerous ways to cover the whole spectrum of problems from blues to psychosis. Throughout the book I will be using the definition of PND already outlined in Chapter 1 (see Box on p. 3).

This definition excludes the blues, which last only about two weeks and do not require medical treatment. It also excludes the condition of those who have previously needed psychiatric treatment—this means those who have previously had a breakdown and needed medication for depression, schizophrenia, manic depression, drug abuse or alcoholism, or any other psychiatric illness. It should be noted that the definition does not specifically require depression, but covers any psychiatric symptom, which might include exhaustion (Chapter 6), irritability (Chapter 7), as well as the severe symptoms of psychosis (Chapter 9), and infanticide or homicide (Chapter 10). Of course women who have previously had a breakdown can suffer from PND, but it is easier for doctors to have a restrictive definition when trying to study and identify the exact cause, symptoms, and ideal treatment.

Postnatal depression

is the first occurrence of psychiatric symptoms, severe enough to require medical help, occurring after childbirth and before the return of menstruation.

In those who have had a previous psychiatric breakdown, an illness experienced after childbirth may be either a recurrence of their previous illness or the result of the abrupt hormonal changes of childbirth, and it is up to the doctor to decide the probable cause or causes for each individual woman, for there may well be more than one causative factor.

In some research studies the definition of PND is limited to six months after childbirth, which is more restrictive than the legal definition given in the Infanticide Act of 1939, which allows twelve months for the mother to recover from the effects of giving birth. The advantage of limiting it to six months lies in a better ability to analyse the common characteristics shared by this group of women. It seems likely that these women are particularly prone to develop a psychiatric illness at times when their hormone levels are abruptly changed at the end of pregnancy, on stopping breastfeeding, on starting oral contraception, and on the resumption of menstruation.

Depression, an emotion of sadness

Depression can be a healthy emotion of sadness or a sickness. It is a normal physiological emotion which all healthy, normal people experience in the course of their lives. If we learn that one of our family has been killed in a road accident or that a friend's house has been burnt down, we would naturally feel depressed, sad, and unhappy, but we would not necessarily be ill or suffering from the loss of any abilities or function. We would not need treatment with antidepressants, although counselling may well help.

Depressive illness

Depression is also the name given to an illness which occurs in men, women, and children at all ages. It is characterized by gloom, despondency, and despair. Depression has been described as a 'disease of loss', and indeed it really is so, for there is loss of happiness, pleasure, interest, and enthusiasm, as well as the loss of the ability to concentrate, to remember, and to think clearly, and also the loss of bodily functions such as sleep, appetite, weight control, and bowel movement (Fig. 14).

Sometimes depression is divided into two types of illness: it is called 'reactive' if it is the result of an obvious cause of sadness, such as bereavement, redundancy, or divorce, and 'endogenous' when it occurs for no apparent reason. But, despite this differentiation, both types may require the same methods of treatment—antidepressants, psychotherapy, or counselling.

The medical fraternity appreciate the confusion caused by the word 'depression' and sometimes prefer to talk about a 'depressive illness'

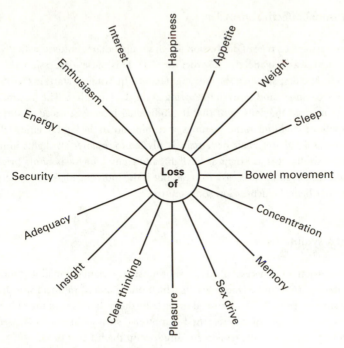

Fig. 14 Depression is a disease of loss

instead. Until the early part of the twentieth century doctors used the word 'melancholia' to describe a depressive illness. Psychiatrists also recognize that, while most sufferers of depression have all the typical symptoms of loss shown in Fig. 14, there is also a smaller group of sufferers whose depression is quite different; this is called 'atypical depression', meaning 'not typical'. This is an important distinction, as we will see later, because the commonly prescribed antidepressant drugs are effective for typical depression, but other drugs are more effective for the treatment of atypical depression, which includes PND (Chapter 15).

Women in certain cultures regard the use of the word 'depression' as an insult. It is rather like referring to someone as a slut or lazy or dirty—so the word is best avoided. If necessary, it is better to speak of a depressive illness or melancholia.

Seasonal affective disorder

One recognized type of depression which should not be confused with PND is called 'seasonal affective disorder' or SAD. This causes depression, desolation, and despair when the long nights come. In Britain it starts in October and November, and eases in the spring as the days lengthen. The treatment is to increase the daily light that the individual receives. Instead of sitting in subdued lighting in the evenings or turning down the light to enjoy television, the sufferer, male or female, is advised to brighten the lights in the home so that it is as bright as daylight, and enjoy four to six hours bright light each evening. It is easy to treat, but if the individual has a few nights of poor light the depression soon returns.

First symptoms

Depression is not necessarily the first or most important complaint of those suffering from PND. One study in which one hundred mothers who had all suffered from PND were asked to describe the earliest days of their illness revealed a variety of different first symptoms, such as insomnia, anxiety, and agitation, with depression coming low on the list (see Box).

These first symptoms frequently started within hours or days of the birth, and then increased in severity, with other new complaints being added over the next few weeks. In other cases the illness started gradually, and it was only when a listening health visitor or doctor heard the full story and diagnosed PND that the mother appreciated that, although she was not crying all the time, her intolerable panics and impatience could be PND.

One midwife, who had herself suffered, explained:

> People with postnatal depression haven't a clue that they're suffering from it, whereas with normal depression you jolly well know you're ill and suffering depression.

Sleep

Sleep is often different after childbirth, which is partly due to the mother's natural instinct to listen out for her baby's cry and be ever ready to sooth

---

First symptoms of postnatal depression or psychosis

Selective hearing and anxiety

Insomnia

Agitation

Irritability

Confusion

Rejection of the baby

Delusions

Hallucinations

Feelings of unreality

Depression

Suicidal thoughts

Changed personality

---

and calm her baby. There are instances when a mother can go to sleep in spite of noisy surroundings—living in a busy road or with the television blaring out—but is awake immediately if the baby so much as whimpers or chatters quietly. The mother has developed selective hearing, cutting out unimportant noises but consciously listening for what matters to her most—her baby.

In typical depression the patient has difficulty in sleeping. He or she may get off to sleep easily but then, characteristically, wakes in the early morning between 3 a.m. and 5 a.m., and either lies awake in utter despair or may get up, walk about the house, make a cup of tea, or start reading until it is time to get up. On the other hand, women with PND may also wake up during the night, despite a yearning for sleep. They don't get up at night unless it is to help the baby, and they would rather stay in bed forever; they can sleep throughout the morning, and indeed any time of the day.

The early mornings are usually the worst time of the day for those with typical depression, and then they improve as the day goes on. By contrast, women with PND are often at their best in the morning, but the depression and inability to cope with the routine work come on during the day. They feel worse in the evenings and want to go to bed early.

Increased appetite

Typical depression is characterized by a loss of appetite with a revulsion to food, which in turn leads to loss of weight, often 5–12 kilos (or 1 or 2 stones) in a matter of months. This is such a common finding that in treating depression the doctor will gauge the success or failure of treatment by the amount of weight the patient has gained. With PND the problem is different. The sufferer's appetite is increased and she is always thirsty, continually tucking into fattening foods and drinking mugs of tea or coffee to while away her hours of solitude. She often has odd cravings, gorging on bars of chocolate, stacks of toast and honey, or piles of doughnuts or sticky buns, A Canadian mother described

> . . . the solitude [sic] of my friends and relations over my quaint eating habits. There is complete disinterest in foods at certain times but binges invariably follow. I wake up at night hungry and grab whatever is in sight. I hide fudge about the house so that I know where to find it when it's needed. I can't help gorging it even when I'm ready to burst.

The result of this increased appetite is that sufferers of PND rapidly gain weight. Within a month or two they may be heavier than when their final weight was taken at the clinic a day or two before the baby was born. This is known as 'maternal obesity', with the fat centred especially around the abdomen, but with thin ankles and wrists. Some women refer to this increasing girth as 'bloatedness' or 'water retention', but this fluid retention is true fat or adiposity. One woman described how 'nowadays I feel like a waterlogged hag—like death warmed up'.

Failure to appreciate that this abnormal appetite and weight gain are part of PND may be another cause of marital disharmony, for there is always the thoughtless husband who declares bluntly: 'I don't like fat women.'

The increased weight brings with it an urge to diet, which too often means going long intervals without food so that the blood sugar drops. As described on page 33 this leads to an adrenalin surge and water retention. Asking sufferers to detail the time and type of food eaten on the day before the first consultation has revealed that most sufferers have missed meals and have long food gaps, which cause unnecessary symptoms.

Unnecessary breast milk

One physical sign, which is not always present, but which, if seen, is positively diagnostic of PND, is the presence of milk in the breasts several months after breastfeeding has finished. This does not occur in typical depression. Such milk in the breast is called 'galactorrhoea' or 'inappropriate lactation'. One mother of a 4-year-old daughter asked: 'What about the milk which is still oozing out of my breasts?'

Galactorrhoea occurs when there is too much of one of the pituitary hormones called 'prolactin'. One of the many functions of prolactin is to prepare the breasts for lactation during pregnancy; another is to respond to the baby's sucking at the breast to stimulate milk production. So in pregnancy and during breastfeeding there is a high level of prolactin in the blood. But when breastfeeding stops this should diminish and return to the level of a non-pregnant woman. A blood test can show if a woman has a high level of prolactin in the blood, even though she is not breastfeeding. Treatment is with the drug bromocriptine (see p. 136). A high prolactin level may also occur when a patient is taking certain antidepressant drugs, but in this case it does not matter. Some over-anxious women like to ensure that their breasts are returning to normal after stopping breastfeeding, and test the breasts each night by squeezing the nipples. This may be misinterpreted by the body as continual breastfeeding and prolactin will continue.

An atypical depression

By now it is hoped that the reader will appreciate that PND is not the same as typical depression, but is a special type of depression which needs special treatment. Irritability is a marked feature of PND, but is not necessarily present in typical depression (see Chapter 7). The most common components of PND are shown in Fig. 15.

Of course it is always possible for a woman who has previously had a typical depressive illness when not pregnant to become ill again after the birth of a baby. It is then up to the doctor to decide whether she has more characteristics of a typical or an atypical depression, for the choice of treatment will depend on the type of depression. Many symptoms are common to both types.

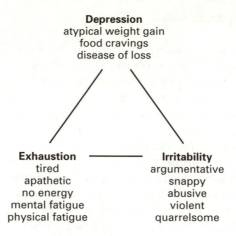

Fig. 15 Components of postnatal depression

Loss of confidence

The loss of confidence which occurs in depression is noticed by those who were previously leaders in their spheres and were extroverts. Olive, a science teacher, explained:

> I have completely lost all my confidence in looking after my baby, and of course I could not breastfeed her, which really upset me. I don't seem to cook so well and am frightened of trying out any new recipes. I dare not attempt dress-making any more for fear that I will spoil the material by cutting it out wrongly, yet I have been dressmaking for ten years.

The loss of confidence brings with it a desire to withdraw from one's surroundings, to become detached, to avoid socializing and making contact with other people. Doctors are used to hearing phrases like 'all I want to do is to run away and hide myself in a corner'. An accountant living in Cornwall wrote:

> I have managed not to let it interfere with my life too much, although it has affected my social life. I used to be the secretary of the local bridge club and Women's Institute and was responsible for arranging meetings. Now I avoid

mixing socially and I know this has made me difficult to live with. Everyone thinks it's because I have a babysitting problem, but really it is that I don't want to see anyone any more.

Crying

When the crying continues after the first two weeks it should no longer be considered to be due to the blues but rather a symptom of PND which will benefit from treatment. This includes the new mother who wrote:

> I can't relieve the feeling of sadness. Every item in the newspaper seems to be a sob story and starts me off weeping.

Mary was at the end of her tether when she wrote:

> Everything is closing in on me. No one understands. Mine are tears of anger. I break down into floods of tears in the streets, shops, and other inconvenient places. I feel I have tried everything and am afraid I shall get to the point where I will give up trying and succumb to my violent tendencies, either towards myself or someone else.

Nina, whose baby was by then nine months, showed a mixture of depression, irritability, and physical symptoms when she wrote:

> Suddenly I feel heavy depressions. I'm irritated with my husband and children. I start looking for quarrels; several times I feel hopeless, start weeping on my own, gasping for breath and wish myself dead. Then I'm afraid to be alive. I desire to be dead and start to think how it is possible to die (often I have suicidal feelings). Often I have headaches and pain in the back, particularly when I'm reading, thinking or studying. During the depressions I dislike women and I'm irritated by little things. When these feelings go on for a day and sometimes more days, I'm afraid to meet other people, e.g. the people in my husband's office. Afterwards I do not understand my own behaviour.

Anxiety

Anxiety is another symptom which may occur for the first time after childbirth. It does not seem to occur in those who describe themselves as 'born worriers' but rather in those with a previous reputation for calmness and placidness. Suddenly they start worrying about everything. First the baby. Is the food right? Is the milk too hot? Should the nappy be changed? Is the growth normal? Then gradually the worries spill over to concern for the father, the home, and the family.

It is too easy to forget that the body took nine full months for the pregnancy and then to expect that the return to normal should occur overnight—it doesn't. The new mother may describe panic attacks when she is suddenly overwhelmed with fear, her heart starts to beat rapidly, she shakes, her mouth is parched, and she is sure that death is imminent—but somehow she recovers. After each panic attack she restricts her activities further, fearful of doing anything which might precipitate another terrifying panic attack. Sometimes the panics occur when there is a slight irregularity of heartbeat or an extra beat. There is no cardiac abnormality, it is just the heart returning to its pre-pregnant state (see p. 23).

It is not surprising that many new mothers end up by being frightened of themselves and of their own actions, for they cannot understand what is going on within them. They are frightened of taking their own lives, frightened of going out shopping, frightened of hurting the baby, of dropping him or drowning him in the bath, frightened of their own company, and of being alone. They will not let their partners out of their sight. The young mother will cry when the father attempts to go to work in the morning, and if he succeeds she will phone him and call him home from work. After a while it is only the most patient of employers who can put up with the employee's continual absences. Penny, a mother in this type of predicament, pleaded:

> I don't know what will happen if someone doesn't help me soon. I'm seriously afraid I will lose my husband, he will lose his job. I will wreck the car and damage the children's lives for ever. I am not fit to live with.

Loss of concentration

Even the simplest of household tasks requires concentration, but no one realizes it until the power of concentration is lost. The mother may forget to turn off the oven, to put tea in the pot, to return the phone to its place, to shut the front door, or to remember to take money and keys with her when she goes out. These everyday tasks, which have been accomplished with ease for years, suddenly become mountainous.

The mental confusion poses a problem and makes women frightened of going out, afraid that they will hand out the wrong fares on the buses or absent-mindedly walk out of a shop without paying. In an effort to avoid others noticing their confusion they will rush into a shop, pick up the nearest article, pay for it, and hurry out. Only later do they realize that it is the wrong size, that they have bought too little or too much, or that it is suitable only for cats and dogs and not babies.

A Nigerian mother of two children was found guilty of shoplifting only ten days after having had a Caesarean operation to deliver her baby. It seems she picked up three baby's dresses but paid only for two. One cannot help wondering why a new mother was allowed out shopping alone so soon after a major operation. More importantly, one could ask: 'Was there a woman magistrate on the bench, and had she ever had children?'

Women are all different. They differ genetically; they have also had different childhood experiences and environments, come from different social classes and educational backgrounds, and live in all parts of the world. Women throughout the world can suffer from PND, but it is not surprising that the way they are affected by this 'disease of loss' will vary, some putting greater stress on some losses than others. The descriptions they give of their lowered moods vary, including such statements as:

> A feeling of being detached from everyone and everything around me.
> It's like living in a bubble. I'm near things yet far away.
> It's a cosmic melancholy.
> A strange nastiness over everything and everywhere.

A physical illness

The very word 'depression' inevitably causes confusion, for it suggests that the problem is all in the mind, whereas to the sufferers it is all in the body. They feel physically ill, and are indeed ill; they are sure that theirs must be a real illness which will readily show up in blood tests or X-rays. It is an illness caused by a biochemical abnormality which affects the working of the brain and body, for the biochemical abnormality in the blood permeates all the tissues of the body. In PND it is usual to hear such expressions as:

I ache all over.
There's a continual aching in my muscles and bones.
I'm tender all over, especially in my breasts. I bruise easily and feel generally out of sorts.
It's like never-ending flu.

This is how one young mother described her experiences:

> When I'm depressed I can't sleep enough at night, so I feel I could sleep all day. Really exhausted, very weepy and can't stop crying, can't think straight, nothing goes right, and I'm really terribly irritable and short tempered. I feel I will never get better, everything is in a hopeless mess. I feel very sick and sometimes retch and feel queasy. Don't want to have anything to do or think about, just no energy for this. I get very hot spells at times and feel faint. I hurt everywhere and cannot cope, but all the tests and examinations by my good old family Doc, I am told, are quite alright. So I must be normal.

Dizziness, or vertigo, is another common symptom which makes mothers think they are really physically ill, as suggested by this extract from Janet's letter:

> Suddenly the swimming starts, with the entire room going round. I somehow lose my equilibrium. I hold my head and keep quite still. I never mention this to anyone as I'm terrified I have a brain tumour or something else horrible.

Broken relationships

It is now some thirty years since Relate counsellors recognized that of all the medical causes of marital and relationship breakdowns PND tops the list. It is not just PND, but the illness which goes on for twenty or more years, gradually becoming PMS. How often do counsellors hear at the first interview the statement 'She's never been the same since the baby was born.' When there is a possibility that the disharmony stemmed from the birth of a child, then a full medical interview is needed to exclude the possibility of PND or PMS, as specific treatment rather than further sessions with the counsellor is more likely to heal the rift

Approaching a doctor

Doctors recognize that women rarely come along to the surgery saying they are depressed, but it is possible to get round the problem by careful questioning. They may ask 'Are you as happy as you used to be?' or, more vaguely, 'How's life—are you enjoying things?' These are good opportunities for the young mother to open up and discuss her problems, how the black cloud hangs over her life, how everything is getting on top of her, how difficult it is to cope with the new baby, as well as the housework, shopping, and husband. Or they may ask if they are lonely, allowing young mothers to talk about the difficulties of socializing, getting on with others, getting confused, and saying the wrong things. Or sometimes the more pointed question is asked: 'Have you changed since having the baby?'

All too often the mother feels vaguely different but does not quite know what has happened nor realize she is ill, and is far too unsure of herself to ask for help directly. All she knows is that she behaves differently now compared with the days before her pregnancy. Twenty-nine-year-old Kathleen was in this predicament and told me how she had been to the doctor's surgery on four occasions to ask for help, but somehow had failed. First she asked about the scaling on her baby's scalp, accepted a prescription, and left before realizing that she had not got down to the real problem. A week or two later she went to the health centre and mentioned her cough. Her chest was examined and she was assured that all was well. She tried a more direct approach on her next visit and spoke about her tiredness and desire to sleep all day. She was given the necessary form to take to the local hospital for a blood test. The following week she was told her blood test was 100 per cent—wasn't she lucky? She was not anaemic and would not need to take any more iron tablets. It was nearly a month later, with her son now nine months old, that she burst into tears and flew off the handle because the receptionist had muddled up her appointment. Finally her tears got her message over to the doctor. Roused to anger, Kathleen was able to explain how her whole life had changed; she had lost her *joie de vivre*, felt inadequate and hopeless, and could not make decisions. She confessed: 'I'm a Christian woman and am ashamed of my behaviour. I can't understand what's happening to me.' There had indeed been a change in Kathleen. She had been personal assistant to a company director, one of the jet set, and it had been her task to organize and coordinate arrangements for his international tours. The tours, hotels, tickets, and flights had always been planned flawlessly. Now she found she could not even organize her own life, let alone anyone else's.

In 1964, Dr Stuart Carne, a London general practitioner, spoke at the Royal Society of Medicine about the recognition of depression in a mother who brought a baby with persistent vomiting, for which no cause could be found. The baby was reacting to the mother's tension and bringing up a little milk during or immediately after a feed. Often if the baby is fed by someone else, the infant will no longer bring back the milk. By treatment of the mother's depression the baby's vomiting was stopped.

Many attempts have been made to try to pick up some of the many 'lost' or undiagnosed cases of PND. A simple blood test, alas, will not show PND, neither will X-rays, brain scans, or other diagnostic machines. The usual psychiatric, psychological, or sociological questionnaires, much loved as a tool for diagnosing depression, again draw a blank in the diagnosis of PND. As shown in this chapter, PND is atypical depression and does not conform to the parameters required for these.

Edinburgh Postnatal Depression Scale

In 1987, workers in Edinburgh, led by Professor John Cox, Dr Sagovsky, and Jennifer Holden, constructed a simple questionnaire to assist in diagnosing PND. This has become known as the Edinburgh Postnatal Depression Scale (EPDS) and is used by health visitors and others involved in the care of newly delivered mothers. Not only is this now used in most of Britain automatically at a set time postpartum, but it is also used throughout the world and has been translated into sixteen different languages. It is an excellent tool for all those health care workers who come into contact with new mothers. Its advent has certainly aided identification and therefore help to many thousands of sufferers of PND.

The EPDS is simple to complete—there are just ten statements, each with four choices of answer. It is best done alone, without another person present; when completed the nurse or health visitor is able to quickly score the questionnaire to note whether the mother is suffering from PND. Unfortunately it is usually only undertaken once, commonly around the six-week mark, and so will only be an effective guide to the mother's state at that time. But, as we have said earlier, PND can occur at any time in the first year following childbirth. According to the correspondence we have received, the majority did not feel their PND started until three months after childbirth. All these cases of PND would have been lost with an EPDS undertaken at six weeks.

Some midwives in Hereford (and no doubt other parts of Britain) are now using the EPDS in late pregnancy so that they have a 'standard' for that mother that can be compared with the later EPDS score taken in the puerperium.

In its effort to be simple, easily understood, and completed by the mother alone without outside help, the EPDS is limited to depressive symptoms and does not enquire about the endless exhaustion, irrational irritability, loss of libido, psychosis, or infanticide and homicide. However, these are all symptoms included in the definition of PND, and are dealt with in turn in Chapters 6–10.

CHAPTER 6

Endless exhaustion

A 46-year-old mother of two teenage sons was heard to declare:

> The traumatic effect of the black miseries and tiredness afterwards is worse
> than labour—the memory of them lasts much longer.

When interviewing new patients and asking them about past pregnancies and whether there was any depression afterwards, a doctor often finds them hesitating, and then awkwardly explaining that they felt awful for several months, exhausted because 'the birth took a lot out of me'. This postnatal exhaustion is really a mild form of PND. It may be self-limiting, lasting only three to six months, or it may herald a recognizable depression with irritability.

The mother feels exhausted and physically ill, with no energy or zest for living, and a desire to hide away and just sit without doing anything. She may excuse herself to her partner in the evening by saying that having a new baby is a full-time job, when in fact she crept back to bed after he went to work, didn't wash the breakfast things until four o'clock, and then sat in the lounge all afternoon lethargically watching television, yet hardly knowing which programme had been on. As one mother explained:

> I can't think, can't work, can't laugh, can't play and just want to sit about all
> day. And I couldn't care less.

Another mother recalled those days by saying:

> I can remember feeling so tired I was sure I was really ill, but my temperature
> was always low—most disappointing.

Under the heading 'I suffered too', the popular television personality Esther Rantzen described her distress after childbirth in the magazine *Women*:

Yes, I'm lucky. A great job, a loving husband, nanny to look after the baby . . . but I was utterly defenceless when it happened to me. For a month it was utter hell. I felt as if I was going insane, I have heard myself shouting at my husband in an unforgivable way and yelling that I must see a doctor, that I was going mad. There were awful attacks of shaking, stumbling and trembling.

I suffered from what I call 'mind slip'. I couldn't concentrate. I could not even dictate letters because I was getting my words mixed up. It was as if I had lost part of myself.

I was one of the lucky ones, though. I managed to get out of it by talking over my feelings with everyone from my husband, friends, and family, to my health visitor, who was wonderful, and a marvellous doctor came round and listened. But all the same I felt guilty about taking up so much professional time.

Tiredness

Tiredness covers both mental fatigue and physical exhaustion. It can be either healthy or unhealthy. There is that satisfying tiredness which follows a hard day's mental activity, the completion of a difficult essay, or a stiff three-hour examination, and that same rewarding tiredness after a hard day's decorating, a strenuous round of golf, or jogging in the park. Then there is unhealthy tiredness, which is not the result of hard work and is present in spite of a good night's sleep. It shows itself as mental apathy and a complete lack of physical energy, together with an emotional flatness which reveals itself by the absence of highs and of laughter and an inability to express happiness or pleasure.

Unhealthy tiredness

Unhealthy tiredness, or exhaustion, is the type of tiredness which characterizes PND. Healthy tiredness is soon disposed of with relaxation, whereas all the sleep in the world will not ease the unhealthy variety.

Gail, a graduate laboratory worker until her pregnancy, described unhealthy tiredness by saying:

I'm dead tired all day. There's no energy for unnecessary exertions like picking up a newspaper from the floor. Before I go into the kitchen I think of all the effort it will entail and almost count the steps there (I live in a two-bedroomed flat). I have to push myself. None of my movements is natural and effortless as they used to be. I don't want anything to do or think about. I just can't be bothered. Even to speak is an effort, it's easier to grunt a reply. It's like being in the half-awake, half-asleep state all day long.

Lethargy is a dominant feature of this exhaustion; all the mother's previous energy seems to have become transferred to the baby at the moment of birth and she is no longer able to respond to the demands of everyday life. A letter-writer described it as 'a flatness which took a mighty long time to clear up'.

A hairdresser, a mere six weeks after her daughter was born, apologized for her behaviour, explaining:

> I've got everything I could wish for—a super husband, home, son and daughter—both wanted and planned; I desperately want to get well again— stop feeling so tired and enjoy it all again. The crux of it is that the energy has given up inside.

That is true postnatal exhaustion. The exhaustion is both mental and physical. A woman suffering from it will have problems in counting her change, doubling the ingredients in the recipe, sorting out the times of trains and buses, and finding suitable dates for her holiday. If she is called upon to help with her older child's homework, she will have the greatest difficulty in concentrating and working out any sums correctly. She will feel generally inadequate.

The pharmacies and health-food stores may rely on postnatal exhaustion to boost their 'over-the-counter' sales of iron and vitamin preparations and those natural remedies 'guaranteed to cure the exhaustion', but few of these are really successful because postnatal exhaustion is caused by a biochemical abnormality.

Problems with coping

The recurring phrase heard from mothers with postnatal exhaustion is 'I can't cope'. This is echoed in Helen's letter:

> Even with ordinary things like cooking, changing a nappy, washing, or preparing a meal, I just can't cope. They are tasks of enormous proportions.

And this upsets me and makes me cry. My daughters used to have a clean dress to wear to school each day, now they just have to make do. I can't be bothered, I can't manage to do the cooking and the ironing as well, it has to wait for my husband at weekends. I just muddle through from day to day as best I can.

This inability to cope is part of the exhaustion and is not related to the woman's previous experiences or abilities. The expression 'I just can't cope any more' is heard from those who were previously highly efficient and well organized as well as from those who were always in a muddle with their affairs. A sister in charge of a premature baby unit in a busy provincial hospital worked for four years caring for the smallest of small babies but found she could not cope when it came to her own healthy baby. A normally energetic, extroverted head of a nursery school, who had been responsible for fifty children under five years of age, found it difficult to care for her only one.

One of Helen's worries was that her daughters had to rely on her husband to do the ironing, and she hated not having the energy to ensure that they were in clean dresses every day for school. But the mother herself may also cease to be bothered about her own appearance, and although she may be aware that her standards have deteriorated, she is quite unable to do anything about it. A mother with a healthy son of four months wrote:

My appearance has gone to pot because I can't seem to be bothered, although I know Tom would like to see the old me. Even my tremendous love for Tom does not seem to prod me into action.

When mothers are recalling the days of exhaustion after the birth, their comments are frequently prefaced by the remark: 'But then mine was a crying baby—he never stopped crying day or night.' There can be little doubt that a ceaselessly crying baby is exhausting. When you have done all the things the books tell you to do to stop the baby crying, and he still persists, it can be most frustrating. But a crying baby may be reacting to the exhausted mother. Only too often a mother hands over her baby to someone else for a few hours, or perhaps overnight, for him to be handed back with the innocent comment 'I haven't heard a squeak from him the whole time.' Was the baby reacting to firmness, confidence, and infinite patience?

Wendy Holton, the co-author of this book, remembers well:

> ... the morning some five or six weeks after delivery when my daughter would not settle and by 10.30 a.m. had become ratty and exhausted. Since my husband left for work at 7.30 a.m. my daughter had been crying and on and off the breast continuously. A friend rang at 10.30 a.m. to chat, and on hearing my despair, said not to worry, she would come round and collect us to take us back to her home for the day to use the 'ten-minute rule'. Shortly after 11.00 a.m. she took the carrycot with my crying daughter up to the top floor of her house, shut all the intervening doors, and said I had to finish my cup of coffee before I went up to see her. Of course I could not hear the baby crying and fifteen minutes later I went to see my daughter sleeping peacefully. My friend and I had an enjoyable day chatting and pottering around her garden. I fed my daughter at 2.00 p.m. when she went straight back to sleep peacefully. Later in the afternoon we collected her young children from school and after tea I returned home, feeling calmer and more relaxed myself, and the baby was now her normal happy self.

A baby quickly senses when the mother is tense and as a result can also become tense and irritable. Use the 'ten-minute rule' when necessary; if you can shut away the crying noise you will relax, and so will the baby.

Social workers, health visitors, and community nurses are taught to keep an eye open for mothers showing early signs of PND, and usually this is not a very difficult exercise. A mother should be suspect if she misses her postnatal appointment or the clinic appointment for her baby's injections. Maybe she is confused and cannot organize herself to get to the clinic on time. A home visit might reveal a very different patient from the carefully made-up, well-presented woman who attended the antenatal clinic. Now she may be dishevelled, with no make-up and no recent signs of her normal smartness. The home may be a bit of a muddle, with the baby's clothes on the floor, a pile of nappies waiting for disposal, and several used cups on the draining board. The visitor may be offered a cup of tea or coffee, and the young mother will happily sit down and drink her fourth mug that morning. She will complain of her need for sleep, even though her head hit the pillow at seven the night before and she did not stir until her partner brought tea at nine that morning. She will excuse her unkempt hair, explaining that she has difficulty in getting out with baby, but in reality her favourite hairdresser used to visit her at home anyway. She needs help, and it is the health visitor's task to organize medical treatment and, if possible, some help until she is able to cope by herself.

Medical causes

Sometimes exhaustion may be due to other causes, and this is another reason for seeking medical help early. In Chapter 2 the many hormonal changes which occur during pregnancy, delivery, and lactation were discussed, and the important part played by the pituitary gland was emphasized. Sometimes during the sudden 'switch-round' of hormones at labour there is insufficient stimulus from the pituitary to the thyroid gland by the chemical messenger called the 'thyroid stimulating hormone' or TSH. TSH passes from the pituitary gland to the thyroid gland (situated at the front of the neck) and tells the thyroid gland to produce its special hormone, thyroxine. The thyroxine controls the speed at which the body works. If there is insufficient thyroxine, the body works slowly; the mother can fall asleep at any time of the day or night, she feels cold, has dry skin, lank hair, which tends to fall out, and a slow pulse. A simple blood test will quickly measure the level of TSH and thyroxine, and tell the doctor whether the thyroid gland is working normally. If there is a deficiency, the treatment will also be simple: it consists of taking one to three tablets of thyroxine daily. Such treatment may not necessarily be a permanent requirement, for frequently, as the body readjusts, the thyroid gland starts functioning normally and the extra thyroxine is no longer required.

Another common reason for the mother to feel exhausted after childbirth is anaemia. If there is a haemorrhage at the time of delivery and not enough iron in the mother's body stores to replenish the blood loss, she may develop anaemia. This also is diagnosed simply by a cheap and easy blood test and, if any anaemia exists, this can be corrected by taking iron supplements.

Excessive exhaustion may also be due to the body's supply of potassium being too low. This can result from a poor diet or from the use of certain diuretic pills which encourage the flow of urine and deplete the body of potassium. Diuretics are sometimes given to overcome bloatedness or water retention. Potassium deficiency can also be recognized by a simple blood test and remedied either by increasing the consumption of potassium-rich foods, especially bananas, tomatoes, and orange juice, or by taking potassium tablets.

The exhaustion is the mildest form of PND. It is seen at the grass roots, and is generally treated by general practitioners rather than by psychiatrists. It is usually self-limiting, being eased before the first six months is over, but occasionally it gets worse and other features of PND develop, especially irritability (see Chapter 7) and loss of interest in sex (Chapter 8). A young shop worker recalled the time after her twins were born:

> I was so flaked out and tired I couldn't rise to anger then—I was far too tired and sleepy, but after a few months I was throwing things and hitting the kids and my husband, I didn't want him anywhere near me then—'Get out', I kept shouting. I'm pleased now he didn't.

Irrational irritability

Everybody gets annoyed and irritated at some time in his or her life; this is a natural outlet for frustration and anger, and any violence that may be involved is directed towards the cause of the irritation. In this chapter, however, we are dealing with an irritation which, when it breaks out into violence, is quite indiscriminate in its object of attack and may be difficult or impossible to control. It is, above all, an irritability which is quite out of keeping with the person's character and all too often ends in violence, both verbal and physical, followed by tears,

Symptoms of irritability

Postnatal irritability may be verbal or violent, and is equally hurtful to the mother and to the recipient of her anger. The abuse may include shouting, screaming, shrieking, yelling, or swearing, while the violence may take the form of banging the table, stamping the feet, slamming the door, throwing items across the room, kicking furniture, hitting animals, children, or the partner. Patients may describe themselves as agitated, jittery, intolerant, snappy, fiery, short-tempered, intolerant, impatient, irrational, spiteful, explosive, fault-finding, aggressive, nagging, bitchy, quarrelsome, or vindictive. They will explain that they 'can't suffer fools gladly' and insist that they 'try not to shout at the children'. Invariably they end up emphasizing that this change in character has only occurred or markedly increased since the baby's birth.

A distraught mother described the change in her daughter Susan, who had previously been the head of the Art Department at the school:

> The destructive urge is not limited to self-destruction but includes others, such as her husband and children and also material things like throwing the iron, the saucepan, or even the sewing machine across the room. It includes attempts at arson—setting alight her own home, her favourite books, and her love-letters.

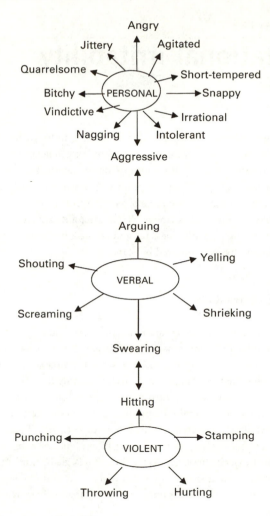

Fig. 16 Symptoms of irritability

Similarity to premenstrual syndrome (PMS)

Irritability is an important diagnostic symptom of PND. The irritability just
described is quite different from that associated with typical depression (as

discussed in Chapter 5) and responds to a quite different treatment. An important aspect is its similarity to the irritability of PMS. PMS is characterized by the triple symptoms of tiredness, depression, and irritability; these combine to make the 'tension' of premenstrual tension and are the most common symptoms of PMS. Premenstrual tension and syndrome are of hormonal origin and can be treated successfully with progesterone, as is further discussed in Chapters 14 and 15. Calmness can also be restored by treatment with progesterone in both PND and PMS (see Chapter 16).

Late onset

Postnatal irritability does not necessarily start immediately after birth, but develops and increases over the next few months, gradually masking the importance of the black depression and endless exhaustion. The irritability itself is variable in intensity in each individual and may show itself as a complete and thoroughly destructive outburst, but whatever the intensity it is not under the patient's power to control it completely. Valerie, a twenty-year-old mother, wrote:

> I am as ratty and quarrelsome as ever, ranging from petty squabbles to the occasional outbursts which affect our home for days. I really do feel guilty about this but it never helps to control my temper. Nothing gets done in the house and my bookwork suffers and I can't concentrate and get confused. I hide myself away in shame, convinced that every other woman in the world is coping splendidly.

A more violent outbreak was described by Tina, whose twins were then fourteen months old. She recalled:

> For quite a while now I have been behaving outrageously. I decided to go to the University Health Centre and get psychiatric help, for after a specially bad crisis I thought I was mad. I had broken the bathroom scales by jumping on them with an incredible rage, then I had taken ten sleeping tablets to quieten me down and slept for sixty hours, and all because the dog had eaten half of my coat.

The irritability is also characterized by emotional swings from anger to distress. These can be seen in Tina's case, for after smashing the bathroom scales she took sleeping tablets to quieten herself, and finished up sleeping for two and a half days. The aggressive outbursts are always a potential danger to other people, especially in the family circle, for the mother seems to try hard to keep the problem within the home. This, in itself, puts an enormous strain on the partner, as is revealed in this husband's description of his wife's emotional swings:

> She is apparently unable to control her reactions and attitudes when we are together, although to the best of my knowledge she had never displayed such extreme symptoms in the presence of other people. However, there are now almost regular and predictable times when we are alone that she will break down completely—displaying the extremes of anger and distress in a most alarming manner. During the past week, she has had four such major outbursts which have involved shouting and screaming, attempted physical violence towards me and very long periods of apparently hysterical and uncontrollable sobbing. Indeed I do not think that the word correctly describes her action as it seems to me not to be crying in the conventional sense of the word. She moves her arms and legs in a rhythmical motion and gasps and gulps uncontrollably. This often happens in the evening or night, though daytime scenes have also occurred when we work together; usually one of these outbursts lasts between half an hour to an hour and a half, always starting with initial anger, leading to violence, and thereafter the inevitable breakdown into tears and sobbing.

No respecter of persons

Frequently these attacks of irritability end up with uncontrollable sobbing which seems to resolve the irritability for a while. The quarrelsome aspect is of particular concern to those women who before pregnancy held down posts calling for administrative and executive ability. The sudden change in temper is alarming to them. Whereas previously they were slow to anger, they now find they flare up at the slightest provocation. They find the simple remedies for self-control no longer work. Here are two examples from civil servants:

> I'm hostile to the world like Dracula, and completely out of control. The least thing upsets me and I don't want to make decisions (not always possible to defer). At times I could literally grind my teeth for no purpose.

> I'm impatient with my elderly father and occasionally break china and glass, although I loathe violence and aggression. I am dissatisfied with my lifestyle

and environment. I find it impossible to overcome this by the conscious effort of trying to count my blessings.

Control is difficult

Control is in fact difficult because the irritability is of a biochemical origin, and the mother soon finds out it is not so easy to control by psychological methods, such as relaxing, counting her blessings, or trying to look upon the bright side. One mother used to count up to ten before giving her daughters, aged six and four, a well-deserved smack. In no time they had learnt the difference between 'nine' and 'ten' and would continue to misbehave until their mother had reached nine . So she started to count in French, then German, and then Dutch. The children had their first language lessons, but I doubt if it really helped their mother.

Blind to the future

Any outburst is limited to the immediate present, with a complete blindness as to its future effect, as reflected by the accounts of two women. One said:

> I'd been crying. I smashed up the kitchen, I screamed in fury and then was shattered.

The other said:

> Pity the dog—I always kick him first.

The one gave no thought to the mess that would have to be cleared up later, the other was not concerned whether the dog would bark less in future.

The stimulus to an outburst

Consideration needs to be given to the factors that act as a stimulus to postnatal irritability. In the background is tiredness, loneliness, a crying baby, and lack of food. Alcohol and smoking, which curb the appetite, may also be relevant. The last straw may be the partner coming in late, an unpleasant remark, an uncalled-for comment, or a slight mishap like spilling the milk or burning the toast. These are all common enough everyday happenings but may be sufficient to spark an outburst. It is often more difficult to avoid the final spark, but easier to deal with the background factors.

The catalyst which finally releases the explosive rage is often the drop in blood sugar. As explained on page 33, after the birth there may be an alteration in the ability of the body to cope with changes in the varying amounts of sugar in the blood. If there has been too long an interval without food (or more particularly without either sugar or starchy foods), then the body reacts and corrects the blood sugar level by spurting out adrenalin to release some extra sugar from the body's stores and raise the blood sugar level. As schoolchildren learn in biology, adrenalin is the hormone of 'fight, flight, and fright'; so when the adrenalin is suddenly poured into the woman's blood, it may cause her to fight in fury. To restore happiness in the home, a mother who is liable to bouts of irritability would be strongly advised to abandon a rigid 'no food between meals' and 'only three meals a day' regime in favour of 'little and often' (see Chapter 19). This is not the time to use a weight-reducing diet which demands long intervals without food or liquid food replacements. Instead lose weight by eating smaller portions, rejecting junk foods for bread or crispbreads, and changing to the three-hourly starch diet which requires a steady blood sugar level (see Chapter 19).

The partner's problems

Postnatal irritability also affects the partner, for too often he is at the wrong end of the mother's bad temper. He finds that she has changed from the elated, vivacious person she was during pregnancy into the ever-moaning bitch of today. Can you blame him if he stops for a quick pick-me-up on his journey home before he faces another irrational flow of verbal abuse or physical danger? All too often the mother knows what is happening but can do little about it. Alison wrote:

> Don is not a terrible ogre—he is a decent man and loves me. He was a salesman for a pharmaceutical firm and understands quite a lot of medical things, but he does not understand why sometimes I pick fights and make him the butt of my bad humour.

Postnatal irritability is a frequent cause of the collapse of a marriage or relationship. She has changed beyond all recognition and he no longer loves this new personality. As this problem is most marked at home, too many men feel it wisest for them to move out. This, in turn, leads to greater stress and irritability and further deterioration of domestic harmony. Can you wonder that PND figures so frequently in the divorce courts?

It is even harder when the mother is left alone to care for her baby. These emotional swings, the quarrelsomeness, violence, and lack of tolerance, create a constant sense of fear in the single parent who recognizes her inability to control these waves of changing emotion and becomes frightened even of herself. In the extreme the condition may lead to infanticidal fears or homicidal actions, which are discussed in Chapter 10.

One concerned grandmother wrote about her daughter:

> Barbara is, I think, slightly better but still suffers bad fits of depression and of course it is not the best situation to be alone with a small child all day and every day—she is an intelligent person and needs some stimulation and conversation. She does love her husband Frank very much—he is also bright and intelligent—but I know she is frightened of herself at times, of these sudden bouts of tempers and going out of control and shouting etc. or striking the child.

If the irritability, quarrels, and aggressive behaviour are not recognized as an illness, they can cause permanent damage to relationships and make lifelong enemies. Perhaps it is the much-maligned mother-in-law who has the greatest difficulty in appreciating the situation. If she sees her son suffer from an apparently jealous and spoilt wife, who expects him to do all the fetching and carrying, so that he has no time to visit his parents, can she really be blamed for speaking her mind and telling her daughter-in-law how lazy and ungrateful she is? Greater understanding of the whole problem of PND is the real answer.

After a later pregnancy

Sometimes PND does not start until a later pregnancy; the older children are already adjusted to a happy family life, and then the mother's character changes. The distress felt by an older child to see their mother crying is enormous. Steps should be taken therefore to ensure that they neither see a crying mother nor quarrelling parents. Getting children to appreciate the problems that the illness brings is indeed difficult and not always successful.

Christine wrote:

> I have two older children and they are suffering from my lack of tolerance and general snappiness. Consequently my eldest child, Graham, who has a problem of his own, has become introverted and withdrawn. It must be dreadful not to have a cheerful Mummy. And yet I try hard, but cannot succeed.

Another wrote in the same vein, ending:

> I now realize that if the downs continue they will not only affect a happy marriage, but they will in all likelihood damage my own daughter's security as well.

If irritability is recognized as part of PND, it can be treated specifically with gratifying results. However, if it is seen in isolation, there is a natural temptation to treat it with sedatives or tranquillizers; indeed it is often the patient who asks for sedation. Unfortunately depression and exhaustion are already present, so nothing is achieved by giving more sedation to a woman who is already over-sedated by her illness. One has sympathy with Elaine who wrote:

> When I take enough sedatives or tranquillizers to calm me down I walk round in a fog like some kind of zombie. I can't get my housework done, much less drive the car. I keep telling the doctor he's treating the symptoms and not the cause. And he just pats my head and smiles. It's maddening.

Too often the last symptom to disappear in PND is the loss of sexual desire, which is discussed in the next chapter.

CHAPTER 8

Not tonight, Josephine

'Not tonight, Josephine' was attributed to Napoleon, and has been considered a classical rejection of nocturnal sexual pleasures. If we can believe all the accounts, Napoleon had good reasons to abstain. They were, however, very different from those that are considered here.

Fully satisfactory sexual activity has been described as 'the cement of a good relationship'. While it is accepted that a happy relationship can exist without sexual activity, there is no escaping the fact that complete sexual satisfaction strengthens and enriches the bond between partners, weaving strong ties of trust and faithfulness within the relationship. Both partners need the contentment and full relaxation that true sexual enjoyment brings.

One of the problems that childbirth can produce in the mother is a loss of sexual pleasure and desire, or a loss of libido, while her partner still keenly desires sexual activity. It is especially true that in those partnerships in which sex was an important cement, the loss of urge after birth can have serious consequences. This loss of interest can be the result of PND, or it can arise from causes unrelated to PND, and so the subject is dealt with separately in this chapter.

For many women the greatest possible insult is for her partner to refer to her as 'frigid' or 'ice cold'. Yet there are many different degrees of loss of sexual desire. There is the woman who recoils the moment she hears her partner's key go into the lock of the front door or as he advances across the lounge. Some women will even object to a mere peck on the cheek or an arm around the shoulder or waist, and will make it quite obvious that there are no opportunities as yet for any sexual activity. Then there are other women who fully enjoy the kisses, caresses, cuddles, and foreplay, but unrealistically would like it all to stop there. Possibly they are frightened of any pain that may be caused or they may feel quite unable to face up to the frustration that a lack of climax or orgasm may bring.

Doctors and counsellors helping partners with relationship problems frequently hear the statements 'Libido is non-existent now' and 'We've had no sex since the last baby was born'. This loss of libido is not found by the

obstetricians, for the same reason that they miss PND: the postnatal examination is usually performed before sexual activity has been resumed or
PND has become apparent. Many books about having a baby suggest that
sexual activities should not be enjoyed until after the postnatal examination, so that brings it out of the obstetrician's responsibility. The *Koran*
forbids sex after childbirth or miscarriage until the puerperium is over; the
maximum period of the puerperium is considered by Muslims to be six
weeks. Loss of libido is therefore likely to be reported to the family doctor,
usually some months after the baby's birth. The doctor may try some treatment before calling a psychiatrist, and so quite a long time may elapse after
the onset before the woman meets a psychiatrist or sexologist. The thera-
pist is seeing the woman too late for a quick resolution of her problem and
the task is therefore much more difficult. Sometimes the woman had low
sexual desire before the pregnancy and is now completely uninterested in
the subject.

Where there was complete sexual fulfilment before the pregnancy, the
cause of the loss of libido can come under one of four headings: postnatal
depression, psychological, hormonal, or physical.

Postnatal depression

Loss of libido is one of the recognized losses that can occur in depression,
or the disease of loss, be it the typical depressive illness or PND. Even
those who are only affected with mild postnatal exhaustion, without black
depression or irritability, may find they are too tired to be aroused. Two
husbands explain:

> Marion falls asleep easily in the day and is always in bed—she is floating on a
> cloud of her own and sex is dead.

> Pat can't make love and is generally sunk in a slough of misery, which pervades
> her whole life and that of everyone around her.

Treatment of depression with some antidepressants may also cause loss
of sexual interest; this includes both the popular tricyclic antidepressants
and the newer SSRIs (see p. 176). It is recognized that one of the possible
side-effects of SSRIs is the loss of libido, so this problem should be discussed
before prescribing this otherwise effective drug. Fortunately, if the cause of

the sexual problem is depression, there will be a return to full sexual desire and arousal once the depression lifts. Perhaps partners should be warned more frequently that the loss of libido experienced in PND is often the last of all symptoms to disappear. Success is more likely, and in the end more speedy, if the man starts wooing the woman afresh, just as he did when they first met. Let him first just kiss occasionally, then cuddle and stroke, and finally, when she is ready, then is the time to complete the act.

Psychological causes

The sexual desires may already have diminished in the early weeks of pregnancy, especially if the child was unwanted and there were thoughts or discussions on the possibility of terminating the pregnancy. Again, symptoms of early pregnancy, such as morning sickness, depression, tiredness, or headaches, may have decreased sexual interest. Occasionally, when there has been a previous difficulty in conception, a history of previous miscarriages (actual or threatened), or unexpected bleeding in the first weeks, the couple may have been advised to abstain during the early months of pregnancy. Many a couple take this advice too seriously and go on to abstain throughout the full nine months. Others find the alteration in the woman's shape in pregnancy a hindrance to their normal position for intercourse, and instead of trying another position they will abstain until the end of pregnancy. When there has been a considerable period of abstention, the resumption of sexual activity may be deferred long after the original cause ended.

Then there are those women who found the pregnancy difficult or labour horrifying, and who are determined not to start another pregnancy: 'never—no—never'. They may claim that they have chatted with women who became pregnant in spite of using good contraception. Women who became pregnant unintentionally need help in building up their confidence with another contraceptive method. However, it is never wise to sterilize one of the partners permanently in the hope that sexual interest will return once the fear of pregnancy has been abolished for ever. There may be other causes for the loss of libido which remain untouched and which do not need such drastic irreversible measures.

Some mothers, especially first-timers, may have their interest too firmly focused upon the baby. A mother who is breastfeeding may find this thoroughly satisfying and may not want to be touched there. It is important to remind couples that breasts are also sex organs, and caressing the breasts stimulates libido, so that the vagina becomes relaxed, moistened, and ready for penetration.

There may also be jealousy. The mother may feel jealous about the baby, who takes up too much of her time, or feel her partner is too devoted to the little one, or even may be suspicious that, while she was away in hospital having the baby, her partner was out having an affair. There are those who feel themselves unlovely because of stretch marks, enlarged breasts, and other physical changes, and cannot believe that the partner can find them attractive. They worry that their partner's love is only a pretence, which raises enormous fears and self-doubt.

Hormonal causes

At the time of the birth of the baby there are tremendous and sudden changes in the level of the mother's hormones. Her body is called upon to adapt to these altered amounts of chemicals flowing in her blood, and sometimes there is difficulty with this adaptation. This is particularly so in respect of the hormones prolactin, oestrogen, progesterone, and testosterone, all of which are involved in the creation of sexual desire. It has already been mentioned in Chapter 2 that when breastfeeding has stopped, the hormone prolactin should normally reduce to its pre-pregnancy level. However, when this is still raised after breastfeeding has ended, it can result in a marked loss of desire. Fortunately this raised level of prolactin can easily be recognized by a blood test, and corrected by one or two tablets of bromocriptine taken daily. In these cases, the bromocriptine is remarkably effective in restoring the normal sexual desires within a matter of weeks. Indeed, a temporary excessive desire, or nymphomania, may be experienced until the hormone balance returns to normal.

Occasionally, even in the absence of PND, there may be a deficiency of testosterone during the upheaval which occurs after delivery. Yes, women require just a small daily amount of the male hormone testosterone, just as men require some daily oestrogen. If the low level of testosterone is the cause of loss of sexual desire, then a short course of testosterone usually rectifies the situation quite easily. There is no need to be frightened of any masculinizing effects if it is used where there is a true testosterone deficiency. Less frequently the fault lies in abnormal levels of oestrogen or progesterone, which can be correctly balanced by the administration of the appropriate hormone.

Sometimes it is the progestogen in the Pill which is responsible for upsetting the normal hormone balance of the body, causing a loss of libido. Fortunately, if this is the cause it is easily remedied and some other form of contraception may be chosen.

Physical changes

After her first child, Sheila asked:

> Why after nine months and receiving such a wonderful reward, am I not ready for sex? Has my vagina altered? Why have I changed?

The answer here is that a considerable number of alterations take place in the vagina during the birth process. To understand these changes fully it is necessary to consider first the alterations which occur in the vagina during orgasm. A normal vagina is a straight passage leading from the outside to the door of the womb, or cervix, and it is into the vagina that the penis is inserted during intercourse. During the foreplay before intercourse the vagina is stimulated and it relaxes and becomes moist. During intercourse with orgasm there is a throbbing at the upper end of the vagina, which dilates, and there is a constriction at the lower end of the vagina.

Now consider the changes which occur during labour in a normal vaginal delivery. Gradually the cervix opens with contractions of the womb. Before labour the cervix is shut, but during labour it opens and stretches wide enough to allow a baby's head, with a diameter of about 10 cm to pass through it, and the vagina as such disappears (Figs. 17 and 18).

If the baby's head comes out suddenly, with a marked propulsive force, there may be a tear of the skin or the vaginal wall, which may need suturing. There is invariably a tear in the cervix, even in apparently normal deliveries, but this does not usually need stitching.

The mechanism of childbirth is remarkable and within a very short time the anatomy is restored: the cervix contracts and the womb, which once held the baby as well as the waters and placenta, shrinks down within six weeks to almost, but never quite, its pre-pregnancy size.

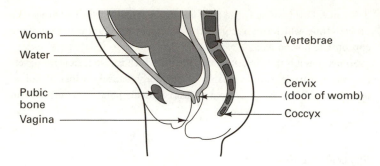

Fig. 17 The baby's head before labour

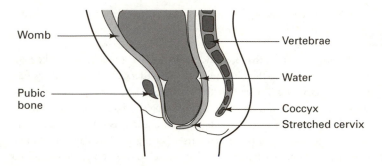

Fig. 18 The baby's head just before birth

This is what happens in a normal vaginal delivery—but there are instances when nature alone does not complete the job. Perhaps instruments or forceps are required to lift out the baby's head, or there may be a tear which has to be stitched. The site of the stitches may become inflamed or even infected and stitches themselves are painful.

Birth is a traumatic process with massive changes in the size and position of these organs, and sometimes when it is all finished it is possible that the nerves which come into action in orgasm are injured. Such injury may be permanent or need a long time to heal. Where this is suspected to be the cause for the loss of desire, the woman should be advised to resume normal activities to allow healing to be expedited.

In other cases women may experience pain at intercourse, when previously, before pregnancy, it was pain-free. Where there is pain on entry, this can be due to painful stitches: the stitching may have made the entrance too small or too rigid, so that it will not stretch. This is only a temporary difficulty and should soon resolve with normal sexual activity. It may be helped by the use of a lubricating jelly before entry. Sometimes the pain may arise from the very fear that entry will be painful.

Pain experienced on thrusting may be caused by pelvic inflammatory disease or by an infection of the bladder or vagina. It needs a full gynaecological examination to decide what the problem is, but once the source of the infection is treated the pain should disappear. Pain may also be caused by endometriosis, in which case the woman will also experience pain with each menstruation.

There are women who claim that the tingling effect of some contraceptive pessaries helps to encourage sexual pleasure. It is a simple tip well worth trying.

Professional help

If all else fails, further help is available from specialized psychiatrists called 'sexologists', who usually like to see the couple together. Tiki worked in a publishing house and wrote:

> I used to be real horny before Tim's arrival. Then I don't know why I had that horrid PND. I'm fine now except that I'm as cold as stone and have had a positive aversion for over twelve months.

Assuming that she is not on any of the SSRI drugs such as fluoxetine (Prozac), paroxetine (Seroxat), or sertraline (Lustral), Tiki sounds like a person who really can be helped by a professional sexologist.

Fathers too

Sometimes it is the new father who has lost his urge following the trauma he has been through watching the daily changes of pregnancy and witnessing the pains of labour. His return to normality may well be prompted by administration of testosterone.

Loss of sexual desire is a tragedy in a woman who has previously had full enjoyment. If it occurs following childbirth, it should be investigated and treated—the sooner, the better. In all cases where the loss of libido has occurred after childbirth, it is necessary for the partner to start again with the whole wooing process. The woman needs to feel she is loved all day long, not only before intercourse. She wants to be kissed and cuddled and spoilt. If she resents any approach, or runs away from intimacy, then no attempt should be made to complete the sex act. She needs more arousal, more love-play, and only when she is relaxed and stimulated should insertion occur.

CHAPTER 9

Psychosis

The most severe form of PND is puerperal (or postnatal) psychosis. This is a mental illness in which the patient has a 'frenzied mind' and loses contact with reality. She may be confused, deluded, and irrational, or have aural or visual hallucinations. She behaves in an odd, peculiar way and is not really 'with it'. It is the type of illness where even the father and family appreciate that the new mother is seriously ill and desperately in need of medical treatment. The medical student learns the difference between depression and psychosis by listening to the remarks of relatives. If they say 'She's having a breakdown', it suggests depression; if they say 'She's going mad', it implies psychosis.

Fortunately it is not as common as the other forms of PND discussed in previous chapters and occurs only in about 1 in every 200–500 births. Lay folk, when they first encounter the disease, often find the name difficult to write.

Pychiatrists divide the psychotic illnesses into organic, schizophrenic, depressive, and manic. In the past there was also the toxic delirium, which included puerperal pyrexia, or childbirth fever—often a fatal illness. Today puerperal pyrexia is rare, as deadly infections no longer occur in our sterile delivery rooms, and if they do we have effective antibiotics with which to control them. Psychotic illnesses may occur in men and women, and do not only happen after childbirth; they may also occur after a surgical operation or unexpectedly out of the blue.

Psychosis is the type of PNI with which psychiatrists are most familiar. They need immediate attention in hospital because the mothers are so acutely ill. Until 1970, most of the surveys into the incidence, age, social class, and other characteristics of those suffering PNI were by psychiatrists studying hospital patients with psychosis, as these were almost the only new mothers they saw. Patients with the milder forms of PND, exhaustion, and irritability were treated by general practitioners or, alas, often left untreated for months.

Hospitalization is essential for all but a few of those women with psychosis. It is needed for the patient's sake, so that she may recover as speedily as possible; for her own safety; and for the protection of others, especially the baby (see Chapter 10). Hopefully the mother will be admitted to a mother and baby unit, so that she need not be separated from her baby. Even if she is in no state to look after or care for her baby when she is first admitted, bonding to the baby will be carefully supervised before she is discharged.

Two days after the birth of her child, 32-year-old Gillian was noticed hammering the baby's head. 'It's the wrong shape. It's too long', she explained, with no thought of the possible damage she may have caused. A 20-year-old mother so adored her child that she thought he was like a turkey and should be roasted in the oven. As some would say, 'They're not in the same world as the rest of us.'

Early onset

Usually there is an acute onset of puerperal psychosis, with a complete change of personality overnight. Indeed half of all psychotic mothers are admitted to hospital within the first fourteen days after birth. Many develop the illness immediately after labour, as the following three women explain:

> After giving birth to both my babies I had the most horrific experience. A dreadful sinking sensation in which I had to fight very hard for control. It was as if I was being pulled down at very great speed.

> The day after the Caesarean operation I woke up and the world looked different and smelt different. Horrible, I was swearing at everyone. Everyone was laughing at me and shouting obscenities. Men entered my room when they shouldn't be there.

> I had to have an anaesthetic because the baby wasn't breathing well. The following day I was ill in the form of hearing imaginary voices talking to me. I was absolutely convinced of this and kept telling the nurses, of course no one believed me. After six days I was transferred to hospital and given teatment.

Early signs

In those patients who develop psychosis in the early days, insomnia and anxiety are often early and worrying signs. Nurses in the postnatal ward are advised to keep a look-out for those mothers who appear agitated, over-active, tense, interfering, complaining, over-demanding, or suspicious; also for those who are sure there is something wrong with their baby, or who accuse nurses of hurting or poisoning their child. These mothers may be in the early stages of psychosis, or it may just be a temporary phase due to the unfamiliar routine of hospital life.

Mothers who appear disturbed or unduly distressed in the first few days after delivery may be advised to go home early in the hope that, by returning to their own familiar surroundings, their mental disturbance will subside, as indeed it sometimes does. However, if the mother continues with her abnormal behaviour at home, then the general practitioner should be called in. The doctor may arrange either direct admission to a psychiatric ward or a home visit by a consultant psychiatrist. This means that the obstetrician does not see many cases of out-and-out psychosis.

Bizarre thoughts

These ill patients are confused and muddled by bizarre thoughts, such as 'I don't know which side is up'. One patient described the condition as 'looking into a room in reverse'. Characteristically there may be sudden changes from normal lucidity to extremely peculiar actions and statements.

Lucy was twenty-two years of age when her daughter was born. Her pregnancy had been normal and the birth easy, but three days later it was noticed she was deluded and she was found running down the hospital corridor crying and shouting 'Look, they've taken my baby away.' It was necessary to admit her to a local psychiatric hospital.

If such a mother is nursed at home, it is essential for both the mother and her baby to be under observation twenty-four hours of the day, every day, by their family or friends. Many of their actions are totally irrational; irreversible damage can occur very quickly while one's back is turned. Fortunately Hazel's baby avoided injury, although she confessed later:

> It was when Hugh looked up at me when I was breastfeeding. Those big blue eyes seemed to hypnotize me. I had a mad urge to stick a pin into those dark, black, circular pupils. Yes, it sounds unbelievable, but the strange urge was there and kept coming back. I loved the baby, yet felt absolutely murderous towards him.

Infanticide and the allied problems of suicide and murder, and the compulsive urges and fears which are among the most severe symptoms of psychosis, are dealt with in Chapter 10.

Fantasy world

The patient may live in her own fantasy world removed from reality and unaware of her surroundings. She may have auditory hallucinations in which she hears voices, music, thunder, marching feet, or snoring. She may have visual hallucinations in which she sees imaginary people, animals, or things. A couple of unidentical twins had pregnancies about two years apart. Both later suffered psychosis, in which the most disturbing feature was seeing, hearing, and smelling large wild animals in their bedroom. One mother recalled:

> The purgatory I experienced and the fear of descending into hell again. I felt the image of Death in a hooded cloak was following me everywhere.

Others have problems with ruminating thoughts, during which they cannot stop thinking about something; the thought keeps going round and round in their mind and they may ask the same question a dozen times. Often there is some slight evidence of reality or word association in which one word or the sight of one person triggers off a whole imaginary sequence. Chapter 11 includes 'Nancy's story', written by a patient, which admirably describes this type of irrational thought disorder.

Isobel, a 24-year-old mother, noticed a small pimple the size of a pinhead on her daughter's face when she was two days old. Isobel was in tears when she asked:

> Could it be a misplaced testis? Do you think Julie has spina bifida? Nobody tells the truth here, everyone is in conspiracy against me. They all say it's nothing, but it is something—I can see it.

Disorientation

The distraught mother may be disorientated in respect of time and place, not knowing the day or month, and unaware that she is in hospital.

Curiously some mothers still think they are pregnant, in spite of having had a traumatic labour. Jane described her illness three years later:

> I remember losing all track of time with a feeling of unreality and unable to relax. I was foulmouthed in a dream world caring for no one at all and feeling blank. The world was passing me by with me not knowing what at all was happening in the world. No sense of reality.

Joyce requested particulars of preventive treatment with her next pregnancy because of her experiences:

> I suffered from various delusions, including the certainty that the hospital staff were trying to kill me. Later I was discharged but then everything culminated in my attack on a neighbour who I was convinced was my husband's first wife and that they were plotting to murder me and run off with my little John.

Sarah's letter recalled:

> In the ambulance I thought we were on TV, in the lifts at the hospital I thought we were being shot at, when we got to the ward I thought we were being gassed. I thought the nurses were going to kill both baby and me.

Sometimes they may not even know who they are. One mother remembered:

> I thought I was the Devil and could stop people getting AIDS.

Rejection of the baby

To normal healthy folk it seems incredible that a mother who has given birth to an adorable healthy baby should sometimes reject that baby. How can she possibly say that she does not love her baby; or that she wants to get rid of her baby or give her baby away? Many have these thoughts but dare not express them, knowing that they will not be believed. Mothers who feel like that are ill, really ill, and in need of urgent help. It is probably their hormone balance which is at fault, not unlike the maternal behaviour in animals discussed in Chapter 12.

One often hears remarks, uttered in the strictest confidence, which explain this predicament. A distraught mother might use such phrases as:

> I don't love her any more.
> I'm emotionally flat about him—he doesn't move me.

> I can't understand—I looked forward so much to his arrival and now I can't stand him. I even attended doctors for five years to have him.
> He's repulsive.
> I wish she'd go away—I don't want my baby.

A Jewess had three daughters without any ensuing problems and then gave birth to her first son. This was followed by an unpleasant psychosis. She explained:

> My greatest wish was to give my husband a son. I've done that now, but I hate him and am even frightened of him.

It used to be thought that the inability to love a baby could lead to illness, but the opposite is true. It is the very illness which blunts the natural love for the much-wanted baby.

When a pregnancy has been happily anticipated and then rejection and loss of love for the baby occur, these are always signs that the mother is ill and in need of medical help. Doctors can help to correct the situation and assist the mother's natural love to return. The feelings of rejection also give rise to unpleasant feelings of guilt—so they become a deep secret, and may be hidden even from nearest and dearest. The situation calls for careful consideration and sympathetic handling by the partner and other members of the family.

Manic behaviour

Not all mothers with psychosis are depressed; some are initally high, elated, and wildly happy and energetic. Jenny, a police officer's wife, was so happy and excited ten days after her first daughter's birth that she decided she would be an interior decorator, for which she had no previous training. She instantly bought over £1000 of material with which to set up shop. Fortunately her husband realized she was ill and she was admitted to hospital before she did any further damage to his bank account.

Kind amnesia

Nature can be kind to such ill patients, for often they are left with no memory of those disturbing days. Karen wrote:

> There came a day a few weeks later when I could not remember what I had
> done for a whole week. They realized I was ill and I was admitted. I have had
> a loss of memory which means that I have forgotten a great deal about my
> son's babyhood.

But fortunately she had also forgotten the many strange, irrational acts
which she committed during those missing days.

I heard one mother relate her experiences at a public meeting on PND.
She described the treatment she received in hospital after the birth of her
first baby as 'barbaric', but then mentioned that she could not remember
much about it. I knew all about her difficult behaviour and how she had
fought first with her husband and mother-in-law, who had brought her
into the ward, and then with the nurses and doctors. She had had to be
sedated and placed in a single room for her own good.

Neither of these mothers received ECT while in hospital, but the few who
do receive it sometimes find they have a slight memory impairment later.

Other psychotic patients

Dr Brockington, and three other psychiatrists from the University Hospital
of South Manchester, studied twenty-six women admitted with puerperal
psychosis and compared them with twenty-nine non-puerperal-psychotic
control women of the same ages and in the same hospital for similar symptoms. They noticed that their puerperal patients were more elated and
sociable, but had lost less weight, were less angry, and showed less verbal
abuse than the control women. Most psychiatrists agree that postnatal
women have a shorter hospital stay compared with other women of the
same age also suffering from psychosis.

Treatment today can restore the mother to normal, but the psychosis,
whilst it lasts, is a very frightening and traumatic experience for all
concerned. Chapter 10 deals with the worst of all scenarios, where the
mother has homicidal fears or tendencies. Chapter 11 includes 'Nancy's
story', written by Nancy to let others know what it was like for her and, to
quote her own words, to:

> ... enlighten those who do not know what it is like to be mentally ill, and to
> entreat them not to exhort those who are at the mercy of violent forces beyond
> their control to 'pull themselves together'.

CHAPTER 10

Infanticide and homicide

Of all the crimes that the public find completely incomprehensible, infanticide tops the list. How can a mother who has gone successfully though nine months of pregnancy kill, or even harm, her own darling baby? It is unthinkable. Rarely do they realize how very ill the unfortunate mother may have been, and how urgently she needed medical help, for she was suffering from the most extreme form of psychosis. Nor is killing her baby the only possibility: the mentally sick mother may kill herself, her partner, family, friends, or strangers .

It was lawyers, rather than doctors, who first appreciated that the mother who killed her own baby was temporarily, mentally abnormal. The offence of infanticide was first introduced into the law of England and Wales in 1922, and later amended in the Infanticide Act of 1938. This states that a mother, who must be at least eighteen years old, who kills her own child, can be charged with the lesser offence of infanticide, rather than murder. This is because, at the time of the offence, 'the balance of her mind was disturbed by reason of her not having recovered from the effect of giving birth to the child or by reason of the effect of lactation consequent upon the birth'. Whereas murder, if proved, must be punished by a prison sentence, the punishment for infanticide is at the judge's discretion. The woman may be freed, placed on probation, or remanded under compulsory psychiatric care. It should be noted that this Act is law only in England and Wales—not in Scotland, nor in the United States. Furthermore it only covers the killing of a child under twelve months and does not extend to other individuals.

The tragedy of Anna Reynolds, who killed her mother a few days after her eighteenth birthday in a frenzied attack during her premenstruum, three months after her baby's birth, was not covered by the Infanticide Act. She was given a life sentence for murder, but was released eighteen months later, as the attack had occurred because of severe PMS. Her full story is vividly described in her own autobiography, *Tightrope*, published by Sedgwick & Jackson.

Infanticide is a very rare offence. Only two offenders were charged with infanticide in 1998, and three in 1997 in England and Wales. However, it is a condition with which I have had an unusual amount of experience. PND is often followed by PMS, a similar progesterone-related disease (see Chapter 14). So, in my practice, specializing for over forty years in PMS, it is not surprising that I have seen an unusual number of women charged with infanticide, and even more women who, when suffering from post-natal psychosis, have very nearly killed their baby.

The tragedies tend to be of three varieties: those occurring shortly after birth, while the mother is in an acute psychotic state; those occurring with the return of menstruation; and, thirdly, the many domestic feuds. It needs to be emphasized that a high proportion do not appear in the press or in law reports and remain hidden from the public for ever.

Six-month-old Tom was first thought to have died from a cot death. His distraught mother had run into her parents' bedroom in the early hours crying and saying that she could not wake the baby. However, the post-mortem showed skull fractures and internal bleeding compatible with the baby having been thrown with considerable force. His mother then admitted that she had thrown him to the ground. She had suffered from depression after Tom's birth, just as she had done after the birth of her first son. She was given a year's probation with medical supervision and treatment.

Hallucinations

Hallucinations are personal and very difficult for outsiders to understand. They may be visual, when the sufferer may see someone or something which is not really present, and which is frequently grotesque and frightening. With auditory hallucinations the sufferer hears sounds which may be compulsive, issuing non-stop instructions which must be obeyed regardless of how absurd or dangerous the action may be. Cathy, aged twenty-three, hurled her eleven-month-old son to his death from the first-floor window. She had heard voices telling her to injure the baby, whom she loved very much and who was very special to her. She obeyed her voices, first by throwing him down the stairs at home. She just watched him falling. When he survived, she calmly carried him back to the first-floor window and flung him head first to his death on the concrete slabs below. She was desperately ill, was given probation, and received medical help.

It is impossible to comprehend the actions of those with hallucinations and they need to be admitted to hospital for their own safety. But there is then the natural desire of the patient, her relatives, and the medical profession for her to return home as soon as possible to live a normal life with her baby. As previously mentioned, a recurrence is likely during the premenstruum, and relatives should be warned of this possibility. If they are not able to arrange a twenty-four-hour surveillance, then admission becomes necessary. This is absolutely essential if lives are to be saved and the baby is to have a mother able to rear her.

Babs threw herself under an express train travelling at a hundred miles an hour and died of multiple injuries. She had suffered from delusions and hallucinations immediately following her baby's birth, and had had a short stay at the mother and baby unit. Her husband stated that at home his wife would just sit around the house, looking vacant, and hardly ever talked or ate. She had previously jumped from a bridge into the river but had been rescued. It must be admitted that continuous surveillance at home, or even in hospital, is extremely difficult to arrange, and occasionally the best efforts go astray. However, the effort must be made and the difficulties overcome.

Infanticidal fears

There do not appear to be any statistics in medical literature giving the frequency of infanticidal fears—that is, of those women who think about or are frightened of harming their child but somehow manage to resist. It is no good asking a new mother if she has such fears, as she will immediately refute the idea, thinking that if she confesses her baby will be taken into care. It is not until the mother is really well and stable, no longer with any fear that social services will step in, that she will confess in confidence.

I receive many letters from pregnant women requesting information on progesterone preventive treatment for PND. My reply requests the name and address of the mother's general practitioner and obstetrician, to whom I send the necessary information and literature (see Chapter 16). Information on previous PND is not required. However, many pregnant women spontaneously give graphic accounts of their previous illness. In 1994–5, one hundred consecutive letters received from pregnant women giving more than requested information were analysed. The results were revealing, surprising, and most instructive. They included one woman who had been charged with an infanticidal attempt and twelve who had had infanticidal fears; in addition, seven had made suicide attempts and eight others had had suicidal fears (Table 1).

The full extent of homicidal fears in PND has not been recognized previously. It is probable that these fears had been dormant after recovery from their PNI, but the memory of them returned when they became pregnant, which is why they urgently sought some method of preventing another PNI.

Half of these letter-writers had been hospitalized for psychosis and eleven had received ECT. Usually the proportion of women suffering from PND who can be treated at home is nearer twenty to one, rather than only 50 per cent as found among the letter-writers. This demonstrates that those requesting progesterone preventive treatment represent women at the severe end of the spectrum of PNI. Among the letter-writers were fifty-one who mentioned how long their illness lasted. Again this is horrifying, with half saying it took more than twelve months to recover (Table 2).

Table 1 Homicidal fears in 100 letter-writers

Infanticidal attempt	1
Infanticidal fears	12*
Murdering	2
Hurting	2
Shaking	2
Hitting	2
Mutilating	1
Drowning	1
Suffocating	1
Stabbing	1
Suicidal attempts	7
Suicidal fears	8*

* Two had both infanticidal and suicidal fears

Table 2 Duration of PNI in 51 letter-writers

Under 1 month	0
Under 3 months	6
Under 6 months	9
Under 12 months	10
Over 12 months	25

Personal accounts

A vivid account of the horror and torment of such fears is contained in Pamela's account in Chapter 11. But many of the other letters were equally heartbreaking, and spoke of the compelling urges and the insistent, repetitive voices that 'had to be obeyed'. If ever such fears are expressed, immediate medical help must be sought. They are rarely spoken of casually, without much thought. More likely, a mother is sincerely frightened of losing control and in her confused state does not know how to call for help.

Included among the numerous letters were the following telling statements:

> A powerful sadness came over me. The greatest fear was that I would lose control and hurt baby, or do something bad to my child.

> There were those voices and urges which wouldn't go away. The whole purpose of my life was to kill myself.

> I'd burst into tears for no reason and when the baby cried I felt like shaking her to make her stop. I really felt like ending it all.

> I had violent thoughts towards my baby—thoughts of mutilating him and murdering him. The thoughts would increase each time I felt any affection for him. The thoughts continued for several weeks.

> I hate this beastly baby and shake her. I feel so guilty. I was trying very hard to love this child, but didn't know how. She would scream for six hours at a go—both of us would be screaming.

> I felt nothing for my baby and even tried to suffocate her. Fortunately I just stopped myself. I had to live with the problem alone. I gradually deteriorated until I took an overdose of 50 tablets, aspirin, valium, and iron tablets. Fortunately you've guessed I survived. That was eleven years ago and now I'm expecting my next child.

> I had such agonizing knifing pains in my breast, so I stopped feeding her. At eight weeks I had to ring the midwife whilst in tears as I wanted to hit Kim to stop her crying. I felt so horribly close to really hurting her.

> I became extremely afraid and anxious with feelings of despair that I would never get better. I felt as if my mind had somehow got into the wrong space—

as if it were out of focus. I had obsessional thoughts about hurting the baby, which tortured me as I loved her more than anything. Depression like a fog would descend. I did despair quite often.

I had restless butterflies—a hyper feeling of being out of control. Also blackness, very unlike me, and violent feelings which were the worst of all—feelings like drowning my baby, etc., etc. I was unable to make decisions, however small, and had a fear of travelling anywhere—what if I threw myself under a train? It sent me into cold sweats.

I shook like a leaf, burst into tears frequently, continually felt tired, very unhappy, nothing pleased me, no joy. I then started to feel suicidal and got hysterical over very little things—also I broke lots of things, dishes and irons— I got terrific strength from somewhere. I felt very black with no end to this unhappiness. I regularly contemplated suicide, but unless you want to involve another individual it is not that easy. I did not want to upset lorry drivers or train drivers by walking out in front of them. I did not want my children to find me hanging in the garage or dead in bed—also tablets are not a guaranteed method of killing oneself. Anyway finally, I am told by my husband, I took lots of tablets and anything I could drink, including methylated spirits, and was rushed into hospital.

Information withheld

Tales of baby battering and infanticide so shock the public that young mothers dare not confide their fears that they have an urge to injure their own child. There is also the constant thought that, if they do express their fears, their baby may be taken away. In medical practice one finds that the truth of whether a mother has ever hurt her child may take some time to reveal; it does not necessarily emerge at the first few meetings. Indeed it was only after Debby had been under my care for twelve months for the treatment of PND, which had merged into PMS, that she thanked me for the greatest benefit the treatment had brought. She had not hit even one of her four children once during the last year. At last she confessed that her children had had many unnecessary bruises on their limbs which had been inflicted by her, and that she had even put her hands around her sixteen-month-old son's neck, but had somehow avoided strangling him at the last minute. Her greatest fear was that the children she loved so much might be taken into care.

It was only recently that a fifty-year-old woman receiving treatment for menopausal problems was able to describe the difficulty she had had in trying to drown her six-week-old son in the bath:

> It's really very difficult to hold down a wet, slippery baby when he's screaming and kicking, so I called his father to help. Instead he saved John, who's been the most wonderful child anyone could wish for.

Homicidal fears or actions appear equally in those with a sincerely wanted baby as in those with an unplanned pregnancy. To the lay person they are quite inexplicable. In July 1995, one press headline read 'IVF mother took her own life after longed-for birth'. This really is something that the public find difficult to understand. A 35-year-old computer supervisor had hanged herself five months after the birth of her baby, whom she had conceived at last after years of failed attempts. At the inquest relatives described how she had changed from a happy-go-lucky individual before the birth to one who worried over trivialities, and how she had stated: 'I am going out of my mind. No one knows what is going on in my head. I don't know how to cope. Even the doctors can't make me love Sam.'

Suicide

Suicide is an ever-present possibility. It is a continual fear to the sufferer, and all those who are close to someone who is in the throes of a depressive illness must be instructed to keep the danger of suicide in the forefront of their minds at all times. It is all too easy to pick up and swallow some readily available tablets. Most attempts are cries for help and can succeed in focusing attention on the real dilemma of the new mother, which leads to positive treatment, adequate help, and a new life. On other occasions the real problem is not considered; the attempt is seen as a foolish act by a stupid woman, a superficial view is taken of the incident, and a recurrence of the attempt is inevitable. Sometimes the end result is worse than the depression, as one mother found out: 'Last year after a stupid suicide effort I ended up with three months in plaster because of a broken leg.' A hazard of aspirin or paracetamol overdose poisoning is kidney failure, with a lifetime of dialysis ahead.

One distraught husband, whose wife had strangled her daughter at seven months, and later took her own life at the second attempt, wrote:

She warned the doctors and the health visitor that she was likely to harm the baby, but was told by the doctors that she just had to pull herself together and get on with it.

Chris had suffered from PND following the birth of her six-month-old twins, and her previously happy marriage had fallen apart. She had made two previous suicide attempts, but then in December, in the early hours of the morning, clad only in her nightgown, she padded barefoot on to a windswept beach and soaked herself in the icy waves. Her body was later found washed out to sea. At the inquest her parents explained all the precautions they had taken. They had locked all the doors at night, hidden all keys, and made sure all pills were hidden, but it seems she must have climbed out of a downstairs window.

Overdose

Whenever antidepressants, tranquillizers, or analgesics are prescribed, there is always a potential for overdose. Whose responsibility is it to see that excess tablets are not taken? If the doctor is going to prescribe enough tablets for them to be lethal if taken all at once, then the doctor must ensure that a responsible adult is given charge of them and that he or she will give the new mother only one day's supply at a time. If no one is available to accept this responsibility, the doctor can either ask the chemist to give out the daily dose or arrange for the patient to be admitted to a place of safety. It is, of course, still possible to take an overdose of paracetamol or aspirin tablets, which are freely available over the counter. Fiona, described in the coroner's court as 'happy and bubbly', took a massive overdose of pills in a hotel room two hundred miles from home, eleven months after the birth of her baby.

The danger of shaking a baby

When a baby's incessant crying puts an ill mother into an intense rage, it is all too easy for her to shake the baby violently without thought for the consequences. Babies have relatively big heads and weak necks, which makes them liable to sustain serious brain injuries and even death. There have been campaigns to educate mothers to avoid shaking their babies. A leaflet 'Don't shake the Baby' was issued in Ohio in 1989–90, and more recently the NSPCC has issued a leaflet, 'Handle with Care', for midwives and health visitors to use as a basis for individual work with parents, aimed at targeting those most at risk.

Successful pregnancy after infanticide

A search of worldwide medical literature until 1995 did not find any reports of women who had committed infanticide and then gone on to have a successful pregnancy.

At a meeting of the international Marcé Society in September 1994, I presented findings on progesterone prevention, mentioning three women who had committed infanticide and had since had a normal pregnancy and puerperium. A psychiatrist commented how unusual it was ever to see more than one woman who had committed infanticide. It was only then that I realized that my experience was unique. The average psychiatrist is concerned with both sexes and all psychiatric diseases, and if the patients keep well they no longer remain under psychiatric care. Thus some psychiatrists may see less than a dozen new cases of postnatal psychosis in one year; when the patients are discharged, the psychiatrists are unlikely to know when the mothers become pregnant again until it is too late.

Women who commit infanticide fall into the category of 'when they are ill they are very, very ill, but when they are well they are perfect'. As with most women suffering from PND, their illness may gradually change to severe PMS . Chapter 14 discusses how PNI gradually changes to PMS. When PMS is adequately treated and they are restored to their normal health with their previous personality, these mothers have a natural desire to have another pregnancy. The following three case histories can give hope to others, their families, and friends.

Case 1. A housewife, thirty-three years old, suffered from pre-eclampsia with her first teenage pregnancy and the son was adopted at birth. She had a second normal pregnancy and labour, but became increasingly depressed during the three months after the second son's birth. She described her misery to her family doctor who arranged for a psychiatrist to visit her at home the next day. The psychiatrist agreed that she was suffering from

PND and promised arrangements would be made for her to attend group therapy at the nearby hospital. She could not wait. A couple of days later her husband left for work as usual at 8.00 a.m. and on returning at 5.30 p.m. found his son drowned in the bath and his wife in a coma on the bed. The mother spent three days in intensive care, where she was noted to be menstruating, and then she was transferred to a psychiatric ward. She pleaded guilty to infanticide and was freed on probation. After discharge she received treatment for PMS with excellent results. She had left school without qualifications, so she returned to college and successfully took 'O' levels and then 'A' level biology. She became pregnant a third time, was well throughout, and had a healthy eight-pound daughter. She received progesterone preventive treatment. There was no evidence of her previous problem and she has continued to live 'happily ever after'.

Case 2. A housewife from Los Angeles gave birth to a perfect son. He was so perfect she was sure he must be the Son of God, so she drowned him, convinced that he would rise again on the third day. Alas this did not happen. Instead she was charged with murder, and was compulsorily admitted for psychiatric care. She subsequently had another son, receiving progesterone in the puerperium. On recovery she devoted her energy to educating others to recognize and treat PND. She was a delegate to the international Marcé Society Conference in York, England, in 1989, determined to spread the word that there is still a good life after severe postnatal psychosis.

Case 3. A secretary gave birth to a son after a normal pregnancy, but she was convinced he would soon die. She took him repeatedly to doctors who could find nothing wrong. She even insisted that he be admitted to hospital overnight for the doctors to see that he was ill. Yet again doctors assured her that the baby was quite normal. The mother was given a note to take to her general practitioner, saying that she was suffering from PND. Two days later she suffocated the baby. When menstruation returned she had severe PMS, which was later successfully treated with progesterone. She pleaded guilty to infanticide and was discharged on probation. She resumed her secretarial career and returned to normal life, but she dearly wanted another child. After she failed to conceive, investigations showed that her only hope was *in vitro* fertilization. Before the obstetrician would agree, she had to have a full psychiatric examination and was pronounced normal. She had successful treatment followed by delivery of a healthy daughter and received progesterone afterwards. Everything was different this time; she enjoyed her baby and she is a devoted mother.

The next story is rather different but it is not included frivolously, as you will see.

Case 4. Sprocket was a healthy, happy Old English Bull Terrier bitch aged four. She was normally pretty well behaved and not at all aggressive, but she was a poor mother and had to be watched every moment she was with her newborn puppies, as she was prone to biting their heads off. This is not unheard of in dogs. Not only is it sad that puppies should be killed in this way, but they are worth several hundred pounds each. However, one day the breeder, Jan, had been watching Sprocket and her young pups for some eighteen hours without a break and could not wait another moment to go to the toilet. There was nobody in the house to take over. Jan returned in just a couple of minutes to find that Sprocket had bitten the head off a puppy. Sprocket knew she had done wrong: she had hidden the head—though not the rest of the body—under her blanket and was showing clear signs of shame and distress. In desperation Jan asked my daughter to ask my advice. I could only suggest that she ask the vet to try progesterone prophylaxis, as one would in humans. The vet had little faith in it but was willing to give it a try, so when Sprocket had her next litter she was given progesterone injections. She was the perfect mother then and subsequently, never again so much as snapping at her beloved pups. Note the infanticide, with confusion and guilt following, and note just how fast the damage can be done if the potentially infanticidal mother is not constantly supervised. All this is so typical of humans. What is really important here, however, is that such a similar problem in a lower animal can be successfully treated with the same hormone. This behaviour goes very deep; it is not under the control of the conscious mind; it is biological and not due to psychological trauma, early experiences, a painful delivery, or similar causes.

This chapter is written in the hope that these many unfortunate mothers will be better understood, and more sympathetically considered; that medical help will be sought at the earliest possible stage; that preventive treatment will become universal; and that ultimately these tragedies can become a thing of the past. Puerperal fever was conquered by medical science. The conquest of PND requires the joint action of the public and the medical profession.

CHAPTER 11

Tales of three mothers

In this chapter the sufferers of PND tell their own unsolicited stories in their own way. They are all different. Sally's tale is one of typical PND. She is now an active member of a PND group, devoting her energies to a problem close to her heart. Nancy and Pamela describe the more severe sufferings of psychosis. I am pleased to say that they have all recovered and are now leading useful lives.

Sally's tale

Sally originally gave this account of her PND at a public meeting in Northern Ireland. It obviously struck a chord with many in the audience, who spoke of the similarity to their own experience. She was good enough to let me include it here.

As I looked after my baby I was only aware that something was not quite right; there was no pleasure in my life, and I seemed to be permanently exhausted. My mother kept reminding me how lucky I was, a good husband, healthy baby, nice house. I knew she was right so therefore I must be the problem. I was ungrateful, I couldn't cope, I was a failure. To make matters worse I had one of THOSE babies, you know, the ones who never read the baby manuals you did!

Holly believed night and day to be interchangeable, routine boring, and sleep non-essential! What little self-confidence I had evaporated rapidly; this baby did nothing right, or maybe it was me.

My feelings of failure escalated as everyone told me how to sort this baby out, especially as all attempts ended in disaster. I was sure I had 'failed mother' stamped all over me and wouldn't even give my baby a bottle or change her nappy in public in case everyone saw how awful I was at this motherhood business. I used to spend hours trying to work out where I could go to escape the rigours of family life. I needed somewhere where someone would care for me and expect nothing in return; no such place existed for me—so I stayed where I was, desperately unhappy and lonely.

I didn't go out unless it was absolutely necessary. I had no energy and was convinced I couldn't even wheel my pram properly, so that it would be obvious to all and sundry what a hopeless case I was, yet home was becoming my prison. Sometimes I wanted to scream and the only thing to hold me back was the fear that if I started to scream I would never be able to stop.

Yet despite all this unhappiness I was, to all intents and purposes, coping—and although I was trotting back and forth to the health centre with tales of headaches and tiredness, not to mention a remedy for Holly's sleeplessness, it was to be six months before what I term the magic question was asked: 'Have you really felt well since your baby was born?' I realized I hadn't, and wept. PND was diagnosed and antidepressants prescribed.

In an ideal world that would have been the end of my story, but it was not to be. While the tablets did provide me with a certain amount of help, I was still none the wiser; all I knew about PND could be summed up in three words: 'I HAD IT.'

I struggled with my loneliness, lack of confidence, and a growing fear that I was going crazy—little did I know that this fear is very common in PND. I didn't dare say the words because, if I did, it might mean that I really was mad and I would be carted off to a mental institution and never be seen again! How silly I was, because, as I never shared my fears, I never received the reassurance I so desperately needed. I remember vividly my GP telling me that he had lots of women on the same medication as me and they were all doing well. I wanted to scream, 'Get them here, let me talk to them!', but I didn't; I just went home and cried some more.

There was so much I needed to know but no one I felt I could ask. How could I waste any more of my GP's time, how could my health visitor understand, how could I tell anyone about my loneliness, my inability to cope and to be a good wife and mother, my fear that I would never be well again, that this was the way my life would be until I died?

My marriage struggled on, sex life non-existent. Holly was still waking several times a night, and in fact was to continue doing so until she was two and a half years old, a fact that I am relieved I didn't know at that time, as goodness knows what I would have done . . . As a result I had neither the energy or the inclination for love-making. In fact I dreaded going to bed, it seemed such a pointless exercise to go to bed and then have to get up time and time again.

Perhaps some of our problems were due to my lack of self-esteem. I didn't like me any more. I was stupid, ugly, pathetic, a failure; how could I be desirable, what was there to desire? I resented the demands made on me; couldn't they see how ill I was, how awful I felt? Yet despite all this my husband was to stay by my side, and not just for this battle with PND, but for the subsequent one too. How I wish we had known that loss of libido is one of the many symptoms of PND, and like the other symptoms will pass too. Instead I was left feeling even more a failure and my poor husband felt not only hurt and rejected but totally confused.

Despite all this, normality did slowly return, and when Holly was two I came off my antidepressants, and six months later became pregnant. We were delighted.

At booking in I mentioned to the staff that I had had a past episode of PND and that I was sure that I had heard that there was some method of preventing it. I knew no more than that and sadly let myself be fobbed off by the reply: 'We don't do that here, we'll keep an eye on you.' OK, I thought, that's fine, I won't need it, anyway. I know about babies now, I couldn't get another one like Holly anyway, and I've got friends. I'll be fine. This tale is proof that positive thinking doesn't prevent PND!

On looking back I feel that the warning bells were ringing even while I was still in hospital after the birth. The problem was that no one, not even me, heard them ringing. I recollect sitting in the dayroom; it was midnight and not a soul was about; I sat and had a cry and then found myself pondering how long it would take them to discover I was missing if I just walked out of that door or jumped over the balcony . . . I wonder now whether, if perhaps someone had found me sitting there in the dark and taken the time really to talk to me, things would have been different. I also find myself wondering whether, if I had received the progesterone preventative therapy I had enquired about, I would have been sitting there at all! We shall never know.

On returning home I became more and more tired, those old feelings returned, and, to add to my problems, I became very irritable, few days went by in which I didn't shout and scream, or throw things across the room. Unfortunately my own GP was away and I saw a locum who prescribed a different antidepressant. Sad to say, I was only to take my tablets for one day. I felt terrible, as if I had died; I could hardly cope, and even now I look back on that day and consider it a miracle that we all survived it. The end result was that I refused to take any more of the pills, phone my health visitor, or even return to the locum.

If anything demonstrates the woolly-minded thinking of the PND sufferer, that does, as my own behaviour effectively cut me off from the help I so badly required.

Life wasn't easy with a constantly crying baby and a bored three-year-old, and with hindsight I can see that I did everything wrong, or nearly everything. I existed on cups of very sweet coffee and cigarettes. Eating was a luxury I didn't seem to have the time or the opportunity for, I kept my worries to myself, and I never did return to the locum or my GP . . . Yet on the plus side I knew that I had survived PND before, so therefore I must be able to do it again. This thought became my security blanket and helped me enormously.

I devised my own strategies, pouring out all my misery and anger into note-books, listing all those 'worst possible days of my entire life' in all their gory detail. This was to be invaluable, as it was through those notebooks that I first started to spot tiny improvements, an extra five minutes in bed, a mother and toddlers' group attended, a neighbour who stopped to chat. At night I would mentally go through my day, seeking five achievements; in the early days there were such silly achievements, ironing a shirt, going to the post box, emptying the ashes to the fire, but they were achievements and I hugged them to me.

Our sex life was non-existent again. I was beyond caring: he was lucky, he got out of this house, talked to people, had a life. Poor man, he never knew what he was coming home to! My mother found me impossible to talk to and I snapped and snarled at the children. Despite all this I began to see the light, only to have it extinguished. What on earth was happening? I was having a good week or two when normality appeared to return, and then suddenly I would descend again into my pit of misery. It was like being given a present, and just as you had unwrapped it and discovered it to be the best present in the world, it was snatched from you. I became angry with myself, how could anyone normal act like this—having PND for two weeks and then not . . .

Months were to pass before I discovered an article on premenstrual syndrome. I checked my diary. So that was it. I had PMS now, not PND! Well at least I had an answer.

Looking back now, I feel maybe what we all need to remember, to hug to us, is that not only does the sun come out from all those grey clouds of postnatal depression, but you can learn to laugh again.

What I would like readers to remember from 'Sally's story' is that there is an end to the miseries. There is a future life after PND.

Pamela's tale

Pamela had her first baby on 16 November. She wrote:

> When I went into labour I was ecstatic, but the feeling of elation started to falter once the baby was born. I felt strangely distant to everyone. I then became depressed and just wanted to cry, but knew I shouldn't. I didn't want Dick at all. After an hour I still hadn't held him at all, and the midwife thrust him upon me.
>
> By the twelfth day I still didn't feel any emotion towards him. I felt empty without him, like there was a big gap that needed filling. It was breaking my heart not being able to feel anything for him. I had felt so close to him while I was pregnant and now I couldn't feel anything for him. I was pacing the room, going mad. I needed sleep. I hadn't slept properly for four days. My midwife called the psychiatrist, who prescribed Trazadone [a sleeping tablet].
>
> On Wednesday, a week later, Dick was asleep and I decided to have a bath. After ten minutes in the bath my stomach felt empty and started to churn and suddenly the voices came out of nowhere, 'Drown yourself, do it, do it.' I remember thinking, 'Oh my God, what are you thinking that for? Get out of the bath, quick.' Still the voices kept coming. I dashed downstairs and rang my nextdoor neighbour. I had to wait for her to walk round from her farm. In the meantime the voices kept coming, telling me to get a breadknife and stab myself in the heart. I was hysterical. My neighbour tried to calm me. Dick woke and wanted a feed. Once I had breastfed him I felt better.
>
> On the Friday I was extremely ill upon getting up. I wanted to kill myself, I felt empty, all I wanted was to be pregnant again. The voices seemed to be coming constantly telling me to stab myself in the heart. At 7 a.m. my Mum rang the doctor, but I waited a horrifying five hours before the psychiatrist came and altered my medication. Within two days my milk started to dry up, so I gave up breastfeeding. I started to recognize when the suicide attacks were coming on. By 29 December my health visitor arranged for my admission to hospital.
>
> On New Year's Day I felt from 10 o'clock I was travelling into the black hole at tremendous speed. I thought I deserved all of this. I was somehow being punished for initially wanting an abortion and that I had had Dick for the wrong reasons. The voices reappeared and I no longer wanted to live. I had no conscious brain to fight back the voices telling me to get a breadknife out of the drawer and stab myself in the heart. The mental torment was unbearable.

I managed to get some tranquillizers and I could have them as and when I needed. I desperately wanted to be knocked out with sedatives. By 12 o'clock I told the nurses I could no longer look after Dick. I don't really remember any more until 5 o'clock. Mum tells me I was doing strange things, but I was out of it. I do remember at 5 o'clock being delirious with the voices still talking to me. I was having conversations with the voices. I no longer wanted to eat. My eating function was totally impaired.

I don't really remember much about those next two weeks except that I receded into a small child who needed her mother. I never stopped crying. I couldn't laugh or even smile. My concentration had been totally impaired on New Year's Day. I couldn't even pass the time of day by watching television or reading. Every minute felt like an hour. I counted every day of that 14 days, knowing that I only had so many to go. I was constantly asking if I was going to get better. I needed endless reassurance that I would.

On Day 11 I was allowed home overnight. On Day 13 the drugs worked. I felt a tremendous rush of maternal love towards Dick, as if someone had turned on a switch. It was marvellous, but knowing I had had a severe mental illness was driving me mad. I didn't have any depression. It was just a numbing of emotions.

Gradually Pamela made a complete recovery, but her illness, like that of so many others, was followed by PMS, which responded to progesterone therapy (see Chapter 15).

Nancy's tale

Nancy was thirty-four years old when she wrote her story. A graduate in one of the top professions, she had continued her profession between her pregnancies. She had puerperal psychosis on four occasions, two so severe that she had to be hospitalized. During her last episode she responded dramatically to progesterone.

Olivia's birth was a particularly traumatic one; she was in a breech position, so it was an emergency Caesarean, six and a half weeks early, my having had an internal haemorrhage, and Jason away in Edinburgh. Whilst waiting for the gynaecologist to arrive I had amused myself by reading a library book which gave an account of a supernatural visit to the author's aunt by her dead cousin. Perhaps this affected me subconsciously—as the pre-med. needle was inserted into the back of my hand I remonstrated jokingly with the anaesthetist that it was one made not by my husband's firm, but by that of a competitor, but somewhere deep down I felt that there was just a chance that I would never wake up again. All I could think of to pray was 'Father, into thy hands I commend my spirit.'

I believe there were six different drugs administered to me for the operation, some of them hallucinogenic. There was a whirling in my head. The spirits of my aborted baby and of my friend's miscarried baby were competing with a dark rush of wings to enter the body of my about-to-be-born baby. I definitely registered the moment that Olivia was born as a whiplash across my brain. Then I saw nothing. It wasn't that I SAW nothing, but that in some way I seemed utterly to UNDERSTAND that nothing, and it was deeply, deeply terrifying. Normally one thinks of 'nothing' as a space between two somethings, but this was not like that. It was a nothing so profound that it was not even an awareness of its own non-existence. I thought then that a knowing hell was greatly to be preferred to this absolute non-existence. Pain—peace, pain—peace, life itself was a mere vibration of pain and peace, and the centre of the pendulum was rest, and rest was death. I became concerned that there was no wickedness left in the world, for how could positive (and it seems I identified myself with positive) exist in the absence of negative and still total nothing? My sister-in-law was with me when I came round, and can testify that I was greatly excited and disturbed.

After three weeks I returned home, leaving the baby still in hospital. I couldn't sleep, and paced about all night. I had had the same reaction after the normal birth of my first child, ten days late, and so we were not unduly worried. That time it lasted about six weeks (as indeed it had the time before, when I had had an early abortion).

That Sunday evening a panel on the television were discussing the question of second marriage, and a saintly looking Church of England monk was being asked his views. They were categorical. The Church did not, and could never, approve second marriages. The sentence was final. God rejected me and I must go to hell, taking Jason with me. This programme was followed by a documentary about the Jewish religion.

That night I lay on the bed in my blue dressing-gown. I had insisted that Jason and I change places; he lay sleeping peacefully on my side of the bed, while I slept (I knew I was asleep) on his side on my back, like a living sacrifice on the pagan altar. The Rabbi stood at my bedside and leant over me. Unzipping my dressing-gown he opened up my body and looked into my soul. 'Where shall we begin?' I whispered to him. 'Let's start at Bethlehem,' I heard him whisper in reply. (I have discovered how this was done—I whispered the words aloud myself, in my sleep.) 'That's funny', my whispers echoed. 'My husband was born in Bethlehem!'

I woke up, I turned to look at Jason amazed. So he was Jesus Christ . . .

* * * * * *

Jason was away and my mother came up to help out. She had brought some apples with her. Apples . . . the fall of man. Whatever happened we mustn't eat them, or we would be expelled from the Garden of Eden. Furtively I took them and frantically buried them under the lilac tree in the furthermost right-hand corner of the back garden. I knew disaster to be overtaking us, and I cast about panic-stricken for the antidote. Death, opposite, life. So get the baby's carry-cot and put it in the right-hand corner of the sitting-room, diagonally opposite the apples, with Charles Dickens' *Great Expectations* in it.

I picked up the baby and went to my neighbour, who I knew had had three breakdowns. When I went out into the street, the houses undulated. I thought that the end of the world would come down the street bouncing from side to side. Yes, that was it, from Ken Lane at No. 33 to us at 22 and then to Rita Simms at 44, and off to the Morrison's at No. 11. 'Pam, I'm in a panic.' She got hold of her psychiatrist, to whom she managed to communicate some urgency, for he squeezed in an appointment for me two days later.

* * * * * *

The disaster was the Flood, that was it. Jason was Noah. I ran up to the bathroom and filled the bath with water. I got the fruit bowl and floated it; in it I put Patrick's plastic farm animals, and a walnut. The nut was me, a nut-case, but also a tough nut to crack.

Jason was away in Italy. Something had happened to him, I was sure. Pam, my neighbour, took me to Heathrow Airport to meet him. The check-out point seemed to be in the bowels. (In fact it is at ground level, but we had parked at first-floor level.) I was afraid to descend. Everyone, including Pam, was smoking. I thought it was Hell, but I was determined to meet him, even if it meant descending into the jaws of Hell itself. The porters wore black uniforms with red bands round the caps and lapels. Yes, Hell indeed, and they the Devil's agents . . . But he came through the barrier, surprised to see me, normal as ever . . .

* * * * * *

Two other neighbours took me to the hospital. The baby had been taken back there as I was quite obviously not able to cope with her. I was convinced that she or I or both of us were about to die, or already dead. I was upset that she hadn't been christened, and wanted to arrange it immediately. Someone called Sister. Sister looked dead white . . .

My neighbours (all true Samaritans indeed) took me on to my appointment with the psychiatrist. I was afraid of one of them (although she is actually one of the most likeable people I have ever met)—because she is barren. Sterility— the end of the world, no more life. I suffered from the other, for I felt her marriage to be imperfect. 'Are you happily married?' I asked her. 'Well, reason-ably,' she replied.

I mustn't get caught alone at the end of the world with a woman. If it was a man, we could have a baby, life could go on. Perhaps it was a trap and the psychiatrist was a woman? I refused to go in to see him. We stood on his doorstep in Harley Street and he came out to me. Deeply suspicious, I refused to shake his hand. 'Hello,' he said. 'Hello,' I said, 'how are you?' (He looked white, like Sister had.) 'Oh, all right,' he said, 'except that I am worried about my investments now that the bottom appears to have fallen out of the property market.' A property speculator! The Devil! I turned and fled. My neighbours chased me. I don't remember the journey home. One phoned my husband, the barren one. I wanted to get away from her.

Eventually Jason arrived, and took me home. I dressed all in white and insisted that he did the same. I was going to be properly married to him, in spite of being rejected by our church because of my having been married before. I went down to the kitchen. I would kill myself with the kitchen knife by plunging it into my heart. I got a red pencil and marked three crosses with it on my white dress over my heart.

My brother-in-law arrived. He was dressed in a blue shirt and blue jeans. But blue was the colour of the water, he would be drowned! He must be in white, the colour of the air! I wanted him to go home and change, but he wouldn't. (A superstition about this lingered and to be on the safe side I gave him a white tie for a wedding present, as I told him, to keep his head above water when the time came.)

* * * * * *

We were in a corridor, following a psychiatrist; he had a cigarette in his mouth. 'I don't think I like him,' I said to Jason. 'Just go with him, he will look after you,' Jason said. 'But he smokes!' I said. 'No I don't,' he said, and put the lighted cigarette in his pocket. (I asked him about this later. It wasn't a cigarette; it was a biro.)

I was met by a handsome coloured man. 'I'm glad it's you,' I said, 'because I believe in . . .' 'The brotherhood of man?' he asked. 'Yes, that's it,' I said, and shook him warmly by the hand.

* * * * * *

I woke up in a strange room, with no memories. I looked out of the window. The place looked like some kind of monastery (The Priory, Roehampton). So I WAS dead, after all! Heaven or hell? Were the nurses angels or devils?

A special nurse was assigned to me, a Chinese girl called Sue, Oh NO! I was God and it was all my fault! If I was God, I would have power. To test my power, I threw my medicine in Sue's eyes. 'Why did you do that?' asked Jason, who was standing by my bedside. 'Because I thought I was God.'

* * * * * *

The colour of the bedspread was of the greatest importance; I must get the sequence right. There was one on the bed and three more in the cupboard. Red: primeval, fire, etc. Brown: mud, earth, life emerging. Blue next: sky, life, free. Then yellow: sun, ultimate release? I worked on it over and over.

* * * * * *

I looked out of the window. There was Jason with his back to me, chatting to two people. He looked older. The baby had been brought to join me by this time. So she and I had died, and we had just waited here whilst the years went by, and finally Jason had died and come to join us. He was older than when I last saw him, but no matter, we were married and I loved him, I would go to him. I picked up the baby and walked out into the garden. When I drew near, they turned around. It wasn't Jason, it was a gardener. 'Hello, do you want something?' I just walked away again.

* * * * * *

My psychosis after Olivia was born was treated by electric shock, drug therapy, and psychoanalysis. I was advised not to have any more children, and it was six months before I began to feel like facing life again, and a year before I felt the return of my old energy and interests in life. For much of the time after I returned from hospital all I could do was sit apathetically on the sitting-room sofa. Even a visit from one of my best friends was a challenge for which I needed a stiff drink, and my hands trembled until she left.

When we discovered that I was pregnant again, the National Childbirth Trust put me in touch with an endocrinologist. I had intended that she should refer me to a psychiatrist who specialized in puerperal conditions, but she told me that there was no need. 'You don't have a mental problem. You have a HORMONAL problem, and we will treat it with hormones.'

It worked, and although I had to fight to hold on to my mind, and though I couldn't sleep and pushed my hospital bed to the window, gulping in the fresh air through the night and trying not to feel claustrophobic, my mind did not take off. Hormone injections were continued for about five weeks as far as I can recall, in fact, just longer than the date that the baby had been due. He was also early, this time by four weeks.

I breastfed him for seven months, and why we did not realize that another hormone change would take place when he was weaned, I'll never know. As it was, I dropped from five feeds to three in three days because I suddenly decided that the breastfeeding business had gone on too long. I immediately took off. I knew I was going under, and I kept meaning to tell Jason, but I kept fighting it, hoping to get over it, as I had done after the birth. Looking back I think this was due to a combination of pride, and fear of rejection. If it ever happens again, I hope that I will have sufficient humility, and sufficient trust in the compassion of others, to seek help earlier.

Just before I cracked up completely we went to a Masked Ball at the Hurlingham Club. I was experiencing that growing feeling of imminent danger, although it was still under control. Jason was in his white dinner jacket (symbolizing Jesus Christ again) and before entering I was given a red mask. I almost refused it, for it made me look diabolic, until I realized the logic of it. God and the Devil, the ultimate and only indissoluble marriage, the one calling into existence the other. I felt that we would be safe together. There was some mix-up over the tables and we were shown to table eleven (eleven, worshipped by some tribal religions as a number with mystical powers) and the man who was double-booked for table eleven—a Mr SLAUGHTER—was shown elsewhere. So we were to escape slaughter, after all. (Who can say that there is not some divine sense of humour behind that coincidence?)

The final collapse was triggered by the penultimate episode of Dickens' *Our Mutual Friend* on television. When the odious schoolteacher attacked the young hero, his screams seemed to go right through me to the marrow of my bones. Lizzie stood rooted to the spot. 'Why doesn't she go to him, why doesn't she help him?' I asked Jason. 'She's paralysed with fear.'

That night as I lay asleep I was in the grip of terrible dreams. I was given three eggs from the fridge (my three children). Which came first, the chicken or the egg? Human flesh, it tastes like chicken, the end of the world, everyone was rushing after each other to eat them up, no, no, hide, under the table, no, rush into the open countryside, listen, you and I will stay together, I won't eat you if you won't eat me, here we are helping each other out of reach of those ravenous mouths, NO, NO, they've got my feet (I struggled to free my feet and legs under the blankets), NO! NO! I was screaming, but no sound was coming out. I was paralysed. Jason lay beside me with his back to me. Why doesn't he help me? Because he's asleep, and anyway he can't hear you. Then I felt the sands rushing off me from the mid-line, and I seemed to come back up into my body from below, like coming up from out of the grave.

CRACK, CRACK, CRACK. Someone outside just above the road on the opposite side was being whipped with incredible ferocity. I counted thirty lashes. So it was Jesus Christ again. 'Alright, alright, I forgive myself, only please,' I pleaded, 'please don't ask me to live without you!'

I was flung back into my body with abrupt contempt. I woke up in my body, sweating. Without whom? What happened? I was sobbing, but I felt some sort of relief, some sort of completion. I looked at Jason beside me. It seemed that all I wanted was to be allowed to be with him. 'Don't ask me to live without you.' Yes, I would be alright so long as he was there.

The next day Jason went to Italy. While he was away I felt an absolute compulsion to get to the bottom of 'What it's all about'. I read *The Book on the Taboo Against Knowing Who You Are,* and when he returned the psychosis had gone too far for prevention. I tried to explain. 'I know the TRUTH,' I sobbed. 'What truth?' 'There's only one of us here. You are me and I am you. Self is everywhere, there's no escape from it, only Self, whichever way you turn.' He rang the doctor.

There were voices in my head. One sobbed and pleaded and seemed to be growing its way up the inside of the back of my head. The other encouraged and comforted and seemed to be seeing the sobbing one through the ordeal. I told the doctor only about the sobbing one, though. It said: 'Mummy, Mummy, you said you were going to look after me, and you're letting them eat me!'

I was immediately admitted to the Psychiatric Unit of St Mary's Hospital.

Jason and the endocrinologist had a terrific fight to get the hospital to agree to give me hormone injections. Even when they reluctantly agreed to do so, it was in conjunction with their own drug therapy. The hormone supplies took three days to get hold of. Once injections were started I got well so rapidly that everyone was astonished. I was discharged after two weeks without medication and returned to work after a further week feeling NORMAL. Energy, normal. Thoughts, normal. Libido, normal. Contrast this with the six months to one year it took me to get over the first episode.

While I was in hospital I saw two things which could not, in reality as we think we know it, have been there. The first was Jason. He was in the next ward, and waved cheerfully to me as he disappeared out of sight round a corner. I struggled with the nurses to be allowed to go after him, and made such a fuss that I was taken through the double doors into the next ward to be shown that he was not there, and that he was at work, and would visit me at visiting time. The other was two suns in the sky. I stood at the window and watched them, fascinated, knowing that the end of the world would come when they merged. (Did they or not? I don't know.)

The most disturbing things that can't be explained were the voices outside the window which cried softly 'NO! NO!'

* * * * * *

Ultimate pain, or ultimate ecstasy? I wasn't sure. And the SMELL. I kept BUMPING INTO it. It smelt like cauterized flesh. I always drew back, immediately, but it seemed to hem me in. I was afraid that I was burning someone when I bumped into it. I always asked a nurse, 'That SMELL—what is it?', and they always replied, 'What smell? I can't smell anything.'

On about the second day, as I sat in the canteen bewildered and terrified, one of the waiters came up to me and muttered: 'Your God is behind you, your God is beside you, your God is in front of you, have no fear.' God bless you, Spanish waiter, wherever you are, for those words! They were something to hold on to, and gave me hope.

I lay on my bed, and my head and my body were two different people. My body was totally relaxed. (The drugs?) My head seemed to be in direct communication with the sun, and all it said was: 'The will to live, the will to live, the will to live . . .'

As I lay there, something fluttered in my body; it beat against its prison, and tried to get out. Now it was over my stomach, now my shoulder, now under my right breast. INSIDE ME, a cock crowed three times (so Peter had betrayed Christ) and my flesh jumped where it crowed. (Muscles twitching? Stomach gurgling?) Suddenly a switch was turned off in my head, just 'Flick!' like that, and I got up. Whatever there was in my body, it was going to rush up through my mouth and pull me inside-out. I must keep it down, at all costs! I began to strangle myself with my belt. The nurse rushed up alarmed and tried to stop me ('You're hurting yourself!'), but it subsided and I let go. My face felt all red, but my head and my body were still different beings, and my body felt fine. (Question: Do your insides feel as though they are corroding? How did you know that, Professor Priest? I'll not give in to THAT and admit it!)

I thought they were hiding Jason and me apart, and that something terrible was happening to him and the children. I began to plot my escape. I took a pillow and tried to smash the window (armour-plated glass.) Then I borrowed Sue's scissors and tried to unscrew the window. Hopeless. So I took a wire coat-hanger, and, holding it like a hook, determined to fight my way out. The first nurse who saw me with it took it off me (I couldn't bring myself to use it, after all). So I decided that the only thing to do was to use my wits. The staff nurse on duty was coloured. I started to shout at him. 'You let me out of here! I have a doll at home, YOU know what I mean, and I'm going to stick a pin in its THROAT! I am the one with the POWER! And when I get up there, I'm going to tell on YOU. I'm going to tell them that you won't let me OUT!'

A whole group of nurses were clucking round me (just like hens, I thought). They seemed afraid to touch me, but eventually they started bundling me back into my room. (One coloured mammy-looking nurse, especially, kept muttering: 'HUH! Jus' who does she think she is?', and days later, when I passed her, she said to one of the other nurses: 'Huh! She oughta wash herself, get rid of the STINK!', which, as I was regaining my senses by that time, amused me in a surprised way.)

A very nice young lady doctor arrived, and she was really sweating. 'Why are you afraid of me?' I asked her. Like a cornered animal I stood up on my bed and contemplated trying to strangle her with her gold necklace, but I hadn't the heart to do it, besides which it was futile—I was outnumbered. 'You want to hurt me! You are going to do something to me!' 'No, I'm not, I'm just going to give you an injection to calm you down, It won't hurt, it's just a little prick . . .'

I was in the road, with no slippers on, just my nightie. It was cold. I saw a lorry with some sacks in it, and I thought if I got into one and hopped along it would keep my feet warm. I seemed to flow effortlessly up into the lorry and got the sack. I started to hobble along in it. A breakdown lorry came along pulling a car. I stopped the man. 'You've got to help me, please, take me home to my hus-band . . .' 'Well, I don't know, love, you'll have to ask the Guvnor 'ere, 'e's in charge.' They moved off, but then it seemed to happen again and they were back.

Of course, this sounds like a dream, but it really did happen, I really did escape from the hospital into the road. No one knows how I managed it, full of Valium and who knows what else, but there were brown stains from the sacking on the soles of my feet to prove it.

I thought that the hospital was electrically charged, and indeed there must be considerable static in there from all those electric shocks that they give people, and from those relentless floor-polishers that are given free rein every day to terrify the germs. When in the reception area, my head really buzzed with disturbance, which it seemed to receive from all over the place. I spilt some water on my canvas shoe and it seemed to take up electricity into the ball of my foot. (Actually, with hindsight, I think it gave me rheumatism.)

More voices. Again one was sobbing (this time with remorse) and one comforting. The sobbing one I identified with myself, the comforting one with Jason. Whether the conversations really took place, or whether they were just in my head, I do not know. All I know is that there, at the bottom of the pit, I found perfect comfort and understanding. I think he really was there when I said: 'I feel that I have a duty to kill myself,' and he replied: 'Well, all I can do, darling, is to ask you, with great humility, not to do it. The children and I need you . . .'

* * * * * *

My recovery was swift and total, and our ardent prayer is that we will never have to go through all that again! I shall never forget the way Jason looked at the end of that two weeks, when he brought the baby up to see me. He looked as though he had spent his last ounce of strength to reach the top step, and was about to collapse.

'Nancy's tale' is a shattering account of her experience of an illness which fortunately is rare. It shows the effect upon her husband, whose behaviour throughout fills one with admiration. A most satisfactory detail of the story, not only for Nancy but also for future potential sufferers, is that once progesterone treatment was under way 'recovery was swift and beautiful'.

CHAPTER 12

Maternal behaviour in animals

Medicine owes much to the work of veterinary scientists, who have solved so many human problems. The Committee of Safety of Medicine rules that all new drugs must be tested and shown to be safe on at least two different animal species before any human trials may begin. This chapter mentions just a few animal studies which are relevant to PND, PMS, and progesterone.

Maternal behaviour

Animals do not attend antenatal classes, nor do they read books on motherhood. The way even the lowliest animals look after their young is fascinating. We have all seen pictures of a row of piglets suckling contentedly from the sow, a bird bringing food to its newly hatched chicks, and the baby elephant walking under mother elephant for protection. It all comes naturally. Scientists have studied the maternal behaviour of vertebrates and the way the new mother looks after her newborn. She keeps them fed and clean, she protects them, and ensures that they are warm and housed.

Maternal behaviour

Feeding

Cleaning

Protecting

Keeping warm

Nest building

Scientists soon realized that such maternal behaviour is present only among female animals who have been pregnant. For instance, if a female monkey, rabbit, sheep, or rodent who has never been pregnant is put next to a newborn litter of the same species, the virgin female does not know what to do with the young. She will neglect them and deal with them as if they were a stone, a tree, or some other inanimate object. On the other hand, an animal who has once been pregnant, if placed near young of the same—or sometimes even of a different—species, will try to protect, feed, clean, and keep them warm.

Nowadays scientists know that they can produce maternal behaviour in virgin female animals—it has been done with monkeys, rabbits, sheep, mice, and rats—by giving them a short course of progesterone and oestrogen in the dose which the placenta would have produced. If the female is then placed near a newborn litter of her own species, she will immediately try to protect the young, giving them warmth, cleaning them, and attempting to feed them.

Maternal behaviour under hormonal control in animals

Absent in virgin animals

Present after pregnancy

Artificially produced in virgin animals given hormones

Abolished if given anti-progesterone injection

Thus we see that, in animals, maternal behaviour is under hormonal control; in particular, progesterone and oestrogen are needed to develop maternal behaviour. This is similar to the maternal instinct and love that develops during human pregnancies. Even when a pregnancy was unplanned and initially unwanted, a mother will usually develop maternal instinct and love for the unborn child long before the nine months of pregnancy are over, such that nothing can persuade her to give the baby away. As a corollary, loss of maternal behaviour in animals may be equated to PND in humans, with the loss of interest and energy, the inability to cope, the rejection of the baby, and even, infanticide.

Drs M.Y. Wang, R.B. Heap, and M.J. Tussig have investigated hormonal influence further. They immunized a group of mice so that they developed progesterone antibodies and left another control group of mice untreated.

Both groups were then mated and it was noted that there was a slight delay in the treated group before becoming fertile, but otherwise both groups had normal pregnancies and normal labours. However, immediately after delivery some mice were moved a short distance away from their litter in their cage. The untreated group showed normal maternal behaviour and immediately set about retrieving their litters, feeding and cleaning them, and making a comfortable nest for them. In contrast, the treated mice, who all had progesterone antibodies, had lost their maternal behaviour; they made no attempt to retrieve their young, they rejected them, or even cannibalized them.

Further experiments on mice demonstrated that maternal behaviour was also lost if mice were immunized to have progesterone receptor antibodies. Even after a second normal pregnancy and birth, mice who had been immunized to produce progesterone antibodies or progesterone receptor antibodies still had no maternal behaviour. PND also has a high recurrence rate. If a new mother has had a depression after her first baby, there is a 68 per cent recurrence rate after the next pregnancy (see p. 127).

Dr Wang and his team published further work in May 1995 in the *Journal of Clinical Endocrinology* demonstrating that in mice maternal behaviour is also abolished if the animals are immunized in early or late pregnancy, but not if immunized during or immediately after delivery. Furthermore, when treated, newborn mice were cross-fostered and given to untreated mothers, and treated mothers given the untreated offspring, it was the treated mothers who suffered the loss of maternal behaviour and not their offspring. Other work showed that the milk of treated mothers was not affected.

Postnatal depression in mice

If given anti-progesterone injection there is:

    No maternal behaviour

    Abandoning of pups

    Killing of pups

Postnatal depression in women

Lack of maternal behaviour

No maternal interest

No maternal instinct

The animals were immunized with the anti-progesterone drug, mifepristone, which is licensed by the Committee of Safety of Medicine for use in early terminations of pregnancy. In the mice experiments it was found to be ineffective if given immediately after delivery, but to abolish maternal behaviour if given before conception or during early or late pregnancy. It remains to be seen if, after a termination in women using mifepristone, the next pregnancy is followed by abolition of maternal behaviour or PND.

This work on mice demonstrates that progesterone is involved in maternal behaviour and strongly supports the hypothesis that progesterone is involved in PND.

Progesterone studies

Much of the work on progesterone receptors has been performed on animals. It was Dr Bruce Nock and his colleagues in New York who first showed that progesterone receptors do not transport molecules of progesterone into the nucleus of cells if adrenalin is present, such as happens when the blood sugar level is too low (see p. 33).

Dr Blaustein and his team working in Amherst, Massachusetts, were the first to demonstrate that, whilst the first dose of progesterone can be very small and still act on the nucleus, the second and subsequent doses need to be some forty times higher to stimulate the same action. In short, after the first dose of progesterone, the subsequent chemical action in the nucleus becomes much less sensitive (or hyposensitive) and needs a much higher dose to stimulate it. This needs to be appreciated when one is using progesterone in treatment (see Chapter 16)

In another study by Professor Goy's team at the Primate Center in Madison, the pellets of food given to pregnant rhesus monkeys were counted daily. The researchers were able to show that monkeys also suffer from morning sickness and that their appetite disappears in the early months of pregnancy but then returns in later pregnancy. These symptoms can be abolished by giving progesterone early on. In short they showed what most sufferers of morning sickness already know, that the dreadful sickness in early pregnancy is due to hormonal imbalance and is not 'all in the mind'.

Similarly, by counting the number of pellets of food eaten, Professor Goy's team showed that the non-pregnant rhesus monkeys ate more (or binged) during the premenstruum and controlled their appetite after menstruation. Numerous women will confirm that their appetite also increases before menstruation.

In a Kenyan study it was noticed that baboons would climb the trees and binge on the fresh shoots during the premenstruum, and then after menstruation would climb down and socialize again with other baboons.

Rhesus monkeys

Suffer from morning sickness in early pregnancy

Their appetite is reduced in early pregnancy

Progesterone relieves morning sickness in early pregnancy

Progesterone improves appetite in early pregnancy

Appetite is increased before menstruation

Appetite is normal after menstruation

Progesterone normalizes appetite before menstruation

This chapter has looked at studies of animal behaviour especially during and after pregnancy. It has shown the various scientific specialties worldwide working together to find an answer to PND. It is all too easy for obstetricians, psychiatrists, and general practitioners who are seeing patients regularly to forget the animals studies that are being undertaken and the relevance of this to their own work.

....

CHAPTER 13

Who is at risk?

Sir William Osler, the great physician and teacher (1849–1919), stated that 'There's never a never in medicine'—and that is particularly true of PND. Doctors are taught early in their training that there is always an exception to every rule in medicine. Although one can recognize certain characteristics or risk factors among pregnant women, it is not yet possible to recognize the individual woman who is doomed to develop PND or psychosis. However, studies are proceeding internationally and it seems that almost weekly original medical studies are published emphasizing new aspects and new risk factors.

Elated in late pregnancy

The North Middlesex Hospital survey published in 1971 showed that it was those women who were happiest, elated, and euphoric during the later months of pregnancy who were at risk—for 64 per cent of such women developed PND, compared with 24 per cent who did not. The mothers who developed PND were also those likely to have been most anxious at their first interview at the antenatal clinic; they were the ones with mood swings, anxious in early pregnancy, elated in later pregnancy, and then depressed after birth. Imagine the pleasure it gave the fourteen doctors who carried out that survey when, in 1994, Dr Brian Harris and his colleagues in Cardiff (see p. 35) showed, with salivary progesterone tests, that the women most likely to develop postnatal blues were those who were well and had higher progesterone levels at the end of pregnancy and a lower than normal level immediately after birth.

Emotions during pregnancy

This North Middlesex Hospital survey used the precise definition of PND, which excluded women who had had a psychiatric episode prior to the delivery of the baby, including depression during pregnancy. Dr Ian Gottlieb and his group at the University of Western Ontario studied 655 women in early pregnancy, who were not then depressed; of these, 75 women became depressed during pregnancy, of whom 54 (72 per cent) recovered after delivery, while 12 remained depressed. Those who recovered reported greater marital satisfaction and less general stress. There are also occasional reports of psychosis starting during pregnancy and increasing in severity postnatally.

Marked maternal characteristics

The mothers studied in the North Middlesex Hospital survey who developed PND also showed a favourable attitude to motherhood. They were the ones who were most likely to welcome pregnancy, who were happy and elated during later pregnancy, and who had few of those annoying pregnancy symptoms like depression, irritability, tiredness, sickness, backache, or headache. When they were asked during the last month of pregnancy whether they wished to breastfeed, 100 per cent answered with a resounding 'Yes'. They had the baby's clothes ready and the nursery prepared, they had decided on baby's names, and probably even knew the school the child would attend.

There were other important findings in the survey which favoured a hormonal, rather than psychological, explanation for the cause of depression. Those who developed PND had no higher incidence of psychiatric illness in their family than did normal women. There were no differences between those who had difficult deliveries and those with easy births; nor in those who had abnormal babies and those who had healthy ones. Again this confirmed the findings of other workers. The earliest was by Dr Mary Martin of Rotunda Hospital in Dublin in 1958, who found that PND was not related to the length of labour, the difficulty of labour, forceps delivery, or the incidence of pre-eclampsia; neither was it related to high blood pressure nor to nausea and vomiting in pregnancy; nor age or marital status; nor the failure to breastfeed. Not all subsequent studies have confirmed these findings, which appear to be more dependent on the day on which the woman is tested—five days or six weeks after birth.

Genetic factors

The influence of a genetic factor in PND is being widely appreciated. There does appear to be a genetically inherited factor in PND, in the same way that some families are more prone to develop a depressive illness than others, but this is not a major causative factor. Sandra and Tracy offer two examples.

Sandra was admitted to a psychiatric hospital after the birth of her daughter Jane and was discharged after an interval of thirty years. Jane had four pregnancies; two required psychiatric admission for psychosis, and a third was followed by depression treated by a psychiatrist. Jane received preventive progesterone treatment for her fourth pregnancy and was well throughout the postnatal period (see Chapter 16).

Tracy's husband had been admitted for depression before her marriage. She had five children and developed postnatal psychosis on each occasion. Her three sons and three grandsons all had a depressive illness between the ages of twenty and thirty-two years, and both daughters and one grand-daughter had postnatal psychosis. One granddaughter escaped depression, but she never became pregnant.

In 1987 I co-authored, with Dr Maureen Dalton and Dr Katherine Guthrie, a paper in the *British Medical Journal* which described the incidence of PMS in identical twins, unidentical twins, and sisters. If one identical twin suffered from PMS severe enough to require medical attention, the chances were 94 per cent that the other twin would also be receiving treatment.

In 1994 Dr Karen Heslington and I published, in the *British Journal of Family Planning*, a study into the incidence of PMS in adoptive and natural mothers whose daughters suffered from severe PMS. There was a significant difference, in that 15 per cent of adoptive mothers suffered from PMS compared with 65 per cent of natural mothers, who were controls. This implies that PMS is not due to childhood upbringing or to antenatal environment, but is dependent on a genetic factor. In view of the close similarity of PMS and PND, a genetic factor is probably also present in PND.

The effect of stillbirth

The *Lancet* in 1979 carried a report by Dr Michael Clarke and Dr Anthony Williams of a study of two groups of 400 women living in Leicestershire. In one group of mothers the baby had been stillborn or had died within seven days of birth; in the other group the mothers all had healthy, normal babies. Their findings were that the incidence of PND at six months after the birth was no greater among mothers who had lost their babies than among those mothers whose babies were healthy. They also found that PND was more marked in younger women of twenty-four years and under. They estimated from their survey that in England and Wales there must be some 23,000 women annually who are at least moderately depressed within six months of their baby's birth.

This report suggests that following the loss of a baby the distressed mother is comforted sympathetically by partner, family, and friends, and she does not need to hide her sadness, as she does with PND.

Social class

Numerous surveys agree that PND is no respecter of class. It is acknowledged that the late Princess Diana was a sufferer—and the consequences of this continued for many years. Those with the support of a lovely home, financial security, and a nanny can suffer PND in the same way as a lonely, single mother living on benefit. On the other hand, housing problems and financial stress increase the risk of a PNI developing. The different results from surveys occur because of different definitions used and different samples of women included or, more importantly, excluded. For instance, a survey in a known deprived area will tend to emphasize poor socio-economic status and lack of support from partner, family, and friends.

A personal study

To study the characteristics of those who develop PND, and particularly to find the incidence of recurrence in subsequent pregnancies, in 1979 I scrutinized the medical records in my own practice and in my hospital clinic of all women who had suffered from PND during the previous ten years and had been seen by me personally. This is probably the largest series of patients with PND personally studied by one doctor. Most of such studies in medical literature have resulted from a search of medical records of hospital patients with the severe form of psychosis, who have been seen by numerous doctors using varying definitions and standards.

The personal study was limited to married women who had suffered their first psychiatric illness within six months of a full-term pregnancy and which was severe enough to require medical treatment. (However it should be recognized that today only 51 per cent of mothers giving birth are married.) The survey covered 413 women, of whom 217 (53 per cent) had required treatment only from their general practitioner and so were classified as 'mild'; 113 women (27 per cent) had needed treatment from a psychiatrist and were classified as having an illness of 'moderate' severity; and 83 (20 per cent) had suffered from psychosis requiring hospital admission and were classified as 'severe'.

Possibility of recurrence

The 413 women had a total of 915 full-term pregnancies; they included 88 women who had only one affected pregnancy (many women said they had been advised to have no further pregnancies because of the risk of a return of their psychiatric illness). There were a further 104 who had had more than one child, but had had no further pregnancy following the one after which they had suffered a postnatal breakdown. This left 221 women who had had a subsequent pregnancy after the affected pregnancy, and among these women as many as two-thirds (68 per cent) had had another PND. Sometimes the second illness was worse than the first, and in others it was of the same severity or not quite so bad, but in every case it was bad enough to require further medical treatment. Furthermore, of those with the severe form of psychosis, over 84 per cent had a recurrence (Fig. 19).

However, the recurrence rate was not 100 per cent and there seemed to be no way in which a recurrence could be predicted. Note the word 'predicted' and not 'prevented'; prevention is discussed in Chapter 16. The survey included five women who each had six normal pregnancies with normal labours, and each time with the delivery of a healthy child. One woman developed PND after every pregnancy; another developed it after each of her first four pregnancies; another had it after her second and fourth only; yet another woman had it only after her last pregnancy (Fig. 20). Mathematicians will tell us that we have not exhausted all the possible combinations and permutations for a woman having PND following one or more of her six pregnancies. So it seems that there is no way of telling what the outcome might be.

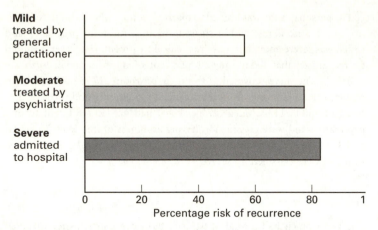

Fig. 19 Recurrence of postnatal depression in 221 subsequent pregnancies

An Italian survey of thirty women hospitalized between 1973 and 1987 for postnatal psychosis, reported by Dr P. Benvenuti and colleagues, showed the same high frequency of psychotic relapses after subsequent pregnancies.

Dr M.N. Marks and a group from the Institute of Psychiatry, London, studied women with a previous history of severe mental illness who were at high risk of a PNI, and also found 51 per cent of the women relapsed.

Age, height, and weight

In 1985, at the San Francisco meeting of the Marce Society, I reported another survey, this one aimed at discovering the type of woman most at risk of developing PND. The 413 women from my practice had all previously suffered from PND according to the definition given on page 3, and had experienced 633 pregnancies, of which 413 had been complicated by PND. Their ages at the time of the normal pregnancy averaged 27.6 years and at the time of their PND 28.4 years—thus they both had the same age range. In short, age was not a factor. Nor was there any relationship between the age at the time of their first pregnancy or their last pregnancy, nor whether the interval between their pregnancies was less than two years or more than ten years. Their recurrence rate remained at 64 per cent.

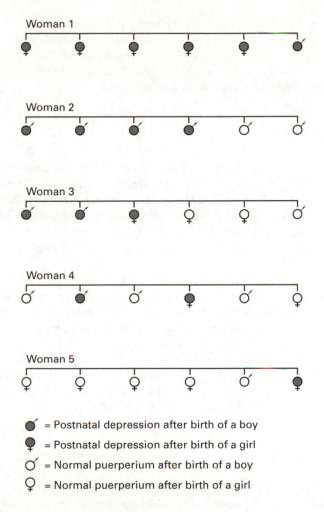

Fig. 20 Occurrence of postnatal depression in five women who each had six pregnancies

Some authors, on flimsy evidence, have suggested that PND is slightly more frequent in women over thirty, and others that it is slightly more frequent in women under twenty. This is then nicely explained by the fact that older women have problems giving up careers, and that younger women are more likely to be socially disadvantaged.

Heights were also studied in my survey and compared with those of normal women of the same age and parity who had normal pregnancies, and again no difference was noted: the short and the tall were equally at risk. In the same way their weight was studied, and again the ultra-slim and the overweight ran equal risks of developing PND.

First pregnancy

There is general agreement that postnatal psychosis is more frequent after the first pregnancy, but this is not so marked for depression. The survey reported at San Francisco noted that PND occurred in 73 per cent following the first pregnancy, with a progressive decline in the incidence after subsequent pregnancies (Fig. 21). All too often, after recovery from the first illness, the woman will be advised by her doctor, relatives, and friends to avoid another pregnancy.

It is interesting that 21 per cent of PND followed termination of a pregnancy, emphasizing the importance of arranging progesterone prevention for those who opt for a termination (see Chapter 16). In Britain, women who have had a termination of pregnancy may feel some measure of guilt and so do not easily seek help for their depression, feeling that they have brought it on themselves, and if they ask for medical help some months later they are apt to 'forget' the incident at their first interview. As a result, figures for the incidence of post-abortal depression in Britain are possible only in respect of those who required hospital admission.

Starting time

The blues develop between the third and fifth day after the birth. They are a short-lived phenomenon and are usually over by the end of the second week. In the early days of the twentieth century it was usual for patients to be kept in hospital, or in bed if it had been a home confinement, for a full fourteen days after the birth to help the mother overcome any emotional problems. Today however many women are discharged within hours and are cared for at home by the midwife. Unfortunately, the new mother is too often expected to resume her share of household work almost immediately, in addition to caring for the new family addition.

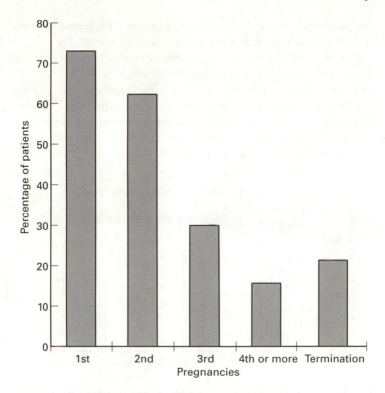

Fig. 21 Postnatal depression after pregnancy in 413 women

PND may start at birth, following on as a continuation of the blues, in which case involuntary tears give way to a general sadness and other symptoms of depression. For other women it does not start immediately and they have a few weeks or months feeling exhilarated and congratulating themselves on their good fortune before the depression sets in.

Those unfortunate women who are prone to psychosis will often find the onset immediately they return from the labour ward or shortly afterwards. In fact, half of all women admitted to hospital with postnatal psychosis will have had the onset within two weeks of birth.

In the study, reported in 1985 at the San Francisco meeting of the Marce Society, of 413 women with PND, it was noted that 51 per cent of those with psychosis had been admitted within fourteen weeks of birth, while in the milder cases, treated by the general practitioner, the reverse was true, with 39 per cent starting between six weeks and six months (Fig. 22).

The 1985 study reported at the Marce Society conference in San Francisco of 413 women revealed that 46 per cent started within two weeks of delivery, 14 per cent between two and six weeks, a further 22 per cent by three months, and 18 per cent between three and six months (Fig. 23). When PND starts after three months it often starts when breastfeeding ends, when menstruation starts again, on starting the Pill, on taking up nightwork, or on adopting a rigorous weight-reducing diet (see Box).

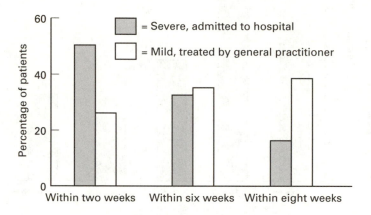

Fig. 22 Time of onset and severity of postnatal depression in 413 women

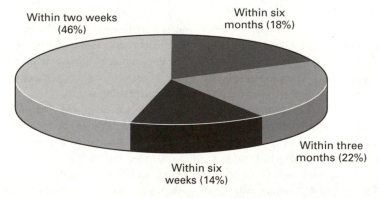

Fig. 23 Time of onset of postnatal depression in 413 women

> ## Postnatal depression starting after three months comes
>
> on stopping breastfeeding
> when menstruation resumes
> on starting the Pill
> on starting nightwork
> on adopting a weight-reduction diet

Symptoms in pregnancy

Not all women thrive in pregnancy. In 1960 I published a survey in the *Lancet* of over 600 women at the Obstetric Department, University College Hospital, London, which revealed that one in four of the expectant mothers who complained of pregnancy symptoms (nausea and vomiting, depression, tiredness, backache, headache, and fainting) during the middle months of pregnancy later required admission to hospital because of high blood pressure or pre-eclampsia (PET). These symptoms, which come out of the blue during pregnancy, may continue and develop into postnatal psychosis or depression after delivery. Doctors studying the hormonal changes of pregnancy and the puerperium have drawn attention to the occasional finding of depression in the last few days of pregnancy which may be heralding a PND and may be due to a decline in placental progesterone.

Vanessa is an example of those women whose depression started during pregnancy, and it is interesting that her mother suffered similarly. Vanessa was born in St Ebba's Hospital, Surrey, in the days when it was called a 'lunatic asylum'. Her mother had become psychotic during the pregnancy and was not discharged until six months after Vanessa was born. During both of her pregnancies Vanessa became depressed, with very strange behaviour, and had to be admitted to hospital. Vanessa's illnesses also eased spontaneously during the first year after the birth of her son and daughter.

Those who become pregnant again before their PND has eased frequently find that the depression lifts immediately the new pregnancy starts, but all too frequently after the next birth there is a return of the old symptoms, often with increased severity.

Rarely, but tragically, one meets a woman who has been struggling for several years to become pregnant but, when she finally succeeds, the pregnancy symptoms, with daily vomiting and deep depression, get too much for her and she pleads for her pregnancy to be ended. Annabelle was thirty-one years old when attending one of the infertility clinics at a London medical school. She asked for such help when she was ten weeks pregnant: 'I can't go on,' she pleaded amid sobs and tears. 'No one knows what it's like. No one told me it would be like this. I'm ready to end it all if you don't help me.'

She needed treatment to ease her frequent vomiting and depression, and agreed to a four-day trial of progesterone. This soon lifted the daily vomiting, and commonsense prevailed. She later was delivered of a fine boy, whom she named after the medical school which had helped her to become pregnant.

Sterilization

Sometimes sterilization is blamed for the onset of a depression. Until 1978 it was thought that such a simple operation as blocking the fallopian tubes could not possibly interfere with the body's hormone balance. However, in 1978 Drs Radwanska, Hammond, and Berger from Illinois University showed that women whose tubes had been blocked subsequently produced less progesterone from their ovaries. Indeed, the lowered progesterone blood level after sterilization has been confirmed by other workers. Today, most women are advised not to have a sterilization operation immediately after birth, but to wait until normal menstruation has returned, and also to avoid sterilization should PMS be present.

Adoption

Depression can occur among adoptive mothers and fathers during the first six months after they receive their adopted child. However, the incidence of depression in adoptive parents is no greater than in the normal population. Psychiatrists are apt to blame the breakdown on the hazards associated with the new baby's arrival, but the fact that adoptive parents are no more prone to depression that non-adoptive adults suggests that it cannot fairly be blamed on such factors as disturbed sleep due to baby's crying, increased work and responsibility, or the divided love of the husband for the child and wife. Furthermore, the illness in an adoptive mother is typical depression, rather than the atypical type of PND.

The Pill

A pilot study was undertaken in my own practice of 100 women who had taken the Pill, compared with a similar number of women who had used some other method of contraception. The results revealed no difference in the incidence of PND in respect of time between stopping the Pill and conceiving, the time interval between pregnancies, or the incidence of side-effects from the Pill.

However, there is some work, still to be confirmed, which suggests that women who start the Pill before the age of twenty-one years and continue for more than five years are at increased risk of developing postnatal psychosis. This suggests that hormonal interference can affect maternal behaviour in both women and animals (see p. 120). In today's society increasingly more women start the Pill at an early age and delay their pregnancies until their late twenties or thirties. It should not be forgotten that many findings in obstetrics, like the effect of thalidomide or rubella, resulted initially from small retrospective studies which were later confirmed prospectively.

Breastfeeding

It has been suggested that there may be a relationship between breastfeeding and the onset of PND. In my 1985 survey reported in San Francisco of 413 women (see Fig. 23) who had suffered from PND, there did not appear to be any relationship between those who did and those who did not breastfeed; nor with the duration of breastfeeding; nor whether they breastfed a particular baby or not. Inevitably in such a large sample, there was the occasional woman who maintained that she had been advised to stop breastfeeding and this had caused her breakdown, and also the occasional woman who claimed she developed PND because she had been advised to continue breastfeeding.

Bromocriptine (Parlodel) is a drug which reduces the prolactin level, and so is occasionally given to stop milk production at the end of breastfeeding, especially if breastfeeding is stopped suddenly. There have been reports of bromocriptine causing a sudden onset of psychosis with hallucinations, but fortunately there is a rapid return to normal as soon as bromocriptine is stopped.

Dieters

There are those who gain excessive weight during pregnancy and naturally want to return to their pre-pregnancy weight with all possible speed. Drastic dieting can cause the onset of PND, but I have not encountered it causing psychosis. It is wisest to wait until the hormones are readjusted before starting a drastic weight-reducing regime, particularly one entailing long intervals of fasting, fluids only, or avoidance of carbohydrates. On the other hand, the three-hourly starch diet, advised on Chapter 19, can be started immediately after birth with benefit, and the extra weight resulting from water retention will rapidly disappear.

The three-hourly starch diet does not involve extra food intake, assuming a good healthy diet is the norm, but divides the total daily food intake into six or seven snacks, each containing some starchy food. This means that no extra calories are involved, and if crispbreads are included the diet can successfully be used in conjunction with a low-calorie weight-reducing diet.

Nightwork

A baby's arrival too often brings with it financial worries, and there is a natural desire for mother to get back to work as soon as possible. This is admirable if suitable daytime work is available, but unfortunately night shifts can cause chaos to the day/night rhythm centre situated in the hypo-thalamus at the base of the brain (see Fig. 1, p. 16). Trying to turn day into night too often leads to sleep deficit and results in an upset of the hormonal balance, with the development of depression or psychosis. This is a partic-ular problem for nurses and airline stewardesses.

Nursing accounted for half of the replies from nightworkers to a survey conducted in 1994 by PMS Help on the effects of premenstrual symptoms on their work. The results included twenty-nine nightworkers, all but three being over thirty. All worked primarily with people and not machinery; 56 per cent reported suffering PND. Of particular interest was that among those who reported violent actions during the premenstrual days, nine out of ten nightworkers reported suffering PND. This violence was directed at the partner in almost all cases, plus some reported additional violence towards property, particularly to crockery, books, and furniture. Fortunately the least violence was against their children.

Different cultures

PND would appear to be worldwide and is certainly not limited to the developed countries, although it is only in developed countries that statistics are relatively easy to come by. In some primitive tribes it is harder to assess, as Dr John Cox discovered in his survey in Uganda. The difficulty was in finding suitable non-pregnant control women in a culture where it is a stigma for a woman to be either single or infertile. Nevertheless Dr Cox did find an incidence of 9.7 per cent among 186 Ganda women attending an antenatal clinic in a semi-rural centre. This is remarkably similar to the incidence of 10 per cent found by Dr Brice Pitt in his study of women attending the antenatal clinic of the Royal London Hospital.

Dr Brazelton of Harvard studied women in Guatemala and Sumatra and also found PND in these primitive tribes. He sees it as a force for doing good—a counterbalance to the physical and psychological tension built up during pregnancy. He suggests that PND is a way of telling the mother to slow down, so that she can gather her energy for looking after the new baby.

Jean Liedhoff, an anthropologist who studied a Stone Age tribe in Venezuela, recalled the absence of PND, which she attributed to the fact that the members of the tribe do not separate the baby from the mother immediately after birth, thus allowing for the normal bonding between the mother and her baby. However, two distinguished anthropologists, Margaret Mead, now based in New York, and Professor Jean la Fontaine, of the London School of Economics, both doubt whether anthropologists have the necessary medical or psychological expertise to detect PND in primitive cultures. They both disagree with the simplistic view that 'back to nature' automatically means all goes well in motherhood: 'doing what comes naturally' may mean that scores of women die in childbirth.

Dr Brice Pitt agrees that contact of the newborn with the mother immediately after birth does have an effect on the mother's behaviour towards the baby and on breastfeeding, but he doubts whether removal of the baby immediately after birth has the effect of causing PND, which may begin many weeks later. In home confinements in England the mother is usually given the baby to hold immediately after delivery, to encourage pair bonding after delivery. There is little difference in the incidence of PND among those having home or hospital deliveries.

Suggestions have been made in medical literature that there is a high incidence of postnatal psychosis among those of the Jewish faith, but in 1957 Dr Marvin Foundeur of New York reported a survey of religious faiths of those admitted to psychiatric hospitals following childbirth. He produced evidence that the incidence was the same for Protestants, Jewesses, Roman Catholics, and others (which included Christian Scientists, Fundamentalists, and Greek Orthodox).

Premenstrual syndrome

In view of the fact that PND so often develops into premenstrual syndrome (PMS), the survey reported at the 1985 Marce Society meeting in San Francisco was further analysed to find whether PMS had started before or after the PND. Before the pregnancy that was followed by PND, 20 per cent of the women reported having recognized PMS recurring with each cycle, which is a similar percentage to that present in the general population. However, a completely different picture emerged on analysing the incidence of PMS after PND: as many as 84 per cent of the women suffered from PMS afterwards. The commonest premenstrual symptoms before PND were tension (depression, irritability, and tiredness) and headaches, whereas after PND, epilepsy, asthma, and somatic symptoms were often mentioned, but they were cared for by other specialists and not by psychiatrists.

The finding that PND gradually changes to PMS suggests a common pathology, and it is probable that both illnesses represent a failure at cellular level of progesterone receptors at different times in a woman's reproductive life—namely, after delivery and after ovulation. PMS is the subject of the next chapter.

CHAPTER 14

Premenstrual syndrome

The next question to be answered about PND is 'When will it ever end?' The relevance of the question is illustrated by the following comments from two women:

> After four years there is still no sign of the depression, which started so suddenly and without invitation after my baby's arrival, making a permanent exit.

> I am now 42 years of age and have been plagued by a multitude of physical and emotional symptoms that started and became worse after the birth of my son and daughter.

While the blues and postnatal exhaustion are self-limiting, depression and psychosis can go on for years. Psychosis is treated in hospital sufficiently to allow the woman to function in the community, and the majority are usually discharged within a few months. But too often they are far from well and need continuous drug therapy.

There may be a lapse of up to nine months after birth before menstruation returns naturally, and even then there is not necessarily a regular interval between menstruations. There is usually a warning that menstruation is returning, with the mother's mental state deteriorating for up to fourteen days before the onset. Then, after the first menstruation is over, there may be some relief of depression and tension for a few days. Gradually the depression eases, with the relief and improvement occurring during the few days after menstruation (known as the **postmenstruum**), but there is a rapid return of the unpleasant symptoms in the days before menstruation (known as the **premenstruum**). This is represented as Stage 2 in Fig. 24, and the patient may remain in this stage for many years, with continuous depression and other symptoms increasing in the premenstruum. This stage is known as 'menstrual distress' or 'menstrual magnification'.

If improvement continues, full relief will come imperceptibly, with a return of normality during the postmenstrual days; such a pattern represents PMS, or Stage 3 in Fig. 24. As improvement continues the episode of premenstrual depression may slowly decrease, not lasting so long and not being quite so incapacitating, until perhaps it only lasts for one or two days before menstruation This stage has been described by one husband:

> She has a lot of up and down aspects to her character, and at the moment they really seem to have settled into monthly glooms and highs.

However, these mood swings, with normality in the postmenstruum but deep despair in the premenstruum, do not necessarily improve and they can continue for twenty or more years, until the menstruating years end with the menopause. This must be recognized as PMS, which can be treated successfully.

Early recognition of the effect of menstruation

The observation that PND may increase with the first menstruation after childbirth was made by Dr Marcé, a French physician, as long ago as 1855. He noted that women whose PND increased with the return of their menstruation frequently complained of vagueness, poor memory, weakness, pallor, anaemia, and menstrual irregularity. Across the Atlantic, in Mississippi, Major Alfred Blumberg and Dr Otto Billig reported in 1942 that hospital patients with puerperal psychosis showed these same swings in their psychotic behaviour, becoming worse after ovulation until menstruation and then improving following menstruation. These findings were confirmed by Dr Harry Schmidt of Los Angeles, and the American doctors came to the conclusion that puerperal psychosis must be of hormonal origin, or have a hormonal component, and they started treatment with progesterone, the hormone of pregnancy. This will be discussed further in Chapter 16.

This association of puerperal psychosis and PMS was noted by Dr Joan Malleson in 1953 when she wrote: 'It is commonly found that if menstruation returns before the psychosis is resolved, exacerbations occur repeatedly in the premenstrual phase.'

This caused Dr A.B. Hegarty to suggest, in a letter to the *British Medical Journal* in 1955, the name 'postpuerperal recurrent depression' for the recurrent depression, irritability, and tension during an attack of mild, but typical puerperal depression, whose symptoms were in the premenstrual phase. However, this title would exclude those women with PMS whose

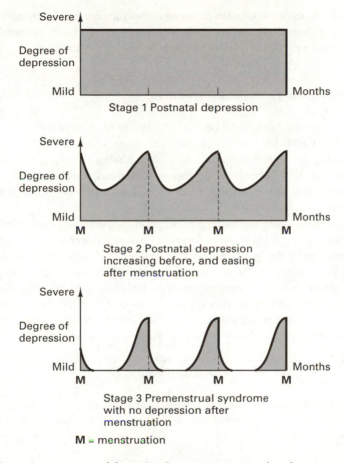

Stage 1 Postnatal depression

Stage 2 Postnatal depression increasing before, and easing after menstruation

Stage 3 Premenstrual syndrome with no depression after menstruation

M = menstruation

Fig. 24 Stages as postnatal depression changes to premenstrual syndrome

onset was not related to puerperal depression, so his suggestion did not win wide acclaim.

In one hundred consecutive patients seen at the Premenstrual Syndrome Clinic at University College Hospital, London, in 1979, there had been fifty-nine pregnancies (including six miscarriages) and it was found that PND of sufficient severity to require medical or psychiatric treatment had occurred in 73 per cent. In the survey reported at the 1985 Marcé Society meeting in

San Francisco, it was found that, among a cohort of more than four hundred women who had suffered from PND, as many as 84 per cent had subsequently suffered from PMS, as revealed by a three-monthly menstrual chart.

Definition of premenstrual syndrome

It is important to know the correct definition of PMS, because the phrase is often used loosely and frequently in the wrong context (see Box).

Using this definition, you will understand why Stage 2 in Fig. 24 could never be PMS, because the depression continues during the postmenstruum. It is only in Stage 3, when there is no depression in the postmenstruum, that the title PMS can be used.

The word 'syndrome' means a collection of symptoms which commonly occur together. In PMS there are over one hundred and fifty different symptoms; among this great variety of symptoms are headaches, migraine, backache, joint pains, bloatedness, asthma, hay fever, and epilepsy. These symptoms occur in different organs of the body and, of course, occur also in men and children, but they are only included in PMS if there is a close time relationship with menstruation and if there are a few days completely without symptoms, always in the same phase of the menstrual cycle.

Premenstrual syndrome

is the presence of recurrent severe symptoms which occur before menstruation, with complete absence of symptoms after menstruation.

Warning symptoms

Before normal bodily functions there are valuable warning sensations. These sensations tell us when our bladder is full or our bowels need emptying; before sneezing there is a nasal tickling; and thirst when we are dehydrated. Each individual woman has her own warning sensations before menstruation. These are not symptoms, but may be regarded as Nature's gifts. This does account for some surveys reporting the incidence of PMS being as high as 90 per cent. The symptoms of PMS need to be severe enough to require medical help.

Tension, which includes tiredness, depression, and irritability, is a very common symptom complex in PMS, so much so that when only tiredness, depression, and irritability occur in relationship to menstruation it is called 'premenstrual tension'.

Occasionally the symptoms of PMS include short-lived episodes of psychosis, with confusion, hallucinations, and delusions occurring just before menstruation. A survey in 1983, published in *Premenstrual Syndrome and Progesterone Therapy*, analysed 1096 women who had received progesterone therapy for PMS. It included sixteen women who had premenstrual psychosis, of whom fifteen (96 per cent) had previously suffered from postnatal psychosis.

The more one appreciates the characteristics and common symptoms of PMS, the easier it is to understand the similarities between this syndrome and PND. Tiredness, depression, and irritability are also common symptoms of PND. Water retention occurs in PMS, which results in bloatedness and weight gain, and can be responsible for the generalized aching of bones, muscles, and joints, and also for headaches.

There is altered glucose tolerance during the premenstruum, so that the individual becomes more sensitive to a reduced blood sugar level. When a low blood sugar level occurs, it is automatically restored by the outpouring of adrenalin into the blood, which can account for the sudden panics, aggressive outbursts and irritability, faintness, and migraine. This helps us to understand the increased appetite and longing for sweet things, the binges, and the food cravings (see p. 33).

There is a remarkable similarity of symptoms in both PMS and PND. In fact many of the quotations given earlier could also apply to women suffering from PMS, so long as the symptoms occur only before menstruation and completely disappear after menstruation has finished.

Fuller descriptions of the many symptoms of PMS are to be found in our books *The PMS Bible* published by Ebury Press (2000) and *Once a Month* (sixth edition), published by Hunter House Books of California (1999).

Diagnosis of premenstrual syndrome

Deciding whether an individual woman suffers from PMS depends not on the many and different symptoms she can recount, but on the timing of the symptoms in relationship to menstruation. Therefore it is no good going to a doctor and asking for help for PMS unless you can take with you an accurate record of the presence and absence of your troubles, and the dates of menstruation. Our menstrual patterns are all different. Sometimes menstruation comes every three weeks and sometimes every five weeks; in some women menstruation only lasts two days and in others it lasts seven or eight days; so a menstrual record is essential.

Although there are many different kinds of charts on which such records can be kept, the most useful for the purpose are shown in Fig. 25. All that is necessary is for you to mark with an 'M' the days of menstruation (or 'P' for period if that is what you call it), and then devise other symbols to denote your various symptoms, such as 'H' for headaches, 'Q' for quarrels and loss of temper, 'T' for those days when you are flaked out with tiredness. Capital letters can be used for severe symptoms and lower case for mild symptoms. These charts can also be useful for PND, to record the gradual change to PMS, as shown in Belinda's chart in Fig. 26.

Belinda had her first baby in January. Previously she had suffered from PMS, so she was used to recording the days of her tensions, which before pregnancy lasted for only two days. She was entirely free from the blues, but then depression started in early April, rapidly becoming worse. She had her first menstruation after childbirth in May, which was preceded by an increase in depression, and she became very irritable for six days, but there was some improvement after menstruation. The progress continued and after her July menstruation she had a few days when she felt really well for the first time in three months. It was not long before the gloom descended again. But gradually the brighter days lasted longer and the premenstrual tension was not too bad. She at last sought treatment in November, and her problem was solved.

Women plagued with PMS naturally seek a permanent solution to their monthly problems. It is all too easy to imagine that the removal of the womb, the source of the menstrual bleeding, will end their recurring miseries. After all, a hysterectomy is relatively safe and frequently performed, and although it is a major operation most women leave hospital within a few days. Unfortunately a hysterectomy, with or without the removal of the ovaries, and whether or not it is followed by hormone replacement therapy (HRT), is not the answer to PMS. The menstrual hormones are controlled by the menstrual clock, situated at the base of the brain (see p. 18), and whether the womb is present or absent the menstrual clock and the pituitary will continue methodically to produce the stimulation that pours the menstrual hormones into the bloodstream. If there is an imbalance of menstrual

	Jan.	Feb.	Mar.	Apr.	May
1			T	T	T
2			T	T	M
3			T	T	M
4			T	T	M
5			TQ	T	M
6	T		TQ	MQ	
7	T		TQ	M	
8	TQ		MT	M	
9	T	T	MT	M	
10	T	T	M		
11	T	T	M		
12	T	T			
13	T	M			
14	T	MQ			
15	TQ	M			
16	TQ	M			
17	MT	M			
18	M				
19	M				
20					
21					
22					
23					
24					
25					
26					
27				T	
28				T	
29				T	
30				T	
31					

	Jan.	Feb.	Mar.	Apr.	May
1					
2					
3					
4					
5					
6					
7					
8					
9					
10					
11					
12				T	
13				T	T
14	T	T		T	
15				T	T
16	T		T	T	T
17	T	TH	T	T	T
18		T	T	TH	MT
19	TH	TH	T	TH	M
20	TH	M	T	TM	MH
21	T	M	TH	HM	MH
22	TM	M	T	M	M
23	M	M	MH	M	M
24	M	M	M	M	M
25	M	M	M		
26	M		M		
27			M		
28			M		
29					
30					

M = Menstruation   T = Extra tired

Q = Quarrels   H = Headache

Fig. 25 Charts showing premenstrual syndrome

hormones sufficient to cause the symptoms of PMS, then even after a hysterectomy the same imbalance of menstrual hormones will persist and produce regular symptoms at monthly intervals without menstruation. There is a better treatment for PMS than hysterectomy—correcting the hormone balance with progesterone, and consideration for progesterone receptors.

Day	Jan.	Feb.	Mar.	Apr.	May	Jun.	Jul.	Aug.	Sep.	Oct.	Nov.	Dec.
1					x	XM	•		•	•		
2					x	XM	•		•	•	•	
3				•	x	x	•		•	•	•	
4				•	x	•	•		•	•	X	
5				•	x	•	•		•	•	X	
6				•	x	•	•	•	•	•	X	
7				•	x	•	•	•	•	X	X	
8					x	x	•	•	•	X	X	M
9		Birth			x	x	•	•	•	X	X	M
10					x	x	•	x	•	X	X	M
11					x	x	•	x	X	X	Mx	M
12					x	x	x	x	X	X	Mx	
13					x	x	x	x	X	X	M	
14					x	x	x	x	X	X	M	M
15					x	x	x	x	X	X	M	
16					x	x	x	x	X	M	M	
17					x	x	x	X	X	Mx		
18					x	x	x	X	X	Mx		
19					x	x	X	X	xM	Mx		
20					x	x	X	X	xM	Mx		
21					x	x	X	X	xM	•		
22					x	X	X	xM	xM			
23					x	X	X	xM	xM			
24					x	X	X	xM				
25					x	X	xM	xM				
26					x	X	xM	xM				
27					x	X	xM	xM				
28					x	XM	xM					
29					x	XM	x					
30					x	XM	x					
31					XM			•				

M = Menstruation   • = Mild depression

x = Moderate depression   X = Severe depression

Fig. 26 Chart showing change from postnatal depression to premenstrual syndrome

Recognition of the similarities between PND and PMS will open the door to more successful treatment of PND, but it does require an understanding of the modern knowledge of the hormonal changes of menstruation, pregnancy, and the puerperium, which have been discussed in Chapters 2 and 3.

CHAPTER 15

Treat the cause not the symptoms

It is the doctor's task to discover the cause of each illness, although it is often easiest to treat the symptoms and forget the cause. In minor and one-off accidents it may not be necessary to pursue the cause, as it does not really matter. If someone has had a slight fall down the stairs and feels some stiffness the next day, symptomatic treatment with a pain reliever may be all that is necessary without considering whether the stairs are safe or need a banister. But in recurrent or severe illnesses finding the cause is important to the doctor who will need to know if the fall was due to a sudden attack of giddiness or slipping on a banana skin. The doctor may then treat the patient differently.

Patients arrive at the surgery complaining of symptoms and are satisfied if they have relief of those symptoms. They do not always know the difference between 'symptoms' and 'illness'; they will often confuse the two. For example, the symptom 'jaundice' could be due to a viral infection or to gallstones blocking the gall duct. These two conditions need entirely different treatment. Another example is 'peritonitis', which may be caused by appendicitis or a perforated gastric ulcer, again the treatment is quite different depending on the cause

---

Patients tend to

complain of symptoms

be satisfied with relief of symptoms

Doctors tend to

listen to symptoms

search for cause of symptoms

treat the cause of symptoms

This is very important when considering postnatal exhaustion, depression, and psychosis. These are all symptoms and can result from many different causes, each cause needing a different treatment. Exhaustion may result from thyroid deficiency, anaemia, or overwork with lack of sleep; depression may result from a recent bereavement or malnutrition; whilst psychosis may result from schizophrenia or drug abuse. The symptoms of depression can easily be treated with antidepressants, and there are valuable psychiatric drugs to relieve the symptoms of psychosis. Unless the cause of the symptom is appreciated patients with PND will need treatment indefinitely. Many women with PND in the 1970s and 1980s are still receiving benzodiazepines over twenty years later. The cause of their symptoms was never sought.

Ruth is an example of the many whose psychotic symptoms received prolonged treatment because the cause was forgotten or ignored. Ruth travelled three hundred miles for her first consultation with me in August 1996. She was thirty-three years old and had been a nursery nurse before her daughter's birth in 1990. Her second daughter was born in 1991 and within two weeks she was hallucinating, confused, and blank. Admission was essential, and she received forty-eight sessions of ECT and anti-psychotic medication. She was discharged on heavy medication, moved to another part of Britain, and continued with the same heavy psychiatric medication. At our first interview she described the voices she was hearing that told her to harm herself and about her husband's imaginary actions. She was exhausted, depressed, unable to cope with cooking, shopping or cleaning, and spent most of the day in bed. A community psychiatric nurse attended weekly.

With the cooperation of her psychiatrist who had been unaware of the timing of her illness, her medication was reduced and within three months she was free from hallucinations, had lost over two stone in weight, and started menstruating once more. She then realized that the migraines she had suffered from now occurred each month before menstruation. Her premenstrual migraines responded to progesterone therapy. When she was herself once more and free from symptoms she became pregnant again. In January 2000 she gave birth to her third daughter, received prophylactic progesterone, and did not suffer a recurrence of PND.

It needs to be emphasized that the hormonal changes of pregnancy (see p. 21) and maternal behaviour of animals (see p. 118) are subjects not studied by psychiatrists. When a patient who still requires psychiatric medication moves to a new area and changes her psychiatrist, he or she does not automatically know how the illness started. Too often it is diagnosed as schizophrenia, a chronic illness which needs long-term psychiatric medication. Unfortunately the problem is increased because the psychiatric drugs used also tend to stop menstruation, so any PMS is missed.

If you move . . .

while taking medication for postnatal depression, make sure your new psychiatrist and GP know how and when your illness started.

There is immense pleasure in seeing women who have received unnecessarily prolonged psychiatric medication because the origin and initial cause of their illness was forgotten, return to the real world and normality.

CHAPTER 16

Progesterone preventive treatment

Stamp collectors would enjoy my daily postbag with its varied colourful stamps from so many different countries, among them stamps from Iceland, New Zealand, Hong Kong, Malawi, Chile, Greenland, Singapore, Finland, Japan, Germany, as well as the continents of North and South America and Australia. The most frequent requests are for preventing a recurrence of PND. Many letters also contain horrifying descriptions of the illness which followed the previous birth. A typical letter came from Louise, who wrote:

> My great problem is my husband's refusal to allow me to have another child, after having a severe breakdown which meant spending three months in hospital after our baby Terry was born.

Prevention of recurrence

Fortunately in most cases it is now possible to prevent a recurrence of PND, especially in those women whose only psychiatric illness followed a birth. Countless patients, having suffered once from PND, have asked for, and received, particulars of progesterone preventive treatment starting at the completion of labour.

The numerous letters of thanks received after successful progesterone preventive treatment describe the relief at having avoided this unpleasant complication. The phrases used include 'wonderful', 'great', 'marvellous', 'positive', 'unbelievable', 'too easy for words', 'so completely different', 'feel first rate', 'confident and coping again', 'a startling contrast', ' very contented', 'wonderful to appreciate being a Mum', 'completely normal', 'no voices or terrors this time round', and 'didn't have those silly excitable days'. Many said they hoped their letter would reach me, emphasizing that they had had no one else to turn to or that they had tried everyone else. The many letters of thanks included:

> I cannot thank you enough for enabling me to have such a fantastic pregnancy and birth. After four children I have at last known the joy of seeing my babe's first smile. It's wonderful to be in full control and completely normal. This babe has been an absolute enjoyment from the moment he was born. The feelings of PND (inability to cope and worry) were replaced by those of pleasure and fulfilment. Being able to breastfeed was an added bonus.

> This is the first of my three babies I have really been able fully to enjoy. I felt like me the whole time, and was able to cope with them all. I didn't even have a single Baby Blues Day. There was this pleasant sense of well-being and I loved the bonding process.

> This was so completely different. After three previous suicide attempts and being hospitalized after my previous three births, it was lovely getting to know my daughter. There were none of those voices that you just can't get away from.

> I still cannot believe the contrasts between the two births. Every day was filled with relief and joy that the terrible unhappy time before had not come back. Nothing seems too difficult to do. I now feel cheated of the closeness and happiness that I could have enjoyed with my first baby. It's been a totally different experience.

> Absolutely fine. Much better than I ever expected. I'm thrilled to be able to breastfeed this time and I have coped amazingly well compared with last time. I have felt so very happy.

> Having Helen was a wonderful experience, so completely unlike the nightmare that plagued Richard's first six months.

> Marvellous—I felt normal—just like my old self. Because I was happy, my children were happy and my husband was happy.

Similarity of postnatal depression and premenstrual syndrome

The many similarities between PND and PMS and the gradual change from PND to PMS have been dealt with in Chapter 14. In fact, 84 per cent of women who have once suffered from PND subsequently develop PMS.

PND occurs when there is a precipitous drop in progesterone level at delivery (see Chapters 2 and 3); similarly PMS occurs when there is a drop in progesterone level prior to menstruation. Both illnesses get worse if sufferers are given the Pill; both increase following sterilization; both start at times of hormonal upheaval; and both depend for their diagnosis on the timing of symptoms, rather than on the exact nature of the symptoms.

Similarity of PMS and PND

Both have symptoms of depression, lethargy, and irritability predominating

Both are related to a drop in progesterone blood level

Both rely on timing for diagnosis

Both worsen on the Pill

Both respond to treatment with progesterone

Both respond to consideration of progesterone receptors

Suicide is an ever-present danger in both

The common symptoms of exhaustion, depression, irritability, headaches, and the occasional psychosis can occur equally in PND and PMS. The changes in personality and mood which occur after delivery can equally occur in the premenstruum. Both PND and PMS may be seen as a spectrum with a gradual merging from the blues to exhaustion and on to depression and finally psychosis. Suicide attempts, violence, and loss of control can occur in both illnesses.

PMS can be successfully treated with progesterone, although for it to be effective progesterone must be given before the onset of symptoms, which means that normally it is administered from ovulation to menstruation. Therefore it is no surprise to find that PND can be prevented by using progesterone in the same way, giving it immediately after the completion of delivery and before the onset of symptoms. The aim is to control the sudden drop in progesterone which normally occurs at delivery, and convert it into a more gradual and slow fall over the subsequent weeks until the return of menstruation (Fig. 27).

The use of progesterone in the prevention of a recurrence of PND was first reported in 1964 and found to be quite successful, but how could that

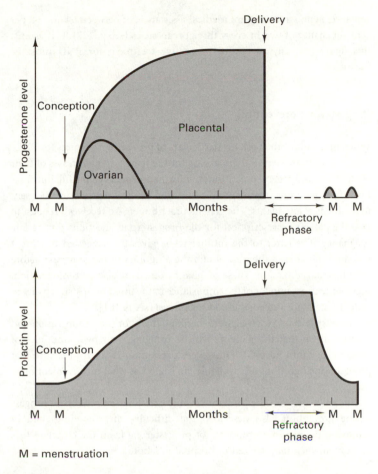

Fig. 27 Blood levels of progesterone and prolactin in menstruation, pregnancy, and the refractory phase

success be measured? If a woman has once had PND, the chances of a recurrence are not 100 per cent, and a search through medical literature gave only vague and variable estimates in regard to the chances of the disease recurring after the next delivery. It was for this reason that the survey reported at the 1985 Marcé Society meeting in San Francisco was undertaken. This showed an overall chance of recurrence, in those whose PND was severe enough to require medical assistance, of between 64 and 68 per cent—a chance of two in every three pregnancies (see p. 127). It is against this figure that any successful preventive treatment for PND must be measured.

Progesterone prevention

When pregnant women ask for particulars of preventive measures for PND, routine letters are sent to them asking for the names and addresses of their obstetrician and general practitioner. Information packs giving full information of progesterone treatment schedules and medical reprints are then sent to the medical attendants. The general practitioner also receives a request to give the patient a prescription for the progesterone injections during late pregnancy. The letter to the mother-to-be gives the suggested treatment schedule and advises them to obtain the ampoules of progesterone before their hospital admission. These pregnant women are also sent information, together with a reminder of the importance of the three-hourly starch diet in order to maintain a steadier blood sugar level (see p. 181).

The obstetricians receive letters thanking them for their cooperation and advising them that the patients will be bringing their own ampoules of progesterone into hospital. Thus every precaution is taken to ensure that progesterone injections are available, no matter at what inconvenient hour the delivery should occur.

One midwife from the Midlands, while extolling the benefits of progesterone prevention, also described the difficulty she sometimes had in removing the precious ampoules of progesterone from the clenched fists of women when they arrived in hospital in labour.

Treatment schedule

The treatment schedule advises that from the completion of labour the patient is given 100 mg of progesterone by injection daily for seven days, followed by a 400-mg progesterone suppository twice daily until the return of menstruation. As the women have all previously experienced symptoms of PND, they are advised that, should there be any suggestion of a return of mild early symptoms, they may increase their daily dose of suppositories to four or six daily, or even return to daily injections if preferred (see Box). All women are different and so too are their early warning signs, but each woman will recognize her own constellation of symptoms.

Progesterone prevention

100-mg progesterone injections daily for seven days, followed by

400-mg progesterone suppositories twice daily for two months or until menstruation returns.

If any symptoms appear, the dose of 400-mg suppositories should be increased to four or six daily, or the patient should return to 100-mg injections daily.

At the end of two months, if menstruation has not restarted and the woman is feeling well, the suppositories can be reduced and stopped. If at any time before menstruation returns and while still breastfeeding she has a return of symptoms, progesterone can be restarted. If menstruation has started and symptoms are worse in the premenstruum, then progesterone should be given from day 14 of the cycle until menstruation.

Progesterone does not interfere with breastfeeding. Indeed, when progesterone was first isolated in the 1930s, it was believed that its main function was the preparation of the breast for lactation. Only one suppository should be used at a time, as if two are used there is a build up of wax which prevents adequate absorption of the progesterone. A second suppository should not be used for at least two hours.

Progesterone preventive surveys

It was at the second Marcé Conference in 1983 that I first spoke of the 90 per cent success of progesterone in preventing a recurrence of PND. In 1985 full details were published in *The Practitioner* of a survey of one hundred pregnant women who had all suffered from a previous PND severe enough to require medical help, had all been offered progesterone prevention, and were then followed up for six months after delivery by letters to the patient, general practitioner, and obstetrician. Most of the women came from England, but the survey also included three from Wales, two from

Scotland, and one each from Northern Ireland, Belgium, Spain, and Switzerland. Six of the one hundred women had decided, for a variety of reasons, not to have progesterone treatment, and four of them unfortunately again suffered from psychosis and had had to be admitted to hospital, producing the expected recurrence rate of 68 per cent. However, of the ninety-four who did receive progesterone, nine women had a recurrence, giving a recurrence rate of under 10 per cent. In fact two of the failures did not receive the full course of progesterone, suggesting that other doctors may be able to improve on these successful results.

This survey was followed by another worldwide one published in the *International Journal of Prenatal and Postnatal Studies* in 1989. The success rate of preventive progesterone was 92 per cent among two hundred women from all the five continents who had all previously suffered PND. This compared with the rate among twenty-one women who enquired about it and did not receive progesterone after birth, of whom only 32 per cent avoided a recurrence.

A follow-up of pregnant women enquiring about progesterone prevention has continued since 1989, with the results being reported at international conferences in England, Germany, the United States, and Australia in 1994 and 1995. Again, the prevention of a recurrence is between 90 and 92 per cent successful. This last survey, in which more questions were asked of the patients, has emphasized the high proportion of these women whose previous illness was postnatal psychosis (50 per cent) compared with depression (Chapters 9 and 10). Usually one expects one case of psychosis for every twenty women suffering from depression. Most important is the finding that psychosis can also be prevented by progesterone treatment.

These successes are not seen by psychiatrists, who only see the failures. On the other hand, once a general practitioner or obstetrician has seen this success, he is likely to give progesterone treatment to other patients without my knowledge. Obstetricians already use, and are familiar with, progesterone for *in vitro* fertilization and assisted conception. A survey in 1995 revealed that 50 per cent of general practitioners already use progesterone for PMS, so they too are familiar with its use. Several hospitals already routinely question all women attending antenatal clinics about any previous PNI, and if there is a previous history they are offered preventive progesterone. The Royal Berkshire and Battle Hospital NHS Trust has information leaflets on Dalton's regime for PND.

As mentioned earlier it is satisfying when, having arranged preventive treatment for some unseen patient, in cooperation with all the doctors involved, one receives letters several months later. Of interest is Mandy's story, which suggests that progesterone prevention also helped her over a major stress event.

Mandy, thirty-one years of age, had suffered from premenstrual tension since her teens. She was well during her first pregnancy and had a 'small-for-dates' baby weighing just 2 kilos. This was immediately followed by psychosis, for which she required drug therapy for three years, after which she received progesterone treatment for PMS. All drugs were gradually stopped over the next six months. When her first daughter was four years old, she again became pregnant, and felt very well throughout her normal pregnancy. She received progesterone in hospital and later at home and there was no recurrence of PND or psychosis. Tragically, when the baby was three months old he died suddenly in a cot death, but Mandy, although naturally emotionally upset, did not develop depression. She was again treated with progesterone from mid-cycle until menstruation and all was well.

Progesterone treatment

Natural progesterone cannot be adequately utilized if given by mouth because it passes via the stomach to the liver, where it is broken down before reaching the systemic circulation and the brain (see p. 29). However, natural progesterone is highly effective if given by injections or suppositories. The suppositories are pellets of pure wax impregnated with progesterone, which can be inserted into either the rectum or the vagina. They are made to melt at body temperature and as the wax melts the progesterone passes through the mucous membrane of the rectum or vagina and into the blood. The melted wax does not go into the bloodstream but passes out of the body, either mixed with faeces if used rectally, or from the vagina, lubricating it on the way. Many women have learnt that to prevent the wax being messy all day, it is worthwhile using a panty liner for half an hour or so, then wipe and wash and all the mess is forgotten. However, it is important not to use two or more suppositories at the same time, as the excess wax then blocks the absorption of progesterone.

Although suppositories are most convenient and can be self-administered, about 10 per cent of women do not absorb progesterone sufficiently through the rectum or vagina, and these women need continuous daily injections, or may require alternate days of injections and days of suppositories.

The injections are highly effective and well absorbed. They need to be given into the buttock muscles where there are fat cells intermingled with muscle fibres. The progesterone is initially absorbed into the fat cells and then gradually released into the bloodstream. Injections may be given anywhere in the buttocks where there is a one-inch pinch of flesh, but never in the thighs, nor in an area which is red, hot, or hard. When an injection is given into the buttock the sciatic nerve is protected by the pelvic bones, but the nerve is unprotected in the thighs (see Fig. 28). So injection may not be given into the thigh or other parts of the body. Many women administer their own injections; alternatively they may be given by the midwife, community or practice nurse, or partner. The advantage of self-injections is that they can be given immediately before taking a bath, as sitting in warm water helps the absorption of the oil.

Rules of progesterone therapy

Progesterone has been used since 1934 and over that time doctors have appreciated that to get its full value certain rules are important. Our new knowledge of the functions of progesterone receptors helps us understand why oral administration is not as effective as rectal, vaginal, or intramuscular (p. 39), why progestogens are no substitute for the natural progesterone (p. 32), why high doses of progesterone are needed (p. 29), and the importance of avoiding drops in the blood sugar level (p. 33).

Experience has taught us that to be effective progesterone must be administered early and before symptoms develop. Progesterone is preventive. For instance, in *in vitro* fertilization progesterone must be used as soon as the egg is transferred; in habitual abortion progesterone is used as soon as the pregnancy is diagnosed; and in PMS it is given from ovulation until menstruation. So, too, in PND it must be started immediately after labour and before any symptoms appear (see Box).

If there is any vaginal thrush or candida infection when progesterone is used, it will tend to exacerbate the irritation. Fortunately today it is possible to eradicate thrush easily, within a few days, by giving the woman and her partner a single dose of Diflucan.

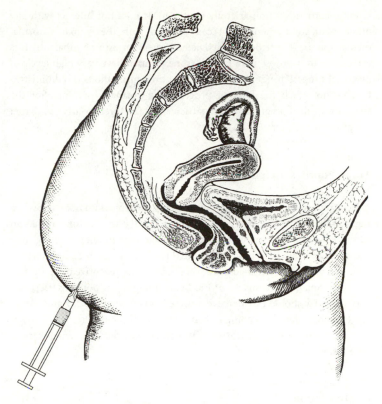

Fig. 28 Injection site—anywhere in the buttocks where there is a one-inch pinch of flesh

Rules of progesterone treatment
Ensure three-hourly starch diet is being followed
Start before symptoms are expected
Use a high dose
Use vaginally, rectally, or intramuscularly
Breastfeeding is enhanced with progesterone
Eradicate any thrush infection

Progesterone is a user-friendly treatment. It does not interact with any other medication, therefore it can be used with the woman's normal medication, be it anticonvulsants, beta blockers, or asthma inhalants. It is impossible to overdose with progesterone: women have very high levels of placental progesterone in pregnancy, and present methods of administration cannot reach the level of progesterone normally present after the sixteenth week of pregnancy. Full particulars of the three-hourly starch diet are given in Chapter 19.

Three-hourly starch diet

A more recent finding shows that progesterone receptors do not work when sugar in the cells is low (see p. 33). This means that the doctor now has an additional responsibility to make sure that the new mother is eating little and often to avoid long food gaps. The three-hourly starch diet, advocated by sufferers of PMS, is also ideal for those receiving preventive progesterone for PND. Small starch snacks of food containing flour, potatoes, rice, rye, oats, or maize should be eaten every three hours during the day and within one hour of waking and going to bed (see Box). If the mother wakes to see to her baby or to give a night feed, it is important that she remembers to have a starchy snack herself.

Contraception

Progesterone can be used as a contraceptive quite safely for women who have severe PMS or are at risk of PND following delivery. The contraceptive dose is half a 200-mg progesterone suppository daily from Day 8 until Day 14, when it should be increased to the patient's usual dose: 400 mg two, three, or four times daily until menstruation. This is specially useful for those women who cannot tolerate the oral contraceptive pill and are considering what form of contraception to use in the postnatal months (see Box).

The efficacy of progesterone as a contraceptive is equal to that of the progestogen-only pill; Dr Mark Steward and I have reported on this in the *British Journal of Family Planning* in 1995.

Progesterone can be used for contraception

if 100-mg suppository given daily from Day 8, increased on Day 14 to usual dose needed for PMS, and continued until menstruation.

Women at risk

In antenatal clinics, the women who should be offered progesterone prevention are those who have previously suffered from PND, those whose sisters or mothers have suffered PND, and all who are planning to be sterilized at or shortly after delivery. Many women who have suffered from PMS of sufficient severity to require progesterone therapy will benefit from progesterone after delivery, as it helps their chances that PMS will no longer trouble them, but in fact they are at no greater risk of developing PND than any other mother. Indeed, in view of the total safety of preventive progesterone, there would seem to be no reason to refuse to give it to any pregnant mother requesting it (see Box).

Although it is only a possibility at present, and more research is needed, in view of Dr Wang's work (see p. 120) on maternal behaviour in mice, one wonders if women who have had a previous termination in which mifepristone was given should be considered for progesterone prevention.

All who require or are requesting prophylactic progesterone in the antenatal clinic should also be given full information about the three-hourly starch diet.

Progesterone prevention should be offered

to previous PND sufferers

if mother, sisters, or aunts suffered PND

to severe PMS sufferers

if sterilization is planned after delivery

if there has been a previous termination of pregnancy

if they have been on the Pill for five or more years

Oestrogen therapy

As both oestrogen and progesterone are produced by the ovaries, and both have increased blood levels in pregnancy, no doubt there are some readers wondering why oestrogen is not used as prevention against PND. The two hormones, oestrogen and progesterone, are complementary, but have different functions. Oestrogen is essentially the feminizing hormone and is necessary for ovulation. At puberty it is oestrogen which is responsible for the growth of the womb, the breasts, and the rounded, feminine body shape. Later it is the oestrogen surge which stimulates the luteinizing hormone (LH) from the pituitary, and this results in ovulation; and it is also oestrogen which restores the lining of the womb after it has been shed at menstruation. So oestrogen is a very important hormone, and without it pregnancy is not possible. Unlike progesterone, oestrogen has the additional advantage that it can be administered by tablet or skin patches.

However, oestrogen also has the ability to cause clotting of the blood, which is necessary at delivery when the placenta separates from the lining of the womb. But oestrogen is not required after delivery, as its clotting powers may cause blood clots to form in the lungs (leading to a pulmonary embolism) or in the brain (resulting in a stroke) or in the veins (producing deep-vein thrombosis). At one time oestrogen was used to dry up the milk when breastfeeding was stopped prematurely but, when the connection between oestrogen and blood clots was appreciated, the Royal College of Obstetricians and Gynaecologists advised obstetricians against its use during the first six weeks after delivery, and since then there have been no maternal deaths due to pulmonary embolism or strokes in the puerperium in England or Wales.

Oestrogen has been used for treatment of PND persisting six months after birth in mothers who have stopped breastfeeding. By this time many mothers have restarted menstruation and are suffering from Stage 2 PND, menstrual distress, or PMS (see p. 141). Looking through the many letters of thanks from patients who have been treated with progesterone prevention, I am convinced that not many would have wished to have waited six weeks, or even months, before commencing preventive treatment.

One way round the clotting property of oestrogen is to give it immediately after delivery, and at the same time give anti-coagulant therapy to ensure that the blood does not clot. This, however, needs careful supervision and daily blood tests to ensure that the blood is maintained at exactly the right level to avoid clotting and also unnecessary bleeding from the womb.

One looks forward to the day when all women attending antenatal clinics are systematically asked about their previous puerperium, and progesterone prevention is automatically arranged when required or requested. This is already the accepted routine in many hospitals in Britain, and some throughout Europe, America, and Australia. It is to be hoped that recognition of the benefit which preventive progesterone can bring will spread throughout the world as more doctors, midwives, and health visitors appreciate the importance of knowing who is at risk.

CHAPTER 17

Stress—can we ease it ?

It has become a habit to blame life's difficulties on stress and then to wash our hands of the problem: 'There is nothing I can do about it!' But what is stress? Is there really nothing we can do to ease stress? Is it an excuse for anything; a way of offloading the problem?

The word stress is used to cover those circumstances when the hormones adrenalin, noradrenalin, and corticosterones rush through our veins. These cause the heart to pump faster, muscles to tense, and our arteries to constrict to reduce blood loss should wounding occur. The digestion shuts down to allow more blood to flow to the muscles. This is a primeval reflex from our 'hunter/gatherer' days to allow us to cope with emergencies, to fight or flee from foes. Adrenaline is an important hormone, secreted by the adrenal glands.

! DANGER ! **Adrenalin rush**	⇒ Fright
	⇒ Fight
	⇒ Flight

Some of the most common symptoms of too much stress are the oft-reported irritability, agitation, anxiety, panic attacks, heart palpitations, dizziness, nausea or lack of appetite, headaches, insomnia, lack of energy, continual tiredness, or lack of libido. When seen as a response to crisis the symptoms are understandable. Having fought or flown from the situation there will be a reduction in energy and resulting tiredness. However when the stress is continuous or present for the majority of time, these symptoms become part of your life and can cause medical conditions such as depression, headaches, high blood pressure, heart disease, and skin sensitivities. In fact stress can be related to many health problems of today.

Stress can be positive

On the other hand, to lead a totally stress-free life would be only an existence as there would be no motivation to even lift yourself from the bed in the morning. Life would be a monotonous, boring, blank, without incentive or purpose. Stress gives us the motivation to do things and to rise to the challenges we find stimulating, to turn negatives into positives, when there are too many of the former in our lives. As with so much today, it is 'moderation' that is required; a little is good, but too much is bad. We need enough stress to enable us to lead a fulfilling and interesting life, but not so much as to make us feel in a continual rush.

As we are all different, our ability to cope with varying levels of stress differs. What is challenging to one person may make another feel totally panicky and overwhelmed. It is important to know your optimum stress levels, where life is stimulating, challenging, and a pleasure, then ensure that you do not regularly overstress yourself.

Endorphin is a positive stress hormone which occurs on exercise. It is beneficial to the body as a whole and can relieve certain levels of pain. Good physical exercise will tone and tire muscles so that sleep will come more readily, and ensure a healthy person. It is thus important to undertake regular exercise, even if it is walking instead of taking the car, or using the stairs instead of the lift. Obviously in the postnatal weeks it is doubly important to get sufficient exercise to help retone the body and to aid sleep. If you do some brisk walking, with the baby strapped to your body or in a pram or buggy, both you and the child will benefit from being outside and sleep better. Others may prefer a trip to the gym where they can compete with others and socialize. There are many types of exercise to suit all people and all pockets.

Major causes of stress

Death of spouse

Divorce or separation

Jail term

House move

Causes of stress

American researchers have drawn up a list of various stresses, rating each out of one hundred. At the top of the list unsurprisingly is the death of a spouse, followed by divorce, separation, a jail term, and house move.

Lower in the list are changes in various situations, such as a spouse starting or ceasing work, altered working hours, eating habits, living conditions, or social activities, family get-togethers, holidays, Christmas, and so on. It is easy to forget that change is a cause of stress, both to those involved intimately in the change and those with less direct involvement. So when you cease work even temporarily on maternity leave, this will affect your partner. A new member in the family will cause change to you all, not just the mother, but to father, siblings, grandparents, friends, and neighbours.

Causes of stress after childbirth

Extreme tiredness following labour

Broken nights causing more continual tiredness

New role as parent

Loss of financial security

Failure to be a 'super mum'

Ease the stress

There are many causes of stress which are outside our remit, and we are unable to do much about, but there are also many that we can change, with a little reorganization to our lives. Look at your new way of life and see where you can make changes, perhaps prepare food early in the day, so that night-times, when you are exhausted and want to spend time with your partner, are not such a rush. Women with PND often find that in the morning they have plenty of energy but it is in the late afternoon and evenings that they are totally exhausted. So plan accordingly. Why not change to eating ready-prepared food if you are really too tired to do anything, or perhaps your partner will take his turn in the kitchen? When you are cooking, do a double batch and put one in the freezer for use when you are feeling less able to prepare a meal.

Some quite simple steps can lower your stress levels in the home environment. Net curtains or, better still, lining curtains, can reduce the level of noise and light coming through windows. Perhaps you can put on some calming music to hide the noise of the traffic outside. Even placing the pile of ironing or old papers in a cupboard or somewhere else out of sight can be helpful. Decorating the room in a restful way may help. If the higgledy-piggledy stack of books irritates you, spend a half hour or so getting them in order to suit you.

Accept all offers

If others offer to do things for you, do not get agitated if they do them differently—sit back and be grateful this is one job you don't have to do. Try not to criticize or moan that the shirts need to be hung this way, or that you *always* vacuum from the windows to the door. Accept that there are various different ways of doing things and appreciate the offer of someone to ease your load. Too many women make a rod for their own back by not allowing others to do jobs for them because they do them differently, and yet complain that they have to do everything and nobody helps them.

Involve older siblings

If you have another child as well as the newborn baby it is often difficult giving time to them both. When you sit down to feed the baby ensure that the other child has some of your time too. Sit together on the sofa and look at a storybook; let them, too, have a biscuit or a piece of fruit and a drink. Depending on the age of the older children it is possible to involve them in the care of the newest addition. Asking for their help when changing the nappy, or getting a toy for the baby or a drink of water for mummy whilst she is feeding makes them feel important too.

If the older child is ready for school or to attend a toddler group, nursery, or playgroup, this will allow you time on your own with the baby. You will need to ensure that the older child gets your attention when the baby is sleeping so they do not feel neglected. Mature mothers may encounter the situation of teenage siblings who will react differently to the new arrival. This is a particular problem with stepfamilies. It is important that they too have time with you on your own, and that they are allowed to give the baby attention and care—but this must be to meet their requirements, and not your own.

Rest when you can

Ensure that you get plenty of rest. This sounds so simple but is much harder to achieve. When the baby is sleeping it seems an opportunity to rush round doing all the jobs you haven't done, but if you are tired you should use this time to sleep or to relax with a good book or the newspaper, lying horizontally. You can do the tidying up or washing when the baby is awake by strapping him into a baby sling. That way the baby will be stimulated as well.

Look at your diary, there are many things that you can combine in one outing, or if you find being confined within the home difficult, then divide your trips so that you go out each day. The secret is to look at your life and to decide what are the major stresses or irritations that you need to work on. By reducing these life will be calmer and easier, and you can then move on to other stresses and deal with those.

If you are missing the camaraderie and companionship of work, remember that any time you go out is an opportunity to meet others and talk. Many people will stop and talk to a new mother with her baby in the buggy, particularly other new mothers, and this is a chance to find out about local mother and baby groups, babysitting circles, and so on. New mothers often find that they want to converse with other mothers about minor problems and situations; it is difficult to confide in old friends who are working and probably cannot understand your current concerns. Work friends are often unable to be as enthusiastic as you are about baby's first smile or tooth, whereas another mother can remember that milestone vividly herself and share the pleasure with you. Sometimes you will crave the stimulating conversation of pre-baby times, whilst at other times you need to nurture the maternal side and talk with young mothers.

Share your worries

Do not let yourself be worn down by small worries about the baby—share these with your partner, health visitor, or other new mothers. It is sometimes forgotten that grandparents have experienced many of these or similar worries and are able to give comfort and advice. Many grandparents, wary of being seen as interfering, step back, but long for a worry to be shared with them. This is a great opportunity to learn from them. Don't forget they are there.

Share your worries/concerns with:	⇒	your partner
	⇒	your health visitor
	⇒	your GP
	⇒	the grandparents
	⇒	other new mothers

It is important that you and your partner share time together, just the two of you again; perhaps you can get a babysitter, or even take your baby round to another new mother. Your roles as parents should not consume your previous relationship of friends and lovers.

Relaxation

There are many relaxation techniques which may ease the stress of modern life. There are those you can do in a group, such as meditation, yoga, or Tai Chi (to name but a few). These will give you an opportunity to meet others and encourage you to participate. Attending a class on a set day and time is probably easier than having to find the time yourself to sit quietly—that can be put off till tomorrow or the next day. You should find details of these classes in your local paper, medical centre, pharmacy, or health store.

Relaxation can also be learnt alone, or with just your partner. It is always useful to know how to relax your muscles; so often you are not aware that you are keeping your shoulders tense or your hands clenched in a tight fist.

To relax your muscles you need to sit or lie down in a comfortable position, wearing loose clothing. Slowly tense and then relax one set of muscles, for example, those in your left foot, and repeat this several times, clenching the toes and relaxing them. You can then move to the right foot, then up to your left leg, right leg, left hand, right hand, tummy, shoulders, and face until you have tensed and relaxed the many different muscle groups in your body several times, and it is fully relaxed. Stay in this state for a few minutes before getting up and resuming your normal life. Eventually you will find that you can relax appropriate muscle groups when you are feeling tense in outside situations, such as in traffic jams, queuing to pay for petrol, or commuting on the train or bus.

Visualization

There are various visualization methods which you can do yourself or in a small group. You need to ensure that you are sitting or lying down comfortably and breathing gently but deeply, with your diaphragm (since shallow breathing causes body stress). Then close your eyes and imagine a restful picture—perhaps a painting or a place you know and love. Some people prefer to make up a peaceful picture, for example, a summer meadow with a river flowing gently through, with a pretty bridge or some trees alongside. Others may favour a sea view with a beach or boats bobbing on the water, or high hills with clouds scudding across. As you gradually build up the picture in your mind's eye, bring in appropriate sounds (the bird song, lapping water, or whatever) and smells. When you have built up your picture, look at it for several minutes, enjoying it, and then put a frame around it. You can even pretend it is a postcard and move it back in your mind till it is the right size and then commit it to memory. Don't rush up; slowly close down the picture and whilst you are breathing gently, begin to move your arms and legs before getting up. You will find that you are far more relaxed.

At times of further stress you will be able to recall that picture from memory, and by fixing on it for a few moments, with some gentle breathing, find that you are relaxing and better able to cope with the situation. I have even recalled a relaxing picture whilst waiting in a queue, infuriated at the slow checkout assistant in the supermarket; it enables me to deal with the weekly shop much easier.

Breathing

Invariably as we become more and more stressed, we tend to develop shallow breathing. This can develop into hyperventilation and panic attacks if allowed to carry on for too long. It is difficult to think about how to breathe—you just do it. However you need to think about it if your stress is resulting in fast, shallow breathing.

Initially you will find it easier to sit or lie down comfortably and just think of your breathing. Lightly place your hands on your abdomen and feel them move gently with your breathing. Breathe deeply in and hold it for the count of two before gently breathing out. As you continue with this deep breathing you will feel your body relaxing and becoming calm.

One part of the body which slows down when highly stressed is the digestive system. The desire for food is reduced. Therefore you just grab anything to eat and end up with a poor diet, which only further increases the stresses your body is under. By changing to a healthy, balanced diet (see Chapter 19) you will feel better and fitter. Maybe your taste buds are feeling jaded or you are one who does not enjoy cooking. If so, why not look at a cookery book or one of the many available videos of cookery shows until you feel stimulated to try something different; you don't necessarily need to follow the complicated recipe, but often you will feel tempted to eat something.

CHAPTER 18

The medical team

Today the general practitioner is no longer the only one to treat PND. There is a team of professionals with different skills, ready to help and liaise with each other, with the sole intention of ensuring that the new mother does not suffer and is restored to health as quickly as possible. The team may include the midwife, health visitor, practice nurse, psychiatrist, psychotherapist, community psychiatric nurse, and counsellor. Also always ready to help are the social workers. Many of these will visit the home, so not all consultations will necessarily be in the doctor's surgery.

Education

The first essential is the education of all team members to ensure that they are thoroughly familiar with the many diverse presentations of PND and have a good understanding of the vital part played by the precise balance of the hormones of pregnancy. In turn they will need to communicate this message to the new mother, the father, family, and friends, so that they, in turn, also understand that this is a hormonal illness over which the patient has no control. The old platitudes of 'pull yourself together' and 'don't be so lazy' should be a thing of the past. There is no need to find a reason for her illness, to delve below the surface and ask about possible child abuse or hidden guilt feelings. This will be necessary in only a few cases, and then at a much later stage in the illness, and initially by psychiatrists or psychotherapists.

Practical help

Discussion with the father or nearest helper may suggest ways in which the team can make life easier for the new mother. Can they suggest someone to take care of the baby for an hour or two each day to allow the mother to have a daytime nap to make up for lost sleep? Is too much being expected of the new mother in the way of housework, cooking, or shopping? Could an older child join a playgroup to ease the mother's load? Is there a local MAMA, NCT group, or mother/parent and baby group for the new mother to attend?

Practical advice has its place, but it must be individually tailored for the mother: everyone is different. Heather, a thirty-year-old secretary, suffered from too much advice. She meticulously listed the suggested treatments that had been given to her, which included 'move house', 'go back to work', 'give up work', 'you're working too hard', 'take a whisky: relax', 'see a marriage counsellor', and 'snap out of it', when—as she said—'all I WANT to do is to snap out of it!'

Even if the mother is only suffering from the blues, it is important to remind the partner not to let her crying be seen by other children.

All team members should also appreciate the importance of regular eating to prevent drops in the blood sugar level, and of a diet for general good health which includes daily protein and fresh fruit and vegetables. They should know, and be able to explain to the father, family, and friends, the benefit of the three-hourly starch diet (see Chapter 19).

If any team member hears a remark which might indicate suicidal or infanticidal thoughts, there is an immediate responsibility to summon medical help and to ensure that the mother is not left alone or alone with the baby. Lynette's story is a case in point. She and John were lying together, with the baby between them, on the morning that an 'At Risk' meeting was planned for 10.00 a.m. Lynette got up to wash and dress, then asked John for the baby so that she could get him ready. Twenty minutes later she returned to tell John she had drowned the baby instead.

Similarly each member should know when there is a need for medication and doctor's help. The midwife conducting the antenatal clinic has a special responsibility to ensure that preventive progesterone is arranged during pregnancy for any mother who has previously suffered from PND or psychosis, for anyone at risk, and indeed for anyone who requests it. Hers is also the responsibility to be ever alert to any change in personality or early signs of depression. She needs to be able to distinguish the blues from the more serious signs of PND.

Call for help

Deep down in everyone is the very natural desire to enjoy the best of health, and generally we feel that nobody understands our problems better than ourselves. When we are unwell, as opposed to being ill, there is always a favourite personal remedy to restore us to our usual state of well-being. There is always the satisfaction of curing ourselves without bothering the doctor. Some people, even when they are really ill, cling to a desire to avoid the doctor, and never is this desire greater than when there is a lurking fear that a simple visit to the health centre will result in confirmation of the unspoken fear that there really is a mental disturbance and a need to see a psychiatrist, or to have a much-loved baby removed from one's own care. Nevertheless, it is better, indeed vital, to overcome this fear and to ask for help. These sentiments were expressed by Elizabeth, whose carefully penned letter said:

> As a rule I am opposed to chemicals and a believer in mind over matter. I prefer to sort myself out without assistance unless I run out of steam. Desperation causes me to seek out an alternative that might end in a solution of my problem. I have exhausted them all. Sometimes a statement only sounds so dramatic because it is true.

That part of Elizabeth's letter might seem sensible enough, but she was in desperate need of help. There is another letter, this time from a husband, who asked apologetically for help:

> I very much regret that my attitude during these scenes has obviously, with hindsight, been the wrong one and may well have exaggerated the problem, as normally I have only been able to manage frequent exhortations to pull yourself together; also at times of anger and violence I am ashamed to say that I, too, have been so angry that I have unfortunately made remarks about her mental health which naturally I now bitterly regret. The result of such remarks seems to have been to increase the number and intensity of hysterical outbursts to such an extent that I am now desperately worried as to what now we can do for the best. There have been occasions when I have considered sending for an ambulance or trying to get her to the nearest hospital.

The health visitor

Whereas at one time health visitors were concerned solely with children's health, today they are responsible for the whole community, young and old alike, helping to ensure good health in all. This has coincided with the remarkable change in the general understanding of PND and with it a desire to recognize the illness at the earliest possible stage.

Many health visitors now use the Edinburgh Postnatal Depression Scale (EPDS) to screen mothers six weeks after the birth (see p. 75). It is quick to complete and to score and, more importantly, it has been shown to have a high sensitivity. It helps health visitors to decide which mothers need help immediately and those who are borderline and need more frequent visiting. Some health visitors have been given special training in non-directive counselling, which when used on mildly depressed mothers has proved remarkably successful. Hopefully the use of the EPDS and the counselling training will be extended to all health visitors.

The general practitioner

The family is often known to the general practitioner, who is in an excellent position to note any change in the new mother's personality, for the same doctor was probably also responsible for her antenatal care and the care of other family members. Once the doctor has seen and examined the mother, he can help with a crying baby, ensuring that the feeding is adequate and there is no colic or nappy rash. Maybe there is an indication for the baby to be given a sedative to help him sleep for longer intervals during the night.

More importantly, the doctor has a selection of medications which can prove helpful. If insomnia is an important problem, he can solve this with non-addictive sleeping tablets, making sure that there is someone available to care for the baby when the crying starts at night. Panics, anxiety, and palpitations often respond well to beta-blockers. Sometimes an analgesic may be needed to help relieve the pain of stitches. A blood test may reveal that exhaustion is caused by anaemia or a low thyroid function—both conditions which respond easily to iron or thyroxine tablets respectively.

Antidepressants

If depression is the prime symptom, then there is a wide range of antidepressants from which to choose. In general practice most patients—men, women, and children—are likely to suffer from typical depression, so the doctor's first choice may well be a favourite antidepressant in the tricyclic group. Unfortunately, as previously mentioned, PND is not a typical depression (see Chapter 5), so that choice is not necessarily the best. The tricyclic group is the good old standby, generally safe and effective. These drugs have the snag that they take about two weeks to be fully effective, although sleep usually improves within a day or two, followed by a quickening in thought, speech, and activity, and a final lift in mood. They include amitriptyline, nortryptiline, imipramine, chloripramine, lofepramine, trimipramine, and dothiapin. Even if taken at night, they tend to cause drowsiness in the daytime, so driving should be avoided, and some patients complain of a dry mouth and constipation.

Selective serotonin re-uptake inhibitors (SSRIs)

Within the last few years a group of drugs has been introduced, designed specifically to correct the brain-cell chemistry and the part played by 'serotonin', a neurotransmitter. These drugs are known as the selective serotonin re-uptake inhibitors or SSRIs.

As mentioned in Chapter 4, progesterone has many various functions on different cells of the body, such as the womb, bones, lungs, skin, and hair. In the brain, progesterone takes part in the dopamine pathway and acts on serotonin in much the same way as the SSRIs, so these are excellent drugs for women with PND, but not if there are any signs of psychosis. They are quick-acting and include fluoxetine (Prozac), paroxetine (Seroxat), citalopram (Cipramil), and sertraline (Lustral). Once again one is reminded that all women are different. Some find the SSRIs make them feel alert and prevent sleep, so medication should be taken on waking. Others find they cause drowsiness, so for them the medication needs to be given at night, when it will ensure a good night's sleep. It is a useful practice to start with only half the dose for one week while the patient discovers which time of the day suits her best; then she can increase the dose without problems. They are better tolerated than tricyclic antidepressants, are less sedative, and safer in overdose. Side-effects may include nausea, headache, and loss of libido.

It is now appreciated that women who suffer PMS tend to be those who have a rapid response to these drugs. Once the correct dose of SSRIs has been established, women with PMS only need to use them from ovulation until menstruation. A systematic review of SSRIs in PMS in 904 women reported in the *Lancet*, September 2000 by Paul Dimmock and colleagues from Keele University, concluded that SSRIs were an effective first line treatment for severe PMS, the side effects at low doses were generally acceptable.

Monoamine oxidase inhibitors (MAOIs)

Another group of antidepressants, known as the 'monoamine oxidase inhibitors' or MAOIs, are especially helpful in the treatment of atypical depression, such as PND, but they have been superseded by the SSRIs. In 1994 a team from Illinois University, including Professors Y.C. Lin, H. Kono, F.P. Zuspan, A. Yajima, and Dr A.C. Lee, succeeded in culturing human placental cells and demonstrated that progesterone inhibited monoamine oxidase activity on the cells. In short, they showed that in placental cells progesterone had the same antidepressant action as MAOIs, which may explain why so many women blossom in pregnancy and why the MAOIs had been the drugs of choice for PND.

The advantage of the MAOIs is that they do not cause drowsiness; indeed they may cause wakefulness at night, so patients are advised to take them on rising, and some patients may also need night sedation. This lack of sleep is important as it interferes with the function of progesterone receptors. Also they lift depression within two or three days. However the downside of MAOIs is that they interact with many other drugs, including ephedrine, amphetamines, morphia, pethidine, and certain tricyclic antidepressants. They enhance the effects of alcohol, barbiturates, insulin, and hypertensives, among others, and should be avoided in those with heart failure, liver disease, and epilepsy. This all means that care needs to be taken with their use, and if patients are already on certain tricyclics, then they must first be weaned off them for two weeks before starting MAOIs, or the MAOIs need to be stopped for two weeks before starting other drugs.

While patients are on MAOIs, there are certain foods which are forbidden, the most important of which are cheese, Marmite, Bovril, and broad beans. Alcohol is allowed, but only in very moderate amounts. This means that MAOIs can be given only to patients who can be relied on to abide with the list of forbidden foods, which they collect with their first prescription. If they transgress and take even a smaller than average portion of forbidden food, they are likely to be punished with a severe headache, due to a sudden rise in blood pressure. In the early days of using MAOIs, before the food restrictions were understood, there were isolated cases of brain haemorrhages after a good pub lunch of alcohol and an 200-gram portion of cheese.

Progesterone

Most importantly, the doctor can start the mother on progesterone therapy, although it will not be as dramatically effective as preventive progesterone started at the completion of labour. Progesterone can be given with any other medication which may be used to bring the immediate symptoms under control. It can be given even if the woman is still breastfeeding, and should be continued until menstruation, when it can be stopped for fourteen days and then restarted. The minimum effective dose is 400-mg suppositories twice daily or injections of 50 mg daily, but these doses can be increased to 400-mg suppositories up to six times daily or injections of 100 mg daily. (See pp. 158–9 for the rules of progesterone treatment.) The most important rule is that the blood sugar must be kept steady, and for this the mother is advised to keep to the three-hourly starch diet (see Chapter 19).

Psychiatric help

If there are any worries about the safety of the baby or the mother, the general practitioner can either ask a consultant psychiatrist to visit the mother at home or arrange immediate admission to hospital. Twenty-four-hour supervision is very difficult to arrange at home, and if this is not possible then hospital admission is essential. Maybe the psychiatrist will give the mother a trial of medication at home while keeping a close eye on her, or arrange for the community psychiatric nurse (CPN) to supervise her closely. If the mother is lucky and living in the right part of the country, she may be able to attend a mother and baby unit as an out-patient—but such units are few and far between. On the other hand, unless there is very good social support at home, most cases of psychosis need admission to hospital, preferably to a mother and baby unit.

Mother and baby units

It still depends on where the patient lives as to whether or not there is a mother and baby unit with a bed available. At present it seems that there are mother and baby units only in Britain and some Commonwealth countries. Some areas have good mother and baby units, and are ready to admit mothers from outside their area, but there are also some black spots where no facilities exist. It is a great comfort to the mother to be able to take her baby with her into hospital, even if at the time of admission she is rejecting the baby. The nurses have midwifery and/or paediatric experience and are ready to give all the tender loving care to the baby which the mother is temporarily unable to give. Admission with the baby has been found to entail risks to the baby of infection and injury from other patients. On the other hand, admission without the baby also has its drawbacks, particularly if there is no one ready to care for the baby and fostering is needed. The mother's progress is usually slower, and the psychological development of the baby may suffer if they are separated in the early days.

Gradually the mother is united with the baby, and very slowly the bonding process takes place. As she improves, she will be allowed out of hospital for a few hours during the day, first alone and later with the baby. Then she may spend the odd night at home, and gradually leave is extended for weekends or longer. As she leaves hospital there may be a day centre for her to attend for the first few weeks while she adjusts to her new life at home with her family. Otherwise she will be visited regularly by the CPN and discharged back into the care of the general practitioner.

Hospital help

If the mother is confused, deluded, or having hallucinations, it is surprising how quickly these ghastly symptoms can be brought under control with modern drugs. Within a few days she will be a different person, although she will still be far from well. She will need to stay in hospital until the medication is stabilized and the psychotic symptoms have all disappeared. If she is considered suitable, she may join in group therapy or have individual therapy. Before discharge she will be able to cope with her own needs and those of her baby, and preferably she will be well bonded to her baby. Nowadays it is only very rarely that ECT is required to bring a rapid end to the mother's sufferings, but it is usually most effective, although there may be a short-term memory loss.

At the end

It is useful for the partner to join in the final visit of the mother to the family doctor. There are many loose ends to be tied up. Discussion will cover the return of menstruation and whether there have been any signs of PMS. She should be advised to keep a menstrual chart (see Figs. 25 and 26, pp. 145–6) to check the possibility of PMS occurring and, if it is present, to ask for help. The return of sexual desire is often the last symptom to clear up (see Chapter 8), and the partner may appreciate help here. Another problem area is often the choice of contraception. The mother would be wise to avoid hormonal contraceptives, which all contain progestogens (yes, even the long-acting injections and contraceptive implants or rods such as Norplant). Sterilization is likely to increase any PMS and is best avoided. However, progesterone suppositories can be used as contraceptives, using half a 200-mg progesterone suppository from Day 8 until ovulation, when a higher dose of progesterone may be used until menstruation if PMS is being treated (see p. 161).

Finally, there need be no recurrence of the present illness. Progesterone prevention is now easily available in Britain and its use is gradually extending round the globe.

While the many different skills of the medical team can help the unfortunate mother, one must not forget the importance of the understanding and help which can be offered by the partner, family, and friends, which is dealt with in Chapters 21 and 22.

CHAPTER 19

The three-hourly starch diet

For all mothers in the first few months after childbirth, and particularly sufferers of PND, a steady blood sugar level is required for general health and well-being. We therefore unequivocally recommend the three-hourly starch diet.

This entails eating small portions of starchy food every three hours of the waking day; within one hour of waking and one hour of going to bed at night. It is important to remember to eat some kind of starchy snack when feeding the baby in the night.

The three-hourly starch diet entails:

Small portions of starchy food every three hours—
throughout your waking day
within one hour of waking each morning
within one hour of retiring to bed at night
when/if you wake at night to feed or settle the baby
every single day

The starchy foods are those containing flour, rice, oats, potato, maize, or rye. They are cheap to buy and all are low calorie—*on their own*! It is the fat the chips are cooked in that makes them high in calories; similarly the cream and sugar in the cakes, the honey we put in the porridge, and so on. These basic starch foods are not fattening.

It is important to combine the three-hourly starch diet with a diet for good general health—that is, three daily portions of protein (fish, meat, eggs, cheese, pulses, nuts) and five daily portions of fresh fruit or vegetables.

> The starchy foods are those containing ⇒ flour
> ⇒ rice
> ⇒ potato
> ⇒ oats
> ⇒ maize
> ⇒ rye
>
> You don't need to eat much; a *small quantity* is all that is required.

One way to do this is to divide your usual daily food intake into seven or eight snacks, each containing some starch (assuming you follow a healthy diet in the first place). So you could have a small bowl of cereal or a slice of toast for breakfast, with another slice of toast at mid-morning. For lunch have only half a sandwich, with some yoghurt or some fruit, and have the other half mid-afternoon. For your evening meal have your main portion of protein, vegetables, and potatoes or whatever, and a piece of fruit or something similar. Then before bed have a slice of apple pie, piece of cake, or anything with a bit of starch in it. In other words, you are eating no more but sharing it throughout the day.

> Divide your usual food intake into six or seven snacks
> Each snack should contain some starchy food

Crispbreads are a good alternative snack. Eat smaller portions of your usual meals, and then have a crispbread (Ryvita, Scandacrisp, or similar) or rice cake mid-morning and mid-afternoon, with two before bed. This way you will eat less than a hundred extra calories daily, but as you will no longer feel so hungry, you will be satisfied with smaller portions of your main meals, and the bingeing on chocolate or sweets will disappear. Your total monthly calorie intake is likely to be far less.

There is a huge variety of crispbreads available. Some you will like as they are, whilst others will need something on them to liven them up. There is a great selection of healthy things to put on crispbread—Marmite, cottage cheese, cold meat, tomato, cucumber, for example—and they do not need a spread as well. I keep a box of assorted crispbreads in the kitchen cupboard and eat them as others would sweet biscuits, but mine are lower in calories!

Why every three hours?

The three-hourly starchy diet will ensure that your blood sugar level remains steady all the time. The bloodstream is a transport system whereby the various hormones and nutrients that the body requires are transported to the target cells. The energy supply for all our living cells is transported in the blood, therefore the body's finely-tuned mechanisms ensure that the level of sugar in the blood does not exceed or drop below certain pre-set levels. If there is too much sugar then insulin removes the excess into the urine to be excreted. If the level drops too low, then a surge of adrenalin converts the stored glycogen into sugar to be transported via the bloodstream through-out the body. In the usual course of events the blood sugar level does not drop until five hours after a meal. However in the postnatal weeks and in the premenstruum this time is often reduced to three hours. If no starchy food is taken to maintain the blood sugar level there will be another surge of adrenalin and the whole cycle will repeat itself until you next have a meal.

Whilst men can in general go up to five hours without food before their blood sugar level drops, there are many who could also benefit from eating starchy foods little and often. It is particularly helpful if they too eat some starchy food when you do, so that you are eating together and you do not feel guilty about your snacking.

If you have just some sugar, a sweet, or some chocolate the blood sugar level will rise rapidly and soon fall back again abruptly; then there will be another adrenalin surge with all that that entails. However, if you have some starchy food, the sugars in which take much longer to be fully absorbed into the blood, there is a gentler rise which is maintained for longer, then a smoother decrease. So if you do want to eat some chocolate go for a Kit-Kat, Penguin, or Twix which also contain some biscuit, rather than have pure chocolate.

Adrenalin is also the hormone of fight, fright, and flight, so that in an emergency we are able to cope, to run away, shout, scream, or draw attention to the danger. However the fight, fright, and flight triad also gives rise to those PND symptoms of agitation, irritability, panic, withdrawal, and tiredness that are so often expressed.

When adrenalin is present these symptoms tend to become apparent, but although you may eat quickly and allow the blood sugar to stabilize, the adrenalin has a half-life of ten days and the symptoms may continue for well over a week.

	Adrenalin	
Fight	**Flight**	**Fright**
Aggression	Withdrawal	Panic
Rage	Depression	Anxiety
Irritability	Caution	Apprehension

Progesterone has many functions within the body, those involving reproduction being only part of the story (see Chapter 3). It also has an important role to play with regard to glucose regulation. When there has been a drop in blood sugar levels the adrenalin in the nucleus prevents the action of progesterone receptors. These transport molecules of progesterone to the target cells and then on through the cell wall to the nucleus. You therefore are inadvertently suspending the full utilization of progesterone within your body. However, in ensuring that the blood sugar level is maintained at a steady level by eating small portions of starchy foods every three hours of your waking day, you are doing your very best to ensure that the progesterone can be fully utilized.

Although we have said earlier that following delivery of the placenta your progesterone level drops drastically, and that the levels of progesterone are minute until the reproductive cycle recommences once more, there are still almost unmeasurably small amounts which fulfil the many other functions of progesterone unrelated to reproduction. These same incredibly small, but vital amounts of progesterone are present in men, postmenopausal women and children (see Chapter 3).

One afternoon recently I received a telephone call from a desperate mother begging me to contact her GP and 'tell him to increase my medication'. I had never met this lady, nor had I any details of her medical history, yet she had total faith that I could make a quick telephone call and ask her doctor, who did know her, to alter her medication. After talking to her for some time I learnt that she had PND following the birth of her daughter, Zoe, now four months old. Among her symptoms were tiredness, feeling weak and faint, panic attacks, and a feeling of uselessness as she couldn't seem to do anything right. As it was 3.30 p.m. I asked her what she had eaten that day, and she replied 'nothing'.

On further questioning it transpired that she had drunk five cups of herbal tea and had had one Snickers bar. She would ask her partner to bring in a pizza for tea—the only food she would eat that day! I explained what a good healthy diet required: protein, three servings daily; and fresh fruit or vegetables, at least five portions daily, which she was totally lacking. I particularly talked to her about the three-hourly starch diet and suggested that before any change to medication she should start to eat properly. I also asked her to keep me informed of how she was.

Two days later she rang to say that she was feeling full of energy and a lot better. A week later she rang to thank me for my help and to tell me that she was feeling so well she wanted to start reducing her medication. Her so-called PND was self-inflicted, caused by her very poor diet.

Breastfeeding

If you are breastfeeding you need to ensure that you take plenty of liquid together with your healthy three-hourly starch diet. This liquid should include sufficient water, milk, and fruit juices, with not too much in the way of caffeine-laden drinks such as coffee, tea, or cola. Your breasts will take the best vitamins and proteins to ensure that your milk is providing sufficient for your growing baby, and your own body will have to make do with what is left. It follows that if you start by having a poor diet then your own body will receive little of what it needs and you cannot begin to return to full health with decent energy levels.

Breastfeeding will also help your body to return to its pre-pregnancy shape; whilst the baby is suckling the uterus contracts and the abdominal muscles are automatically gaining a workout.

It is important whilst breastfeeding to have plenty of calcium-rich foods, to ensure that not only does the baby receive a good level of calcium, but that you do too. Women need to build up good bone mineral density to prevent osteoporosis later in life. The recommended intake of calcium for a breastfeeding mother is 1,250 mg daily. A pint of milk will give 700 mg, as does a portion of spinach with a medium-sized cheese and tomato pizza and yoghurt. By law in England, white bread must still contain added calcium. It was originally included in white bread and flour during the Second World War to ensure children had sufficient calcium for their growing bones. Other foods high in calcium are all dairy foods, canned fish, spinach and other green vegetables, tofu, bread (your starchy food), figs, rhubarb, and that delight, chocolate. For a non-breastfeeding mother the recommended daily intake of calcium is 700 mg.

Larger portions today

Until the middle of the last century, when large numbers of women entered the employment market, and before fridges and freezers were common, women were at home all day. They spent much of their day in the kitchen baking bread, cakes, biscuits, and cooking soups and stews, and since 'good cooks always taste', women inevitably ate little and often. The well-to-do had their breakfast, mid-morning coffee, lunch, afternoon tea, and supper, and everyone enjoyed a bedtime snack to stop night starvation. When the family sat down for their evening meal the mother would serve large helpings to the men and labourers, but smaller helpings to the women, and even smaller portions to the young children and elderly.

Today there is only one size portion, and the fast food outlets serve the same sized portion of food to everybody. It is important to remember that men do require a higher daily total calorie intake than women and we should serve smaller portions to ourselves.

Vitamins and other supplements

It is some people's belief that rather than simply eating a good, balanced diet, they can get away with a bad diet and supplement it with vitamin tablets and the like. This does not give any kind of balanced diet, although some vitamin levels will be raised.

Our body is an extremely complex, integrated machine and 'balance' in all things is required to keep it performing at its very best. Along the great length of the alimentary canal the digestive system removes different elements of our diet at those specific points where they can best be utilized. If you take your vitamins and minerals in tablet form they are not available for use at the correct points along the tract and the most effective usage cannot be obtained. As these supplements are in tablet form, any overdosage of a specific vitamin or mineral is not necessarily excreted in the urine, but may be retained within the body and can cause unnecessary ill-health.

The secret is to have variety and to balance your diet to your particular food preferences. By taking your vitamins in their natural form, any excess vitamins are unlikely to be taken up by the body but will pass out unabsorbed. It is only in cases of major consumption of a particular food item that damage occurs, for example, over-consumption of carrots over a prolonged period can cause the skin and body parts to turn orange, whereas reasonable portions of carrots are particularly good for your general health.

We strongly advise all women not to take vitamin B6, also known as pyridoxine. Although some have suggested it for PND, any benefits have been totally unproven. The body's daily requirement of vitamin B6 is 1.2 mg, which is easily obtainable in any diet containing meat, fish, breakfast cereal, beans, lentils, spinach, or bananas. Drs K. Dalton and M.J.T. Dalton have studied 172 women who were taking vitamin B6, all of whom had a raised pyridoxine blood level. It was noted that 60 per cent of these women already had signs of nerve damage and pyridoxine overdose neuropathy. Their work showed that as little as 50 mg of pyridoxine daily, taken for six months or more, can cause these symptoms. The early symptoms include headache, puffy eyes, irritability, shooting pains in the head, chest, arms, or legs, sensitive skin, and weakness of the limbs, particularly fingers. These symptoms disappear on stopping the vitamin B6, but can reappear later if vitamin B6 is again taken in increased quantities, such as in a multivitamin supplement.

We are also concerned by current work which shows that St John's Wort can adversely affect medications taken for a variety of reasons. Thus it should never be taken with any medication or without your doctor's knowledge. However, St John's Wort should not be stopped abruptly but gradually tailed off if you are taking any other medication.

There are many other vitamins, minerals, and herbal remedies which are advocated by their manufacturers for a multiplicity of symptoms (rather than the causes), although evidence of efficacy is poor or non-existent. It should be remembered that as vitamins and mineral supplements are considered 'foodstuffs', the health claims do not need to be substantiated; nor do they need licencing by the Committee of Safety of Medicines.

There is no substitute for a healthy balanced, varied diet, with starchy foods every three hours and protein, fresh fruit, and vegetables.

Slimming and weight loss

Whilst a few mothers with PND will feel a need to binge, the majority will find the desire to regain their pre-pregnant figure of sufficient importance to deny themselves a healthy diet. However, you can still lose weight by eating a good healthy diet as outlined in this chapter, particularly by including the three-hourly starch diet—these filling starchy foods are low calorie in themselves.

Those mothers with PND need to avoid long periods without food, particularly the starchy foods. Thus the various diets which involve fasting for twelve hours or even a day should be discarded, as well as those which require you to eat only one or two types of fruit for a day or replace meals with liquid supplements. This will cause the blood sugar level to drop repeatedly and the adrenalin symptoms will be present for over a week.

Whilst we eat more these days, particularly the fatty foods, we do less physical exercise, and therefore tend to gain more weight than our predecessors. So the first priority is to ensure both that you have a healthy diet and also that the portions are smaller. Cut down on those fatty foods and also on extra sugar. Maybe it does taste nice—but it is not good food, and it will neither help you to lose weight nor aid your PND.

For those who are anxious to lose weight, breastfeeding is a great boon. Not only does the breastfeeding take up to 500 calories per day, but the action of the baby suckling on the breast helps the womb to contract and aids the muscles in the uterus and stomach to revert closer to their pre-pregnancy shape.

Exercise

However tired and lethargic you may feel, it is also important to ensure that you take some exercise. In the days before electric appliances the housewife's day was taken up with vigorous exercise in beating carpets, sweeping stairs and hallways, scrubbing floors, and other domestic chores. The open coal fires produced lots of dust which meant that the housewife had to dust daily, whilst laying the fire and bringing in the coal also involved quite a lot of physical exercise. There are today exercise programmes to help you regain fitness which mimic these 'housework' tasks.

However, a regular good walk with the baby, at a reasonably fast pace, is excellent exercise. Babies love the sling which holds them close to mum and lets them hear her heart sounds. Walking also provides a wonderful opportunity to speak to and get to know other people and the neighbourhood; it is amazing how many people will stop and chat to a new mother. Now you have the time, you don't need to jump in the car.

Many health clubs and gyms have creche facilities where you can leave your precious bundle whilst having a workout. It is important to get yourself into a routine which involves some exercise at least three times weekly. The physical exercise will also help you to sleep better and feel more relaxed.

CHAPTER 20

···

Careers and motherhood

When the midwife handed Lorna her new son, shortly after delivery, Lorna admitted that she had never held a baby before. In her late thirties, with her own PR company, she had had a successful and well-ordered life. She and her partner had a large mortgage on a beautiful penthouse flat, with a nursery fully prepared for their family addition. Yet like so many of her generation she had never held a baby, bottlefed, or changed a nappy. Quite different from her parents' and grandparents' generations who were brought up in large families. For them, with siblings, aunts, uncles, and other close relatives who were always around, there was invariably a young-ster to be looked after. Lorna had never encountered this early learning experience, and although she had read lots of books about her pregnancy and the coming baby, suddenly she felt frightened of holding such a fragile being. The responsibility of this new life and her inexperience overwhelmed her as she lay there, whilst her partner was glowing with pride.

Lorna's experience is not unusual today. There are many successful young women who have ensured that their career is well established before fulfilling their maternal needs. In 1999, the average age of first-time mothers was 28.9 years.

Yet their very success in their career and lifestyle can lead them to expect instant success in motherhood. Whilst they may be responsible for a large staff or millions of pounds worth of financial services, with others refer-ring to them for their expertise and experience, suddenly they are unable to cope with the needs of a small 3-kg person. They are frightened that they may be too robust in handling this fragile being or allow it to flop and harm itself—or a thousand other worries. It is important to appreciate that the exacting standards they have established in their life cannot be achieved instantly and may need to be lowered.

Rebecca left school at fifteen, before her GCSE exams. She had discov-ered she was five months' pregnant and it took another month to tell her mother. She would not now have to worry about a career as in the imme-diate future she had a baby to plan for and a new life ahead of her. The probability of council housing and a guaranteed income, small though it may be, was hers. When she held her baby after delivery it was for her too the first time she had held a baby, yet Rebecca and Lorna's life experiences had been totally different.

Until the late twentieth century, the very much larger families meant that both girls and boys learnt how to handle small babies, to pacify and feed them. If it were not your own sibling, then it would be a niece, nephew, or perhaps a more distant relative. With large families living close to one another there was always a baby or toddler around. However today we live in smaller families, often many miles distant from relatives, and the hands-on experience is no longer available.

Large families

Always a baby or toddler requiring help and attention

Brothers and sisters to offer help

Extended families available to assist

No close family locally

Without siblings, aunts, or grandparents there to support and help you in establishing yourself as a parent, it can sometimes be a lonely and frightening experience. When relatives are living close by they pop in for half an hour or so to help and encourage a new mother. However today, often living many miles away, these people will come for a short intensive period—a few days or a week—and then disappear again, not to be seen for weeks or even months before the next intensive visit.

Motherhood does not come in a day

The first thing to remember is that just as Rome was not built in a day, so parenthood does not descend upon you automatically in the labour suite, but occurs over a period of time. Most grandmothers would agree that however hard you try it is impossible to be a perfect mother.

A newborn baby's cry is designed to gain its parent's attention, so when unable to settle and calm the baby the parent's anxiety levels rapidly rise. Unfortunately the baby too senses your anxiety and the cries become louder and more painful to the parents.

It is pertinent to remember that whilst Lorna's career is now well established there was a time when she was the 'new girl' who did not know anything about the job, but with perseverance and time became proficient and respected. Similarly you cannot be good at handling babies immediately, give it time. Motherhood is a new 'career' and needs to be seen as that. You will need to read, to listen and learn from others, and to allow yourself to make occasional mistakes. Give yourself time to be able to identify the different cries—when baby is wet, needs comforting, or is just making sounds to himself.

It will take time for you to establish a rapport with baby, to have a timetable for sleeping and feeding, for both of you learn from each other. Not forgetting the broken nights and lack of energy following a long labour, this learning process in itself will be tiring for the new mother. Allow yourself to make mistakes, and to learn from them. Remember the small successes of each day—when you were ready when the baby needed feeding, that you had managed to get a load of washing done, or a meal prepared. Please don't believe you can become a 'supermum' at once; it takes time. Sometimes you will feel you are going backwards not forwards.

Many mothers find the first few months of a second child's life more rewarding as they can relax and enjoy it, rather than being tense and overwhelmed as they were with the first baby.

Entertainers warn that you should never work with children or animals, for from their earliest days they will make a fool of you. If you try to show how clever they are, they will not perform; likewise if you tell people how badly behaved they are or how they constantly cry, they will behave as little angels!

No matter how many books you have read, none of them are likely to cover exactly your particular problem or situation. Even when they do, unfortunately your baby will not conform in a 'textbook' way. Sometimes it feels as though you will never get through the 'quicksand' of inexperience in which you feel you are drowning. This feeling is not unique to you; it is shared by many thousands of young mothers.

Returning to work

Today, motherhood is low on the agenda for some women. Foremost in their plans is a successful career, and only when that is established and the right partner found do they perhaps realize that the clock is ticking away and motherhood needs to be fitted into their business timetable. Prior to pregnancy, a successful career woman will have gone through many books on parenthood and will have planned the pregnancy carefully. She may even time conception to suit her career (like Nicola Horlick, who admitted to timing her own pregnancies so that the babies arrived in the Christmas holidays, or the schoolteacher who plans her pregnancy to maximize maternity leave by fitting it on to the long summer holiday).

Women make up almost half the British workforce today, at all levels, from high-powered executives, teachers, health professionals, to factory and shop workers. There is great pressure on women to work, regardless of their family and home commitments. This creates an obligation in women to further their careers regardless of their own preference to stay at home in the early months or years of their child's life. Following a few months' maternity leave, they return to work as normal, leaving the baby with a nanny or other professional carer. They see the few months' absence from work as only a short career break, and are anxious to get back as soon as possible to resume their place on the promotion ladder.

For some the gloss does not last long. In early 2000, a British health magazine surveyed their female readers about their work, and with surprising results. A reported 77 per cent replied that they would quit work if they were given the chance. This was not because they disliked the work itself so much as the inflexibility of working hours and low pay and conditions whilst running a family and home in tandem.

In the few days or weeks between leaving work and the delivery there is much to organize. Working late into pregnancy is exhausting and these last weeks should be a chance to rest, prepare for the forthcoming event, and relax whilst you still can. Once the baby has arrived and you return home, things may perhaps seem easy at first – or do they?

As the countdown to your return to work starts you will have very mixed feelings. Once more you will be able to do something at which you are successful and respected, but this darling little one will have to be left with others. Will they be as sensitive to his every need? Have you found the best available care for baby at a price you can afford? These are worries that naturally fill every working mother's mind. When the day finally comes, is it possible to leave your adored baby in the hands of someone else ?

Returning to work can be a major hurdle for the working mother. There is the emotional upheaval involved in leaving the young baby just as you have established a pattern to suit you both. The relief of returning to a job in which you are highly competent is tempered by a myriad of concerns about leaving the baby. Had you expressed enough milk? Will the carer get the temperature of the milk exactly right? Will she find the skin cream? Will she know the special little cries that you have now learnt to interpret? The worries are endless and natural on leaving your baby.

Having done a full day's work you return to the little one who makes constant demands upon your time just when you long to sit quietly. There seems to be no time that is your own. It is important to ensure that you get sufficient rest if you are to juggle the two careers of work and motherhood. It is not surprising therefore that returning to work is a common time for that cloud of PND to descend on unfortunate women (see p. 132).

Perennial guilt

Often on returning to work the mother finds that her thoughts are centred on her baby and domestic arrangements, not on work. Whilst at home she is constantly filled with thoughts of work and how are they are managing without her. Unfortunately guilt is synonymous with the working mother, no matter what the age of her children. Guilt is something that has to be accepted; you cannot get away from it.

Working mothers often talk of 'quality time' with their children, the child needs time with his parents. Almost all time can become quality time for children; they need to be with you and involved with whatever you are doing. For example, take the baby in the car with you when you visit the bank; if possible allow him to sleep in the same room as the one in which you are working; slip him into a baby sling and carry on with the housework, cleaning, walking, or whatever. Once my husband even repaired the washing machine with our three-month-old daughter strapped across his chest. It took him one and a half hours and she was fast asleep the whole time; absorbed in the job, my husband had forgotten she was there !

As the child gets older they enjoy helping you to clean, to wash—how they love to play with water whilst supposedly helping you ! Of particular benefit for a toddler is to help you cook and to make pastry, cakes, or some other offering, which you can all delight in eating later. They long to share the washing-up with you at this age—although by the time they are teenagers the thrill has worn off! It is this time which is quality time, not necessarily visits to some educational establishment such as a museum or expensive visits to theme parks or 'must-have' toys.

If the baby is used to your company and being with you, then as they become a toddler and more confident they can move away from you, perhaps even out of the room you are in, but return when they need to. This helps to build their confidence, and they do not feel shut out of your life.

It is so easy to expect to give 'quality' time to a baby or toddler, but once that quality time is spent, to expect the child to 'go away' and get on without you. The child does not necessarily want this; he just wants to be with you. The best educational toy you can give your child is your own time—just doing ordinary things with him, sharing jobs, and looking at things together.

'No' to night work

One common solution to ease the financial burden of a young child is for the mother to work on an evening shift, or even to do night work. The father is then able to act as carer and to take an active part in the life of the child, and there is less disturbance to the young child's life.

Working an evening shift means you may not return home till midnight or later, with your mind full of your working life. It takes time to calm down and relax ready for a good night's sleep. So it is often well into the early hours of the morning before you fall asleep, and then you need to wake to feed the baby and attend to his other needs. You are not getting anything like eight hours' sleep per night. If you have to do evening shifts do ensure that you get at least eight hours' sleep in each twenty-four hours, otherwise you cannot expect to keep healthy and well. Night shifts often mean that when you return home in the morning the rest of the family is waking. A few hours' snatched sleep is not equal to a good night's rest (even if broken by a feed or two).

When you try to turn day into night and vice versa, the body's day/night rhythm is greatly disturbed; it does not know when you should be resting/sleeping or up and about. Everyone needs to sleep (or at least rest, lying down) for eight hours a night if they are to be active for the next fourteen or so hours. To complicate matters, the day/night controlling centre of the brain is adjacent to the menstrual controlling centre where signals for the varying hormone levels are sent out (see Fig. 1, p. 16). It is no surprise then that disturbance of one will affect the other, thus worsening or triggering PND.

Sleep

Sleep is essential for us all, for it is a time when the body can revitalize itself. Certain organs especially the kidneys work best when we are resting and lying horizontal.

If you find it difficult to get to sleep then ensure that you are calm and relaxed before lying down. Perhaps a warm, milky drink, along with that starchy snack will do the trick. It is not advisable to take alcohol to help you sleep. Some people find that a warm soothing bath relaxes them ready for bed, whilst others would prefer some calming music. Make sure that the bedroom is at the right temperature—if it is too hot or too cold you will not get to sleep so easily.

If you feed the baby as you get ready for bed, even if this means waking him to do so, you will find that you will have a good few hours of sleep before being woken by a hungry baby demanding another feed. As he gets older and sleeps for longer at night, you will find that you have a better sleep pattern yourself. Chapter 17 includes some relaxation methods to assist sleep which you may find very helpful.

Another way to get to sleep is to lie in bed in your 'sleep position' and to picture a big, blank board. In your imagination draw a figure '99' on the board and put a border around it; look at it for a moment or two before rubbing it away. Now draw the figure '98' and put a border around that, look at it, then rub it out. Continue down through the numbers and you will find that the brain will get bored and you will quickly fall asleep.

If you are unable to get to sleep because your mind is buzzing with ideas, thoughts of jobs to be done, and such like, it is a sign that you have had a rush of adrenalin. Get out of bed, eat some starchy food (this is the only time I personally will eat a couple of sweet biscuits), and calmly return to your bed. You will find that sleep comes easily. If your brain is still rushing after half an hour, eat another biscuit or two before trying to sleep.

Even if you do not 'sleep' in the sense of losing consciousness, it is important for the body to lie horizontal in a relaxed position. Your body can still then undertake its repair and restoration work so that you will be fully revitalized and ready for the morrow.

CHAPTER 21

And fathers too

So far in this book we have discussed PND—its effects, treatment, and prevention. We have persistently emphasized the importance of the partner in helping the new mother and in understanding the tremendous hormonal changes she has experienced over the past year or so. We have discussed the need for the father to be supportive and considerate.

Yet there are men who experience a change in mood, some might even describe it as depression, which can follow the arrival of the baby. It takes two to make a baby, and assuming he has stayed around thus far, both mother and father have achieved a major change in their lives. The fathers too may need help and understanding at this difficult time, and they should not be overlooked in our aim to treat the new mother's depression.

The differences

There are however great differences between maternal and paternal PND. The mother's PND is generally of hormonal origin, and as has been shown it can be prevented by hormonal treatment begun at delivery. The male type of PND is more often brought about by the change in circumstances within his life, and the deprivation of sleep which invariably follows the arrival of a baby into the family unit. Rarely do men with male PND experience a full-blown depression of psychological origin which requires antidepressant medication and psychotherapy/talking therapies. This depression is extremely unusual in comparison to PND which occurs in one of every ten new mothers.

During the nine months of pregnancy and labour the mother has undergone major physical changes, with tremendous increases in her hormonal levels as well as changes in her cardiac, respiratory, and kidney output, to name but a few. In comparison the male has had it easy—or has he? He has had to watch the many physical and psychological changes occurring to his loved one. The financial implications of living on one income are frightening, even if it's only going to be for a short while because she plans to return to work soon. Then there is the cost of all that baby paraphernalia; how it all mounts up and it takes up so much space! There is the overwhelming responsibility, which is only just dawning on him. There may also be issues relating to his relationship with his own mother and father which need dealing with. His 'men's nights' may now be his only refuge.

Supportive partner

The new father has watched his darling change shape into someone with an awkward lump who can't sit still for long, is constantly uncomfortable, and continually wearing the same old clothes. He probably didn't grumble about having to go to the 'open all hours' store in the middle of the night to satisfy her strange food craving. Although it was a planned decision to have a baby, perhaps this was prompted more by the female. Then when she was pregnant there was the nausea to deal with—her not wanting to eat, or feeling sick, or sometimes actually being sick and in the most inconvenient of places.

Once that stage was over things got on to a more even keel; her shape changed and her waist became thicker. Everything seemed more real. Although seeing the scans was interesting it was difficult to make out exactly what you could see in the fuzzy picture, and what it all meant. Remember the excitement when the bump started to show and the father could actually feel the baby kick—a future footballer perhaps!

During the final weeks of pregnancy she was often tired and found it difficult to move around, her usual excitement and energy somewhat dissipated. She had become more careful and cautious, and much of her time and attention was spent in getting all those last-minute baby things just right. Her sleep was disrupted as she plodded off to the bathroom, and no matter what position she lay in, she was uncomfortable after a while. Regardless of how careful she was, his own sleep was also being disturbed. There had been times when he knew he should rouse himself and be comforting and considerate towards her, but all he wanted to do was sleep.

After several false alarms the time had finally arrived and carefully she was placed in the car for the journey to the hospital. There the staff welcomed them and for a while all was hustle and bustle as they examined her and they all got settled into the delivery suite.

This was it. It really was happening. Could he remember all the little jokes he had collected ready for this time? Where was the sponge to wipe her face? What were those breathing exercises they had practised so carefully? The labour may have seemed long to her; to him it lasted a lifetime. Suddenly things quickened and there was this tiny being, all red and crying. Here was their offspring. It was a most amazing moment. It would live with him forever. His partner was glowing as the baby was given to her to hold, and he was bursting with pride and wonder as he gazed at them both. Everyone was congratulating them and smiling. The nurses soon got things tidied up and off they all went to the ward. Later, much later, he left to ring around family and friends and broadcast this amazing moment to everyone. In the silence of home he realized that life would never be the same again.

Home as a family

When he proudly brought mother and child home, there were moments of complete panic as the responsibility of the care and nurturing of this tiny being dawned. The baby was so fragile and tiny. How will he know what its cries mean and how to satisfy its needs? Together they will manage far better than they realized. But they both need to work together and share the care of the baby from the earliest stages; even if she is fully breastfeeding there are still a multitude of things he can do.

Often in those first few weeks one of the proud grandmothers, or some other relative, will come to stay and help. This can leave the new father feeling somewhat left out. He must ensure that he is involved in the care. It is sometimes wisest to take time off work when relatives have left, or best of all arrange for them to come to help once father is back at work. Typically the new mother needs the support and company of female relatives when the baby is a few weeks old, rather than in those first few days of the new family's life.

After a full day's work it is hard for the father to come home and find the home a mess, no food ready, and mother and baby both wanting his attention. He may have to prepare supper, sort washing to put in the washing machine, and tidy up. He longs for the old days when there was just the two of them and they could impetuously go out for a meal or to see friends. Now it is a major excursion to go anywhere. A quick visit to the pub is frowned upon; she too may long for the opportunity to socialize again, but who can take a baby into that smoky atmosphere?

So many changes have happened in a relatively short while. He will be wondering what sort of father he will be. Will he be like his own father? Will he be strong and determined? Will his child feel he was overly strict to him? Will he be able to answer all the child's many questions as he grows up? Will they enjoy the same sports together? He knows that he wants to be a 'hands-on' father, to play his part in the caring role, but when he picks up this tiny, fragile little bundle, suddenly it all becomes a bit scary.

What about me?

These are all normal thoughts and fears experienced by almost all new fathers, particularly with the arrival of the first child. With subsequent children the worries may not be quite so fearsome, although the financial problems can increase. It is important to share these worries and concerns, particularly with your partner, so that together you can overcome them. This is not to give you *carte blanche* to moan about your own problems, but you should both sit down quietly and discuss them together. Sharing is important, and it is too easy for a man to put on a brave front so that everybody thinks he is coping well, when in truth he is crying out for someone to ask 'and how are **you** doing?'

Sleep

Tim sat slumped at his desk. Phew, he was exhausted and felt awful. He had lost another contract that morning and his boss had read him the riot act. Whilst usually he would be charged up and determined, now he just couldn't care less. He almost told his boss what to do with the job, but couldn't summon up the effort. He felt so tired all he wanted to do was to go home and sleep, but even that was now impossible.

One of the major changes in the life of the new father is the lack of sleep and the continually interrupted sleep. This probably started during the last weeks of pregnancy and has continued. It seems that he is always wanting to sleep, and could do it anywhere. It needs to be appreciated that sleep deprivation is a form of torture, and it is important to ensure that whenever the opportunity arises you all do get a good sleep. When the baby sleeps in the day or early evening, this is a chance when both parents should try and sleep, or at least lie down to rest (see p. 196). If there are elder siblings perhaps you could all watch a quiet video, or spend some time reading and resting whilst the baby sleeps. This is not the time to try and rush around doing all the many jobs that need to be done.

Ensure that you each get a chance to sleep in at weekends. It is often sensible for one partner to get up and take the baby out for a walk or drive on Saturday morning whilst the other sleeps; then on Sunday, swap over.

If you find that you wake in the night worrying, your mind active, this is a sign that your blood sugar has dropped, and you would benefit from eating some starchy food such as biscuits or cake (see p. 182) etc.

How to seek help

If you feel you are experiencing more than the usual concerns of being a new father, that you are actually feeling rather depressed, then seek help as soon as possible. If you meet the health visitor when she arrives to do the usual checks, seek an opportunity to discuss your feelings and fears with her. Alternatively see your GP and explain how difficult you are finding things.

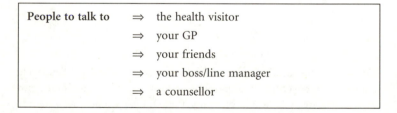

People to talk to	⇒	the health visitor
	⇒	your GP
	⇒	your friends
	⇒	your boss/line manager
	⇒	a counsellor

It is likely that you are not the only father among your group of friends. Talk with another father who has been through those early days with babies; they will often have had the same sort of worries and can help you talk about them. They may have suggestions of how they overcame them.

It may be that you should discuss the matter with your boss or line manager. This is particularly important if you find that the lack of sleep and worries are affecting your work. Perhaps you can take some extra time off, or work part-time for a couple of weeks. The law allows every new parent to take up to thirteen weeks' unpaid leave from work within the child's first five years. Whilst not suggesting you should necessarily take all that in one go, a couple of weeks off when needed will possibly give you a chance to establish a routine and get life back on the tracks. Many companies now understand the upheaval a new arrival causes and will do all they can to help the new parents. Talk with your line manager or boss and explain why you are not working to your usual standards, before they start nagging you to pull up your socks. By being the first to raise the subject you will feel more positive and assertive, rather than pressured.

Some find that the best help can be had from counselling, when you get an opportunity to talk about your apprehensions, concerns for the baby, your feelings towards your own father, perhaps changed feelings towards the new mother, and so on. To talk with someone who is non-judgemental and understanding, who will listen without telling you what you should do, can be very helpful to the new father. This need not involve a long-term commitment, just a few sessions will often be sufficient for you to get things in perspective and enable you to enjoy all those new experiences of fatherhood in a positive nature.

It may be that your GP will feel that you would benefit from a short course of antidepressant therapy; these can often make a great deal of difference. However the number of men who need medication is very small indeed.

A healthy life

The importance of good general health is exactly the same as for the new mother. You need your healthy diet with three portions of protein and five servings of fresh fruit or vegetables. It may be an easy option to collect a pizza on the way home, but ensure that you get your daily allowance of fruit and vegetables. Perhaps you could bring in some fresh fruit as well.

Whilst all new fathers want to 'wet the baby's head' with their friends, alcohol should be taken in moderation. The recommended weekly intake of alcohol for men is 28 units (21 for women).

Again exercise is important and strongly recommended. Choose the types of exercise you personally enjoy. This may be a chance for you to leave the baby with a babysitter so that both you and your partner can partake in sport together, perhaps enjoying a game of squash or tennis. Or perhaps a good run, a workout at the gym, or the local football team are more in your line. If you feel your life is too busy to fit in a special 'exercise session', then ensure you walk to the next bus stop or the station; perhaps park the car a distance from the door at work so that you get the opportunity for a brisk walk. Forgoing the lift and walking up and down the stairs instead will make a tremendous difference to your fitness.

Enjoy fatherhood

Most important of all is to enjoy the new baby, who is constantly changing and within a few months quite different from the tiny, fragile baby you first brought home. Share the many tasks between mother and father, delight in the first smile and early sounds, play and talk to the baby, and watch his reactions. This time is most precious and goes so quickly.

Take pleasure in your new family, for there is no greater source of enjoyment and satisfaction, although we all make many mistakes along the way. To see your own flesh and blood learn to sit, walk, and talk and grow into a person in his own right is fantastic. You will find the companionship of a young toddler following you around and 'assisting' in little jobs is most fulfilling, and all those sleepless nights will recede in your mind. Your life has changed—but the benefits far outweigh the losses.

CHAPTER 22

We all can help

Help for those suffering from depression after childbirth needs to be based on an understanding of the psychological changes in the mother, and the fundamentally different problems facing the father. These factors are dealt with in the first part of this chapter, before some suggested do's and don't's for family members and friends anxious to help the suffering couple.

Understanding the new mother

We all need to be aware of the important and tremendous changes a new mother experiences at the end of pregnancy and with the arrival of the new baby. This is regardless of the normality or otherwise of the pregnancy, whether it had been planned or not, how well she had been during the nine months, or if she had undergone many months of fertility treatment to become pregnant. Each person's experience of childbirth is different; for some unfortunate mothers the horrors of their delivery will haunt them long after. We should remember that she is likely to be tired, and also apprehensive of her new role. She may want our advice, but she is also likely to be frightened by her new responsibilities and wary of any presumed criticism or comment from others.

We need to appreciate these changes, but if a mother's reaction to them is more than would be expected, we do have a responsibility to consider that perhaps this is the onset of PND and to ensure that her partner, family, midwife, health visitor, or family doctor is alert to any differences in her personality.

It must also be appreciated that there are psychological factors which occur after birth. It is a daunting time for a mother when she becomes aware that she is responsible for this small bundle of humanity, who is totally dependent upon her for warmth, food, cleanliness, and psychological well-being, as well as learning slowly how to become an independent individual.

It may be helpful to remind the new mother of all the changes which took place in her body during pregnancy (see Chapter 2) and how the return to her non-pregnant state will be gradual. Having become more aware over the months of the baby inside her and his kicks, the mother must now accept that he is a totally separate entity—one that she must get to know, appreciating his uniqueness. It is frightening to realize how dependent the baby is upon her, yet his own individuality is already making itself known. How do you start a relationship with this tiny human being? One moment he is perhaps sleeping soundly, and the next he is demanding— yes, not asking but **demanding**—food and attention. Suddenly she feels clumsy beside the nurses who pick up her baby so confidently and hand him to her for another feed. The baby struggles and screams whilst she tries to feed him; yet when the nurses hold him and place a bottle to his lips silence ensues and contentedness replaces that scowl. Is the scowl really meant for his mother?

It can be an awesome thought. The enormity of being the main provider of emotional and physical needs can suddenly get too much. With single mothers, particularly teenage mothers, there is the added apprehension of whether they will be able to provide sufficiently, both physically and financially, on their own. The mother may have doubts about her own ability to cope with the demands of motherhood; an overwhelming sense of the responsibility; fears of harming the baby; feelings of emptiness and resentment at baby being the centre of attention.

It is a natural and normal response to the new responsibilities of parenthood. Sometimes the arrival of the new infant unlocks unconscious fears or memories of a mother's own childhood. We all have many different remembrances of our childhood, both good and bad. The holding of one's own child will often be the trigger-factor for the recollection of these memories and can sometimes be a disturbing and frightening occurrence.

There are also some people who find that holding their own baby in their arms suddenly brings back hidden feelings about their own parenting. A new mother may recall the mothering or fathering she had—perhaps the need to please one or both parents—and compare them with her present feelings of inadequacy. Sometimes new parents feel they will be judged by others on how 'good a job' they make of parenting. Or a mother may find that the freedom she previously had has suddenly gone; she is tied to this child for many years to come, and the consequences and responsibilities of parenthood can seem insurmountable.

Some women have a negative reaction towards their femininity which they cannot ignore. They may adopt a quite different, more masculine hair-style, spurn make-up, and try to become 'one of the boys'.

When friends and relatives—especially the new grandmother—give advice on what the mother should do or how she should feed the baby, they should remember that every child is a unique individual and what worked or was needed for one baby is not necessarily right for this one. It is essential to work out what suits both mother and child. Remember that babies do not do everything according to the book. The new mother must not become despondent because at a certain age her child is not doing exactly what he should do—each child is unique, so she must relish and consider that individuality.

If she is breastfeeding she must remember that the baby is taking energy and nutrients from her, so she needs to allow her body both the time and the ingredients to do this. It is easy for the new mother to forget to feed herself whilst concentrating on the small infant, but without the correct food intake the breast milk will not satisfy the baby, and thus a vicious circle of hungry baby and irritable mother is set up.

Teaching motherhood

In Alabama the problem of teenage pregnancies is acute, so some schools have decided to teach the responsibilities of motherhood to their fifteen-year-olds. They are given a doll which cries and needs feeding and changing at regular intervals. They must take the baby doll everywhere with them, even on their evenings out, and they must also attend to the doll when it cries at night. They soon learn the downside of motherhood and become more interested in effective contraception.

Noting changes

If the father thinks there has been a change in a mother's personality or behaviour, he should also realize what has caused it. If it is only mild, he should have patience and all will sort itself out in good time. He should make allowances, help her, and give her every opportunity to sleep as much as possible. He also needs to remember the many bodily changes that occurred during pregnancy, not only those in the womb, but the changes in the heart, kidney, and lungs, which all need to return to normal after the birth. He should also pay special attention to her diet, tempting her with extra delicacies, and ensuring that she is eating little and often and following the three-hourly starch diet (see Chapter 19). It is also important to spend time with her; she is lonely and bewildered by her new responsibility and by her new personality. At the same time he may need to keep an eye open for the unexpected panics, the irrational irritability, or the anger over trivialities which may suggest that PND is developing and the time has come to ask for professional help from the midwife, health visitor, or family doctor.

The new father may even be faced with the other extreme of thought disorder, or psychosis (see Chapter 9), when somehow he cannot get through or communicate on the same wavelength with the new mother. Her thinking may be all askew, or perhaps she is talking non-stop. She may be speeded-up and high, having lost touch with reality. Sometimes she has crazy, irrational, and illogical ideas about people or things; or she may be so muddled that she hears visions, sees smells, and feels sounds. These are all danger signs, and the father's first essential task is to call professional help immediately. While awaiting help he has the responsibility to ensure that his partner and baby are not left alone for a minute, for she may unexpectedly make an attempt on her own life or that of her much-loved baby (see Chapter 10).

The father has a Herculean task when coping with a disturbed mother and newborn baby at the same time. He should not be afraid or ashamed of confiding in other members of the family or friends, so that they too can understand and lend a helping hand. There is no reason why the problem should be hidden; it can happen to anyone, regardless of class, colour, or culture. If there is another child, or children, there will be the greater responsibility of finding additional help and a reliable carer, hopefully a family member or friend. Accept offers of help; the kindness can always be repaid at a later date. If all sources of help fail, then ask the health visitor or social services to help out; they are trained for just such emergencies.

Preparing for parenthood

A baby belongs to both parents. Ideally, future parents should attend antenatal classes together, when they will learn of the possibility of the blues, depression, or even psychosis occurring after the birth. There should be free and open discussion about the hormonal changes which occur during pregnancy, labour, and the puerperium, and the cause of depression after childbirth. It is important for them to appreciate that PND results from the hormonal upheaval, over which the mother has no control, and that it is definitely not 'all in the mind'. The woman should know that she will not be alone, and that she has no need to feel guilty, if she is unfortunate enough to develop problems; it is no disgrace.

It is indeed comforting for the father to learn how he can help his partner with relaxation and breathing throughout labour. To most men it is a never-to-be-forgotten event to hear their own offspring giving their first yell, and many appreciate the opportunity to help and comfort their partner during the birth. A few others may find it disturbing to see their loved one in such pain, and the blood and mess can be very frightening for some fathers.

If a couple expecting their first child feel that the woman has a high risk of developing postnatal problems, either because another member of the family has been stricken, or because she has severe PMS, or because she has a previous history of psychiatric illness, then it is well worthwhile asking for specialist advice and arranging for preventive progesterone to be started on completion of labour (see Chapter 16).

It is important to remember that what we eat may pass to the baby. We learnt this terrible lesson with thalidomide taken during pregnancy. It should remind us to take extra care with over-the-counter drugs, herbs, and excess vitamins and minerals. The Committee of Safety of Medicines keeps an eye on all drugs but not on over-the-counter medications since these are classified as foodstuffs and therefore do not need proven effectiveness for advertising or sales promotion.

It will be an immense help later if the couple start sharing the household chores and shopping during pregnancy, so that when the baby arrives the father does not have to learn how to cope with the temperamental washing machine and already knows which are her favourite shops and where she hides the cleaning materials. When she returns home with the baby, it is the baby who will need all her time and attention, and she will not want to be interrupted or distracted with petty unnecessary queries.

Sleep

It is usually agreed that we need eight hours of sleep each night for good health. If we put our hands on our hips, our thumbs will be pointing to our kidneys. The kidneys are very important organs, their job is to clean the blood and remove impurities. The kidneys do shift work and work best at night when we are lying down. It does not matter if when we are lying down we are asleep or awake. However the kidneys slow down their work if we get up to make a hot drink, or sit and watch television or read. Very few people seem to know this. So we do not have to worry about not sleeping or waking up repeatedly during the night. We can use the extra time by thinking and planning happily, and we won't be tired the next morning. We can even listen to music or the radio, watch television, read, dictate, or do a hundred other tasks so long as we remain horizontal and allow the kidneys to function properly. Incidentally, it does not matter if we get up to urinate as that is a normal kidney function.

Tips for parents

The broken nights of early parenthood can be a tremendous drain on both mother and father. Remember that continually waking someone who is asleep is a recognized form of torture. Experts tend to ignore the way lack of sleep caused by a new baby can affect both parents. Maybe they are having to wake two or three times during the night, and even if only one parent does get up to feed and change baby, both are woken and their sleep pattern is disturbed. It is important, therefore, for both parents to try and get to bed earlier and not have such high expectations of their energy levels. Give time to adapt to the new life with baby.

When either partner gets the chance of a rest during the daytime, they should take it, and not feel guilty. Parents are often faced with the conundrum—when all is quiet and the baby is at last sleeping peacefully, should they get some rest, or should they spend the short time available doing those many jobs awaiting attention? If the opportunity comes, they should opt for rest and relaxation, and do those jobs later when the baby is awake and can be strapped to their chest in a baby sling. Both parents can use the sling to enable them to get on with the odd jobs around the house. Babies love them, and enjoy the endless movement and the closeness to a loved one.

Remember that babies, like animals, are very quick to pick up how you are feeling. They can sense if parents are tense, frightened, irritable, or scared, and they too will become the same. However, if the parents are well rested and calm, then baby will feel so too.

It is normal and natural for a new mother to want to regain her figure as soon as possible after delivery, to be able to get into clothes that fit. By the time the baby finally arrives she can be thoroughly fed up with the look of overused maternity clothes, even if she was so eager to get into them in early pregnancy. However, it must be remembered at this time that the first priority should be the return of her fitness and vitality, for which a good healthy diet is the first essential. It is tempting to try to starve herself, especially when she is too tired to prepare or cook a meal. She may need to be reminded of the importance of eating a good balanced diet. If she is breast-feeding she should avoid any kind of 'slimming diet' which encourages missing meals or taking meal substitutes. How can she expect the baby to thrive if he does not get all the nutrients he requires?

A new mother needs at least three or four portions of some form of quality protein (fish, cheese, eggs, meat, or pulses), together with four or five portions of fruit or vegetables, daily. If there is any sign of PND, then it is vitally important to eat some starchy food every three hours of the waking day, including when she wakes to feed the baby at night (see p. 181) It is also important for new fathers to ensure that they are eating well and heathily.

Again, try and take a walk each day with the baby in the buggy or in a sling. Getting out and enjoying some exercise helps a mother's return to normal, and often the gentle rhythmic movements of walking will soothe the infant—after all, the baby has spent nine months rocked by her move-ments, and often the rocking movement of a walk or a car journey will settle and calm an irritable child.

When out walking with the baby it is amazing how many times there is an opportunity to talk with another mother. The chance to exchange pleasantries will often be an opportunity to further a friendship with someone who may know other new mothers in the area, thus widening a circle of friendship with others in a similar situation. To be able to share concerns and fears with other new parents is often a way of easing worries. There are many local toddler groups, or perhaps there is a welcoming NCT or MAMA group which meets locally. Their informality offers a chance to share experiences with other new parents, which can give the reassurance that others feel the same way. Most local groups now welcome new fathers, giving them an opportunity to share their concerns with others in a similar position.

There may well be very real financial worries with the new arrival, when there are so many unexpected expenses which need to be met. If the mother's income is absent, then these may be of mounting concern. Even if the child is the second or third, there are still added expenses. These worries should not be brushed aside with the stark comment 'we'll manage somehow'; discuss the concerns.

Initially an ideal solution appears to be for the mother to take on an evening or night job, such as waitressing, nursing, or working as a telephonist, enabling the father to take care of the baby and any other children. Unfortunately night work upsets the mother's normal day/night rhythm centre in the hypothalamus and too often triggers depression or an increase in PMS. Thus this solution is one to be avoided if at all possible. Should the mother start an evening job or night work, it is important to be aware of this possibility and for the work to be stopped at the first signs of depression or an increase in PMS.

Whilst hormonal PND may affect new mothers regardless of social standing or financial security, typical depression is more likely to affect those whose security, financial or otherwise, has less solidity. This is the kind that is more likely to occur with single mothers, or those with poor housing conditions or unstable relationships. This will be helped by the support of counsellors, health visitors, and, most important, family and friends.

PND, whether mild or severe, is always a strain on any relationship. The outcome depends very much on how much effort has been put into dealing with the numerous problems and the readiness to forgive and forget the strange, illogical idiosyncrasies of the sick mother. She will need to talk, talk, and talk again, while he will need to listen, listen, and listen again to all the same old things. It is a traumatic time for the relationship and counselling may well be needed before the rift is finally healed. But there is always an end to the illness and with it comes the reward, which is a strengthening of the cement of the relationship, which will then be stronger than ever before.

Where to go for help

Your first port of call should be your local health centre with your GP and health visitor. They are available to all and are fully knowledgeable, fully trained, interested professionals who can share your concerns.

Accept practical help from others, and if this is not readily forthcoming, do go out of your way to enlist help. If you are fortunate enough to be at the right spot at the right time, you may be able to get help from a self-help group. One such is MAMA, the Meet-A-Mum Association. It is a practical organization set up especially to help those mothers with baby blues. It has a nationwide network of mothers' groups, who meet together over a cup of tea to chat about their anxieties, fears, loneliness, and so on with mothers who have the same problems. There is always someone ready to chat, even if it is at the end of a telephone. It is sponsored by *Woman* magazine.

The Association for Postnatal Illness (APNI) is an organization specifically formed to help better understanding of the problem of PNI and to encourage more research into the subject. It has a team of volunteers, all of whom have suffered and recovered from a bout of PND and are ready to help those still in the throes of it, either by phone chats or visits.

Other groups are run by the National Childbirth Trust (NCT); these are also made up of mothers who have been through the problems of childbirth and are ready to lend a listening ear at any time of the day or night.

Home-Start is a voluntary organization offering support, friendship, and practical assistance to parents with children under five who are experiencing difficulties in parenting. The Home-Start volunteers are all parents themselves, and visit families in their own homes and, by the support they give, assist to prevent family crisis and breakdown. The families can be referred by social workers, health visitors, GPs, other family members, or families themselves. There may be a Home-Start branch in your area. If you are that lucky, do contact them if you feel the need.

Family and professional help

The PND which has a psychological basis resulting from stress can be experienced by either or both parents and even by adoptive parents. This is best treated with psychological help, primarily counselling and befriending, with shared help from other members of the family and support from friends and the health visitor, and, if necessary, with antidepressant therapy. However, the PND with a hormonal basis is better treated with progesterone, or the SSRI or MAOI group of antidepressants. Better still it can be successfully prevented with progesterone (see Chapter 16).

In the case of a one-parent family, it is the family or friends on whom the burden of watching and caring for a mother with PND falls. If she shows signs of psychosis or an inability to care for the infant, they must ensure that medical help is found and that practical assistance is offered. They need to be willing to lend a hand, or a listening ear whenever she needs to talk.

The new mother should not be ashamed to ask others to take over the baby when he is crying endlessly; a crying infant can be most disturbing for a mother who is feeling below par. Some social workers have been known to arrange part-time fostering for the baby to help the mother when it is most needed, and to give her the odd hour or two of peace and time alone.

One person the new mother, the father, or worried family members or friends can all talk to is the health visitor. She is there to help and will not think badly of a mother who talks about her worries. Most health visitors are mothers and may perhaps have been through what the new mother is feeling now. They are trained and experienced in helping mothers and they want to help and support them. Unfortunately there is a myth that they are judging a new mother, or perhaps will criticize. This is only a myth; a mother should see them as a friend who can help, and build a relationship with them. Health visitors have a wealth of experience and understanding, so do talk to them, whatever the worries.

If you feel that a new mother may be experiencing PND, or even the severe psychosis, it is important that you ensure that she receives appropriate help. However, there are also some important do's and don't's to remember so that the mother does not feel even more guilty.

Important don't's

Don't try reasoning with someone who is mentally ill. This is a maxim that doctors and all who work with or help the mentally ill learn very early. Mental illness defies all logic and reason. The mentally ill person is no longer capable of reasoning on normal thinking lines. Just cast your mind back to 'Nancy's story' (Chapter 11) and remember that to Nancy's disturbed mind there were coincidences everywhere—in the television programme, the apples her mother brought, the porters in their black uniforms with red bands round their caps and lapels. So don't add to the complications by trying to make the patient see reason where, for her, reason does not exist.

PND is no different in this respect from other depressions. It is no good trying to argue that there is no need to be frightened of spiders, of going out, of staying in, of letting the baby cry, or of going to sleep. It is pointless assuring her that there are no dangers involved, for she will still be frightened. Her thinking has become illogical, and that is that. How reason can be lost in respect of one factor, but not others, is seen in Jenny's story.

Jenny was the wife of a bank manager. She was frightened of travelling in any vehicle which she could not get out of whenever she wanted to. This precluded her from travelling by rail, plane, or boat, although she did not mind going by car if her husband was driving because he would stop when asked. This limited her holidays to British resorts which could be reached by car. One day a lump was noticed in her breast. She knew and fully appreciated what breast cancer was, for her kindly mother and much-loved stepmother had both been nursed by Jenny through the horrifying last stages of breast cancer. The breast cancer in no way frightened her and she accepted the diagnosis without any anxiety, whilst remaining frightened of travelling in enclosed vehicles.

Don't adopt a smug attitude. This could give the mother a feeling of guilt or ingratitude. It is better to let the mother express her own true feelings of anxiety and fear. Kay, after she had recovered, was able to recall:

> I was very irritable to my two other children and my husband. But how could I tell him how I felt? I was thoroughly ashamed and feeling guilty like this, and he would have thought me mad, although I was not (I have felt like it at times, though.) So I covered up except for telling my sister, who understood as she had a boyfriend who had had a breakdown and she has visited quite a few psychiatric hospitals.

Don't nag. This may mean you will need the patience of Job to repeat endlessly: 'No I don't mind that it's a boy, although I said I wanted a girl'; 'The baby is quite all right'; 'I really do understand it's not your fault'. Nagging by outsiders is even worse, particularly if it comes from the older generation who have forgotten the anguish, or from those who have never experienced it.

Don't point out her shortcomings. There may be unfinished jobs, or she may have an unkempt appearance, but it does not help if you are forthright and just say what you think of the new mother's self-indulgence.

Don't use glib or meaningless phrases. It will not help her to be told 'Pull yourself together'; 'You don't know how lucky you are'; 'There are lots worse than you'; 'It's no good moaning, it won't get you anywhere'; or 'Think of others'. There may be times when these comments are appropriate, but not to a new mother possibly experiencing PND.

Don't let her be alone with the baby. This is vital if you feel there is even the slightest possibility of her doing harm to the baby or herself.

Don't let any older children see their mother cry. They see crying as babyish, and to a young child who has held his or her mother in high esteem it is traumatic to see her unexpectedly descend to such babyish habits for no good reason.

Don't let her feel that she is being lazy if she is resting. If she wants to go off to sleep at 7.00 p.m., so much the better. Sleep never did anyone any harm and she probably needs all the sleep that she can get. But if she has been given sleeping tablets, keep a careful count and hide them away. It is much too easy to swallow an extra one, and then just one or two more.

Don't say 'A new baby, my—aren't you lucky' when she feels absolutely frightful, and don't expect to see all new mothers radiating joy and contentment all day long. If you're a visitor, do not stay too long—she may be longing to go to sleep again.

Don't recommend any patent medicine, tonic, vitamin, or mineral preparation to help her overcome her exhaustion. In particular I would strongly advise against the use of vitamin B6, or pyridoxine, which was a popular over-the-counter medication claimed to help exhaustion, depression, irritability, headaches, and many more symptoms until 1983, when Dr Schumberg and his neurological colleagues in New York reported seven cases of nerve poisoning from massive doses of pyridoxine. Until then it was thought that pyridoxine, being a water-soluble vitamin, was quite harmless. However, recent studies have shown that, with even very small doses, 60 per cent of women taking vitamin B6 for six months or more develop symptoms of nerve poisoning causing numbness, pins and needles of the hands and feet, generalized itching, and muscle weakness. The advice should be firmly to avoid vitamin B6 whether alone, in a multivitamin preparation, or with minerals. If your blood has been tested and the blood has been found to be deficient in vitamin B6 (which is excessively rare in Britain), then it is a sign of gross malnutrition and medical help should be sought.

Don't be offended when your offer of help is turned down.

Important don't's

Don't try reasoning with the mentally ill

Don't adopt a smug attitude

Don't nag

Don't leave her alone with her baby

Don't let other children see her cry

Don't admire the new baby too much

Don't recommend tonics or patent medicines

Important do's

Do allow the new mother to talk freely and express her innermost fears, without showing shock or amazement. Often there are no grounds for her fears, but let her talk about them; she needs to get them out of her system.

Do show consideration and sympathy for her in her predicament.

Do have an infinite supply of patience and understanding, even if you find her chatter all beyond your comprehension or feel you cannot condone the illogical behaviour. Listen and listen again; the unfortunate mother may need to get her racing thoughts vocalized.

Do urge her to wait until the depression is over and done with before beginning to make decisions. Once recovery has taken place, that is the time to decide whether to move house, build that extension to the lounge, or plan a holiday.

Do offer practical help, which is usually so desperately needed. She will probably be most grateful for help with shopping, washing, ironing, or the offer of a prepared meal or freshly baked cakes. If there are other children, it would mean a lot if they could be looked after for an hour or two, or be taken to or met from school.

Do see she avoids heavy shopping and housework. Remember those stomach muscles which were so stretched during pregnancy—now is the time to give them a chance to recover. Certainly it is worth her doing post-natal exercises, so long as her energy permits. The worst thing is standing in one spot for too long, like standing while waiting for the kettle to boil, when she could be sitting. In the age before labour-saving devices, a new mother might have been advised to scrub the floor on her hands and knees, which is an excellent exercise for the abdominal muscles.

Do take an interest in any other children. Greet them first before looking at the newborn, or better still ask the child to let you see the baby. In Holland it was a tradition for the baby to bring a gift to the other children in the family; this way it was hoped any sibling jealousy would be avoided. If you intend giving a gift to the new baby, do remember the other children, even if they only get a bar of chocolate.

Do be there for both parents, but particularly the mother, whenever you are needed.

Do ensure that she is having a good balanced diet, containing protein at least two or three times daily, and four or five portions of fresh fruit or vegetables daily, and that, if there is any hint of PND or PMS, she is eating small portions of starchy foods (flour, rice, oats, potato, maize, or rye) every three hours of her waking day, and always within one hour of waking and one hour of going to bed at night, as well as in the middle of the night if she is waking to attend to the baby (see Chapter 19).

Do know—and this is the biggest 'do' of them all for the partner, relatives, and friends—when to call in a doctor. Do not assume that all doctors are too busy to listen, and realize that there is a lot a doctor can do which cannot be achieved by others. If there have been some good days among the darkness, it is well worthwhile the partner diligently making a note of the good and bad days, and also any days of menstruation, if this has restarted. A well-kept record can help the doctor diagnose problems more quickly and more precisely.

When considering a list of do's, mention must be made of the solution discovered by one woman, who wrote: 'After my first breakdown I came to an arrangement with my husband—he agreed to give me unlimited champagne during the second week of my puerperium and all went well.' I suppose it is better to have the head swimming from champagne than from anything else, but the mind boggles.

Important do's

Do allow her to talk freely

Do show consideration and sympathy

Do have infinite patience and understanding

Do urge her to wait before making vital decisions

Do offer practical help

Do take an interest in her other children

Do be there whenever needed

Do encourage her to eat a three-hourly starch diet

Do encourage her to eat a healthy diet

Do ensure she has adequate sleep

Do know when to call medical help

CHAPTER 23

A way ahead

Babies should bring happiness. If they do not, something is wrong. This book is an attempt to help when things do go wrong.

'When endocrinology is fully understood there will be no place for psychiatrists.' Those words were spoken fifty years ago by Hans Selye, an eminent endocrinologist. In this quotation he was reminding his audience that the science of endocrinology was gradually discovering the chemicals in the human body that were producing mental disturbances, irrational behaviour, and so on, which had hitherto been seen as psychological disturbances best dealt with by a psychiatrist. This was not heralding any conflict or contest between the two disciplines, but was a signpost pointing to the distant future, where the study of psychiatry will have evolved into endocrinology like a caterpillar's transformation into a butterfly. It is in this context that this book has been written, in the hope that, by applying a few endocrinological findings and some clinical observation to one small but important aspect of psychiatric illness, PND, human suffering may be relieved and normal health restored.

In the fourth century BC Hippocrates described an illness in his *Third Book of Epidemics* in which there is a reference to a woman who became restless and could not sleep, and became delirious eleven days after giving birth. She became comatose and finally died on the seventeenth day. Hippocrates suggested two causes for her illness. The blood discharge from her womb could have been carried towards her head, resulting in agitation, delirium, and attacks of mania, or 'when blood collects in the breast of a woman, it indicates madness'. These hypotheses were accepted as dogma for the next 2000 years.

The madness aspect placed the condition in the realm of the psychiatrists, who treated the illness on the traditional lines of a typical depressive illness or psychosis. We are at last emerging from that era into a new one, arising out of the development of endocrinology, which is trying to explain not only the interactions and influences of hormones, but also the finer biochemical reactions which take place within the nuclei of cells. It is these actions in the centre of all living cells which affect our behaviour and our lives.

We live in a scientific age with computerized diagnosis and sophisticated biochemical technology, but the age of clinical observation is not yet past. It was clinical observation that spotlighted the foetal damage resulting from rubella and also from the administration of thalidomide in early pregnancy. Again, it is clinical observation that has brought a new understanding and treatment for PND.

Clinical observation

Observation in surgeries, health centres, and clinics will definitely reveal the high incidence of PND and the resultant unhappiness and disruption of marriages, families, and homes. More than forty years of my clinical observation has formed the basis of this book, together with the new work of molecular biologists and veterinary scientists. This has led to a greater appreciation of the hormonal upheaval in pregnancy and the puerperium which, in some women, causes this misery of miseries out of which arises PMS. Paradoxically, it was work on PMS that brought the recognition of its similarity to PND and the relationship between the two. The successful treatment of the former with progesterone has led to the prevention and treatment of the latter. This should be a step forward in lowering the incidence of PNI.

Dr M Clarke and Dr A Williams, writing in the *Lancet* in 1979, estimated that each year 23,000 women in England and Wales suffer from moderate or incapacitating PND, bringing unhappiness and distress to new mothers. The time has now come for an increased awareness of all that is contained in this book and a concerted attempt to eradicate the problem. A greater emphasis at the antenatal clinics of any previous psychiatric illness in the patient or members of her family, and a continuous observation of the psychological well-being of women during pregnancy, would enable potential sufferers to receive treatment at the earliest possible stage. There is also a need for the institution of a three- or six-month postnatal examination designed to detect, diagnose, and help the unfortunate mothers. It is hoped that from this small acorn of observation a mighty oak tree of knowledge will grow.

Rhonda Small and her team from La Trobe University, Australia, reported in the British Medical Journal of 28th October 2000 a study of women who had given birth by caesarean section, forceps or vacuum delivery, of whom 467 were debriefed by midwives before discharge and 450 received standard care. The follow-up at six months showed that debriefing did not influence the incidence of postnatal depression at six months. Such a response

confirms tha PND is a hormonal disease and not influenced by the psychological effect of debriefing immediately after birth.

Who should prevent PND?

The final question remains: which branch of the medical profession should
take over the task of preventing PND? Physicians who treat tuberculosis,
polio, or diphtheria see only cases where prevention has failed; they do not
see the innumerable cases of these diseases which never happened because
they were successfully prevented by vaccination. So psychiatrists may treat
PND, but they do not see the many cases which have been successfully
prevented; they see only those who were not spotted early and missed out
on preventive treatment.

Obstetricians see very few women with PND, and those cases which do
occur in the wards in the early days after birth are likely to be discharged
home early with a pat on the back and 'You'll soon get well once you are
in the familiar surroundings of your own home'. If such women do not
return for their six-week postnatal appointment, there is no further follow-
up, no note on the medical file. Maybe she is receiving treatment, maybe
she has moved, or maybe she has just forgotten the appointment.

It is the general practitioner, who knows the patient's history and her
pre-pregnant state, who is in the ideal position to organize progesterone
prevention during pregnancy and treat the very earliest symptoms after
birth. Some have already accepted this additional task and appreciate the
excellent results.

With the recent changes in the approach to childbirth, mothers and
midwives are more involved in decisions about pregnancy and childbirth.
This gives midwives the responsibility of highlighting those mothers
needing prevention and of ensuring that the treatment is fully carried out.
So it remains with the community physicians, whose prime task is prevention, to ensure that all involved in antenatal care have a full knowledge of
the devastating effects of PND and recognize the importance of selecting
women requiring progesterone prevention.

Physical symptoms

In this book I have shown how our energies can be harnessed to fight for
the recognition of PND and its prevention. This is only the beginning

of our understanding of PNI. Undoubtedly psychiatric symptoms are the commonest, but there are also those who have their first episode of physical symptoms after birth, and gradually improve as they develop PMS. They too can also avoid a recurrence of their PNI with progesterone prevention. I am referring to those who have their first, sudden attack of asthma, migraine, epilepsy, sinusitis, or uveitis after childbirth and then as they improve have recurrences in the premenstruum. They are referred to their appropriate specialist, who recognizes and treats the condition, just as they treat hundreds of other men and women with the same symptoms. With each recurrence the woman's medication is increased. The fact that severe recurrences occur postnatally can be overlooked, and no attempt at prevention is considered. Who can blame the consultant who sees less than one case of PNI annually?

My first patient with physical symptoms of PNI was also my first patient to receive progesterone for premenstrual asthma (a full account is contained in our book *The PMS Bible*). She was a 34-year-old mother with an acute asthma attack, whom I saw in 1948. She had three children and had been admitted to hospital after each of these births with severe asthma, and subsequently had acute attacks before each menstruation. Her acute asthma attacks were treated with adrenalin injections, as it was in the days before steroid therapy for asthma had been discovered. She subsequently received progesterone injections from ovulation until menstruation and became symptom free. Four years later she again became pregnant and 'blossomed in pregnancy'. She had preventive progesterone immediately after her son's delivery and remained free from asthma until last seen in 1968.

Before tackling the large problem of physical symptoms of PNI, let us concentrate our energy and resources in our fight for recognition of PND and its successful prevention.

In tribute to the many women whose sufferings have contributed so much to this book, two of their quotations will provide the ending:

> I feel at last I can see a light at the end of a very long road.

> I've come out of the end of the tunnel—what a wonderful surprise.

Useful addresses

Association for Postnatal Illness (APNI), 25 Jerdan Place, Fulham, London SW6 1BE. Tel. 020 7386 0868. Telephone advice and befriending for PND; supports research and issues newsletters.

Birth Crisis Network, Standlake Manor, Nr Witney, Oxon OX8 7RH. Tel. 01865 300266. Support for mothers who have had a bad or difficult birth.

Home-Start, 2 Salisbury Road, Leicester LE1 7QR. Tel. 0116 233 9955 *www.home-start.org.uk* Offers practical help and emotional support to mothers of children aged under five years.

Meet-A-Mum Association (MAMA), Waterside Centre, 26 Avenue Road, South Norwood, London SE25 4DX. Tel. 020 8771 5595. Helpline tel. 020 8768 0123 (Monday–Friday 7.00 p.m.–10.00 p.m.)

National Childbirth Trust (NCT), Alexandra House, Oldham Terrace, London W3 6NH. Tel. 0890 4448707 *www.nct.online.org.uk* Nationwide organization offering preparation for pregnancy, labour, and breastfeeding as well as coping with PND.

Parentline Plus, National freephone helpline tel. 0808 800 2222 *www.parentline-plus.org.uk* Provides support to anyone—mums, dads, step-parents, or grandparents—with the demands of raising a child. Offer a national network of parenting courses and work with children and adults in families facing divorce and separation.

PMS Help, PO Box 83, Hereford HR4 8YQ *www.pmshelp.org.uk* Offers postal help and advice on PMS and PND to sufferers and their families. Publishes booklets on the three-hourly starch diet.

Serene (BM Cry-Sis), London WC1N 3XX. Tel. 020 7404 5011. Provides support for families with excessively crying, sleepless, and demanding babies.

Twins and Multiple Births Association (TAMBA), Harnott House, 309 Chester Road, Little Sutton, Ellesmere Port CH66 1QQ. Helpline tel. 01732 868000 (7.00 p.m.–11.00 p.m., Monday–Friday; 10.00 a.m.–11.00 p.m., Saturdays and Sundays). Offers support and information to families of twins and multiple children.

Further reading

APTER, T., Why Women Don't Have Wives: Professional Success and Motherhood (Macmillan, London, 1994).

BROCKINGTON, I. F. and KUMAR, R., *Motherhood and Mental Illness* (Academic Press, London, 1982).

BROCKINGTON, I. F. *Motherhood and Mental Health* (Oxford University Press 1996).

COMPORT, M., *Surviving Motherhood: How to Cope with Postnatal Depression* (Ashgrove Press, Bath, 1989).

COMPORT, M., *Towards Happy Motherhood* (Corgi, London, 1987).

COX, J.L., *Postnatal Depression: A Guide for Health Professionals* (Churchill Livingstone, Edinburgh, 1986).

DALTON, K, *Premenstrual Syndrome and Progesterone Therapy*, 2nd edn (William Heinemann Medical Books, London, 1984).

DALTON, K. and HOLTON, D., *PMS: The Essential Guide to Treatment Options* (Thorsons, London, 1994).

DALTON, K. and HOLTON, W. M., *Once a Month*, 6th edn (Hunter House Books, California, 1999).

DALTON, K. and HOLTON, W. M., *The PMS Bible*, (Ebury Press, 2000).

DIX, C., *The New Mother Syndrome: Coping with Postnatal Stress and Depression* (Allen & Unwin, London, 1985).

DIX, C., *The Working Mothers: You, Your Career, Your Child* (Unwin Hyman, London, 1989).

DUNNEWOLD, A. and SANFORD, D. G., *Postpartum Survival Guide* (New Harbinger Publications, Oakland, California, 1994).

HAMILTON, J. and HARBINGER, P., *Postpartum Psychiatric Illness: A Picture Puzzle* (University of Philadelphia, Pa., 1992).

KLOMPENHOUWER, J.-L., *Psychiatric Psychosis* (Horst Publications, Amsterdam, 1992).

MARSHALL, F., *Coping with Postnatal Depression* (Sheldon Press, London, 1993).

Some publications by Katharina Dalton

1953   'The Premenstrual Syndrome', joint authorship with Raymond Greene, *British Medical Journal*, **1**, 1007.

1954   'The Similarity of Symptomatology of Premenstrual Syndrome and Toxaemia of Pregnancy and Their Response to Progesterone', *Bntish Medical Journal*, **2**, 1071. BMA prize essay.

1957   'The Aftermath of Hysterectomy and Oophorectomy', *Proceedings of the Royal Society of Medicine*, **50** (6), 415–18.

1959   'Menstruation and Acute Psychiatric Illnesses', *British Medical Journal*, **1**, 148–9.

1959   'Comparative Trials of the New Oral Progestogenic Compounds in the Treatment of Premenstrual Syndrome', *British Medical Journal*, **2**, 1307–9.

1960   'Early Symptoms of Pre-eclamptic Toxaemia', *Lancet*,198–9.

1960   'Effects of Menstruation on Schoolgirls' Weekly Work', *British Medical Journal*, **1**, 326–8.

1960   'Menstruation and Accidents', *British Medical Journal*, **2**, 1425–6.

1960   'Schoolgirls' Behaviour and Menstruation', *British Medical Journal*, **2**, 1647–9.

1961   'Menstruation and Crime', *British Medical Journal*, **2**, 1752–3.

1962   'Controlled Trials in the Prophylactic Value of Progesterone in the Treatment of Pre-eclamptic Toxaemia', *Journal of Obstetrics and Gynaecology of the British Commonwealth*, **69** (3), 463–8.

1966   'The Influence of Mother's Menstruation on Her Child', *Proceedings of the Royal Society of Medicine*, **59** (10), 1014–16. BMA prize essay.

1967   'The Influence of Menstruation on Glaucoma', *British Journal of Ophthalmology*, **51** (10), 692–5. BMA prize essay.

1968   'Antenatal Progesterone and Intelligence', *British Journal of Psychiatry*, **114**, 1377–82.

1968   'Menstruation and Examinations', *Lancet*, 1386–8.

1970   'Children's Hospital Admissions and Mother's Menstruation', *British Medical Journal* , **2**, 27–8.

1971   'Prospective Study into Puerperal Depression', *British Journal of Psychiatry*, **118** (547), 689–2.

1971   'Puerperal and Premenstrual Depression', *Proceedings of the Royal Society of Medicine*, **64** (**12**), 1249–52.

1973   'Progesterone Suppositories and Pessaries in the Treatment of Menstrual Migraine', *Headache*, **12** (**4**), 151–9.

1973   'Migraine in General Practice' , *Journal of the Royal College of General Practitioners*, **23**, 97–106. Migraine Trust prize essay.

1975   'Food Intake Prior to a Migraine Attack—Study of 2313 Spontaneous Attacks', *Headache*, **15** (3), 188–93.

1976   'Migraine and Oral Contraceptives', *Headache*, **15** (4), 247–51.

1976   'Prenatal Progesterone and Educational Attainments', *British Journal of Psychiatry*, **129**, 438–42. BMA prize essay.

1978   'Menarcheal Age in the Disabled', joint authorship with Maureen Dalton, *British Medical Journal*, **2**, 475.

1979   'Intelligence and Prenatal Progesterone', *Journal of the Royal Society of Medicine*, **72**, 951.

1980   'Cyclical Criminal Acts in Premenstrual Syndrome', *Lancet*, ii, 1070–1.

1985   'Progesterone Prophylaxis Used Successfully in Postnatal Depression', *Practitioner*, **229**, 507–8.

1987   'A Preliminary Study into the Efficacy of Progesterone Suppositories as a Contraceptive for Women with Severe Premenstrual Syndrome', joint authorship with Maureen Dalton and K. Guthrie, *British Journal of Family Planning*, **13**, 87–9

1987   'Characteristics of Pyridoxine Overdose Neuropathy Syndrome', joint authorship with M.J.T. Dalton, *Acta Neurologica Scandinavica*, **11**, 237–41. Cullen Award, Royal Free Hospital.

1987   'Incidence of the Premenstrual Syndrome in Twins', joint authorship with Maureen Dalton and K. Guthrie, *British Medical Journal* , **295**, 1027–8.

1987   'Trial of Progesterone Vaginal Suppositories in the Treatment of Premenstrual Syndrome', letter in *American Journal of Obstetrics and Gynaecology*, **156** (**6**), 1555.

1987   'Commentary on "Premenstrual Syndrome and Thyroid Dysfunction" ', *Integrative Psychiatry*, **5**,179–93.

1988   'Treating Premenstrual Syndrome', *British Medical Journal*, **297**, 490.

1988   'Women's Problems in General Practice', *Stress Medicine*, **4** (3), 183.

1988   'Progesterone for Premenstrual Exacerbations of Asthma', *Lancet*, **2**, 8613–84.

1988   'Premenstrual Syndrome', *Health Visitor*, **61**(7), 199.

1989   'The Aetiology of Premenstrual Syndrome is with the Progesterone Receptors', *Medical Hypotheses*, **31**, 3237.

1989   'Sucessful Prophylactic Progesterone for Idiopathic Postnatal Depression', *International Journal of Prenatal and Perinatal Studies*, 323–7.

1989   'PMS: Critique of a Study'. *Medical Monitor*, 33–4.

1989 'Postpartum Depression and Bonding: Comment', *International Journal of Prenatal and Perinatal Studies*, 225–6.

1990 'Do Progesterone Receptors Have a Role in PMS?', *International Journal of Prenatal and Perinatal Studies*, 215–18.

1990 'Premenstrual Syndrome and Postnatal Depression', *Health and Hygiene*, 11, 199–201.

1991 'Birth of the Blues: Postnatal Depression', *Chemist and Druggist*, 34–6.

1991 'Premenstrual Syndrome: An Alternative View', *British Journal of Hospital Medicine*, 45.

1991 'DMPA and Bone Density', joint authorship with M.J.T. Dalton, letter in *British Medical Journal* , 303, 855.

1992 'Diet of Women With Severe Premenstrual Syndrome and the Effect of Changing to a Three Hourly Starch Diet', joint authorship with W. Holton, *Stress Medicine*, 8, 61–5.

1992 'Early Detection of Pre-Eclampsia', *American Journal of Obstetrics and Gynaecology*, 167 (5), 1479–80.

1993 'Epidemiology of Premenstrual Symptoms', letter in *Journal of Clinical Epidemiology*, 46 (4), 406–7.

1994 'Progesterone and Glucose Metabolism', joint authorship with W. Holton, *British Journal of Family Planning*, 19, Suppl., 4–5.

1994 'Postnatal Depression and Prophylactic Progesterone', *British Journal of Family Planning*, 19, Suppl., 10–12.

1994 'Progesterone as a Contraceptive in Severe PMS Sufferers', joint authorship with M. Steward, *British Journal of Family Planning*, 19, Suppl., 22–3.

1994 'The Incidence of Premenstrual Syndrome in the Adoptive Daughter', joint authorship with K. Hesington, *British Journal of Family Planning*, 19, Suppl., 23–4.

1994 'Progesterone is the Safe Way to Deal With Depression', *General Practitioner*, 24, 59.

1995 'Premenstrual Syndrome and Postnatal Depression', joint authorship with W. Holton, *International Journal of Prenatal and Perinatal Psychology and Medicine*, 714, 451–4.

1996 'Alternatives in Hormone Replacement Therapy', *British Journal of Therapy and Rehabilitation*, June 1996, 3.

1996   'Psychological Implications of the Menopause', *British Journal of Therapy and Rehabilitation,* **June 1996,** 3.

1998   'Premenstrual Syndrome' in *Encyclopaedia of Mental Health,* Academic Press, New York.

1999   'Premenstrual Syndrome' and 'Postnatal Depression' in *New Fontana Dictionary of Modern Thought,* Harper Collins, London.

2000   'PMS: from Myth to Reality', *Sexual Health.* Vol 1, 4, 82–3.

2000   'PMS Bible', Co-author W.M. Holton, Ebury Press.

Publications by Wendy M. Holton

1989 'At Variance on Vitamins', *Health Visitor*, **62**, 258.

1991 'Premenstrual Syndrome and Progesterone Suppositories', joint authorship with N. MacKenzie, *Journal of American Medical Association*, **265/1**, 26.

1992 'Is This PMS?'; 'Can Diet Help My PMS?'; 'Too Young for PMS?', booklets published by PMS Help, Hereford.

1992 *PMS—How to Beat It*, joint authorship with I. Simpson, Peter Andrew Publishers, Droitwich.

1994 'Progesterone and Glucose Metabolism', joint authorship with K. Dalton, *British Journal of Family Planning*, **19** (Suppl.), 4–5.

1995 'Premenstrual Syndrome and Postnatal Depression', joint authorship with K. Dalton, *International Journal of Prenatal and Perinatal Psychology and Medicine*, **7/4**, 451–4.

1996 'Postnatal Depression and Premenstrual Syndrome—the Effect on Marriage' in *Saving the Situation* (ed. J. Nettlefold), Family Practice Press.

1996 *Depression After Childbirth*, 3rd edn, joint authorship with K. Dalton, Oxford University Press.

1996 'PMS—the ripple effect', *BASMT Bulletin*, **12**, 28–9.

1998 'PND—Why Me?' booklet published by PMS Help, Hereford.

1999 *Once A Month*, 6th edn, joint authorship with K. Dalton, Hunter House Books, California.

2000 *The PMS Bible*, joint authorship with K. Dalton, Ebury Press, London.

2000 'PMS: from Myth to Reality', joint authorship with K. Dalton, *Sexual Health*. Vol 1, 4, 82–3.

Glossary of drugs

Drugs, that have been patented, have a capital letter

Aldactone   diuretic
Amitrityline   tricyclic antidepressant
Amytal   barbiturate
Anafranil   tricyclic antidepressant.
analgesic   drug to relieve pain
antidepressant   drug to relieve drpression
antihypertensive   drug to relieve high blood pressure
antipsychotic   drug to relieve psychosis
atenolo   betablocker
Ativan   antianxiety drug, benzodiazipine
barbiturates   hypnotic drugs, that produce tolerance, are liable to abuse and have
   severe withdrawal effects
bendrofluazide   diuretic
benodiazapines   hypnotic drugs with risk of tolerance aand advised use for less than
   two weeks duration
betablockers   reduce the frequency and severity of angina, and lower pressure
bromocriptine   lowers prolactin level
Camcolit   lithoium antidepressant
Depixol   antipsychotic
Diazepam   longacting benzodiazepine
diuretic   increases that amount of urine passed
dothiepen   tricyclic antidepressant
Duphaston   dydrogesterone, progestogen
Dutonin   SSRI antidepressant
Dydrogesterone   progestogen
Fluoxetine   SSRI antidepressant
Gamanil   lofepramine, tricyclic antidepressant
hypnotic   induces sleep
imipramine   tricyclic antidepressant.
iron   needed by red cells, used in anaemia
Largactil   antipsychotic
Lentizol   lofepramine, a tricyclic antidepressant

Levonorgestrel progestogen, contraceptive

Librium antianxiety, long acting benzodiazopine

lithium mineral present in the body in minute amounts, antidepressant most suitable for manic depressants

lofepramine tricyclic antidepressant

Lorazepam benzodiazepine

MAIO monoamine oxidase inhibitor, antidepressant most suitable for atypical depression

medroxyprogesterone progestogen, contraceptive

Nardil MAOI antidepressant

Navidrex thiazide diuretic

Norethisterone progestogen

nortriptyline tricycle antidepressant

Parlodel bromocriptine

Parnate MAOI antidepressant

Paroxetine SSRI antidepressant

Placebo inactive substance that has no curative effect

Priadel lithium antidepressant

Primolut norethisterone, progestogen

progesterone neurosteroid, produced by ovaries and adrenals

progestogen artificial progesterone, which lowers progesterone blood level, used in contraception and HRT

propanolol betablocker

Prothiadin dothiapin, a tricyclic antidepressant

Provera medroxyprogesterone, progestogen

Prozac fluxetine, SSRI antidepressant

pyridoxine vitamin B6

serotonin chemical acting within brain cells

Seroxat SSRI antidepressant

SSRI selective serotonin reuptake inhibitor, a type of antidepressant

Sertraline SSRI antidepressant

Surmontal tricyclic antidepressant

thiazide diuretic

thyroxine produced by the thyroid gland

Tofranil tricyclic antidepressant

tranquillizer drug to bring tranquility

tricycle antidepressant group of antidepressants best for typical depression

Valium long acting benzodiazepine

Xanax long acting benzodiazipine

Glossary

abortion death of foetus.

adrenal glands two glands above the kidney responsible for producing numerous hormones.

adrenalin one of the hormones produced by the adrenal glands.

afterbirth see placenta.

amenorrhoea absence of menstruation.

anaemia insufficient iron in the blood.

anorexia loss of appetite.

antenatal before childbirth.

anus exit from the alimentary tract or back passage.

atypical not typical.

candida a yeast normally present in the alimentary canal.

cervical smear test for the diagnosis of cancer of the neck or door of the womb.

cervix door of the womb.

chromosomes tiny threadlike structures within the cell nucleus containing genes.

conception becoming pregnant by fertilization of the ovum.

contraception prevention of pregnancy.

corticosteroids hormones produced by the cortex of the adrenal glands.

diuretics drugs capable of increasing the amount of urine passed.

dormant sleeping or inactive.

dysmenorrhoea pain with menstruation.

dyspareunia pain on intercourse.

ECT electroconvulsive therapy; a type of therapy in which an electric shock is administered to the brain.

endocrine gland organ releasing hormones into the blood to act on distant cells.

endocrinologist a person who studies the hormones of the body.

endogenous arising from within.

endometrium inner lining of the womb.

exogenous arising from outside.

follicle stimulating hormone hormone produced by the pituitary acting on the ovary to ripen the follicles and produce oestrogen.

follicular phase that part of the menstrual cycle after menstruation and before ovulation.

galactorrhoea fluid in the breast when not breastfeeding.

genes factors controlling heredity carried by chromosomes.

glucose a form of sugar found in the blood.

gonadotrophin hormone produced by the pituitary acting on the gonads, either testes or ovaries.

gonadotrophin releasing hormone (GnRH) hormone from hypothalamus to the pituitary, which stimulates the gonads (ovaries in women).

gonads sexual organs; ovaries in women and testes in men.

gynaecology study of diseases of women.

haemorrhage loss of blood, bleeding.

hormone receptors compounds which transport hormone molecules into the nucleus of cells.

hormones chemical messengers, produced by glands and having an action on cells in another part of the body.

hyperglycaemia raised blood sugar level.

hyperthyroidism excessive thyroid activity.

hypnotic drug to induce sleep.

hypoglycaemia lowered blood sugar level.

hypothalamus specialized part of the base of the brain.

hypothyroidism underactive thyroid function.

infanticide killing of an infant by its mother.

labour birth of baby.

lactation breastfeeding.

lethargy excessive tiredness.

libido sex drive.

luteal phase that part of the menstrual cycle after ovulation and before menstruation.

luteinizing hormone (LH) hormone produced by the pituitary which causes ovulation and the production of progesterone.

manic mental illness with unnatural elation or excessive activity.

maternity elated to pregnancy.

menstrual clock specialized portion of the hypothalamus responsible for the cyclical timing of menstruation.

menstrual controlling centre situated in the hypothalamus and responsible for the cyclical timing of menstruation.

menstrual cycle time from the first day of menstruation to the first day of the next menstruation.

menstruation monthly bleeding from the vagina in women of childbearing age, caused by the disintegration of the lining of the womb.

metabolism building up and breaking down of chemicals in the body.

migraine severe form of headache.

nucleus central vital part of every living organism, where metabolism occurs.

obstetrician specialist in the care of women during pregnancy and labour.

oestrogen hormone released by the ovary.

ovary reproductive organ containing egg cells.

ovulation release of egg cell from the ovary.

ovum egg cell.

paramenstruum days immediately before and during menstruation.

parturition birth of baby.

pituitary gland situated immediately below the brain producing numerous different hormones.

placebo inactive or inert substance which has no curative effect.

placenta sometimes called the 'afterbirth'—organ which develops within the womb responsible for feeding the foetus and for the production of hormones of pregnancy.

postmenstruum days immediately after menstruation.

postnatal after childbirth.

potassium mineral present in blood and cells of the body.

pre-eclampsia illness in late pregnancy in which there is a raised blood pressure, swelling, and albumen in the urine.

premenstruum days immediately before menstruation.

progesterone hormone produced by the ovary for the preparation of the lining of the womb; also the starting point for the production of numerous corticosteroids.

progestogen man-made steroid capable of causing bleeding from the lining of the womb, and having different actions to that of natural progesterone.

prolactin hormone produced by the pituitary gland, the most important action being concerned with breastfeeding.

prophylactic preventive.

psychosis severe mental illness.

puerperium days after childbirth.

pyrexia fever, raised temperature.

pyridoxine vitamin B6.

refractoryvresting, not easily stimulated.

sedative drug to bring calmness.

serotonin a chemical acting within brain cells.

sodium mineral present in the cells and blood of the body.

sterile unable to conceive.

sterilization operation to prevent permanently a person becoming pregnant.

stress the reaction to demands made upon a person.

syndrome collection of symptoms which commonly occur together.

testes two male reproductive organs which produce sperm and testosterone.

testosterone male hormone produced by the testes.

therapy treatment.

thyroid   gland in the neck producing hormones responsible for the speed of metabolism of the body.

thyroxine   hormone produced by the thyroid gland.

tranquillizer   drug to bring tranquillity.

trauma   injury to body or mind.

uterus   womb.

vagina   passage leading from the exterior of the body to the door of the womb.

vasectomy   surgical operation on a man to make him permanently sterile.

vitamins   substances contained in food that are essential in minute quantities for life, growth, and health.

yeast   vegetable micro-organism normally present in the alimentary canal, but can cause thrush if in the mouth or vagina.

Index

Depression After Childbirth